This study constitutes an interesting literary-criti  fourth gospel, and examines the artistic achievem redescribing his story in a creative and poetic way. The book is divided into two parts. Part I is concerned w  criticism appropriate for research on the practice, and concentrates on John 18–1 istorical methodologies can be combi oach to gospel literature.

SOCIETY FOR NEW TESTAMENT STUDIES

MONOGRAPH SERIES

General Editor: Margaret E. Thrall

73

JOHN AS STORYTELLER

John as storyteller

Narrative criticism and the fourth gospel

MARK W. G. STIBBE

*Vicar of St Mark's Church, Grenoside, Sheffield
and part-time Lecturer in the
Department of Biblical Studies,
University of Sheffield*

CAMBRIDGE
UNIVERSITY PRESS

Published by the Press Syndicate of the University of Cambridge
The Pitt Building, Trumpington Street, Cambridge CB2 1RP
40 West 20th Street, New York, NY 10011–4211, USA
10 Stamford Road, Oakleigh, Melbourne 3166, Australia

First published 1992
First paperback edition 1994

Printed in Great Britain at the University Press, Cambridge

A catalogue record for this book is available from the British Library

Library of Congress cataloguing in publication data
Stibbe, Mark W. G.
John as storyteller: narrative criticism and the fourth gospel /
Mark W. G. Stibbe.
        p.   cm.
Includes bibliographical references and index.
ISBN 0 521 47765 4 (paperback)
1. Bible. N. T. John – Criticism, Narrative.   I. Title.
BS2615.2.S744   1992
226.5'066–dc20   91–18214   CIP

ISBN 0 521 47765 4 paperback

200 22 629

226·5

WG

To my father

CONTENTS

PART II   AN APPLICATION OF THE METHOD OF NARRATIVE CRITICISM TO JOHN 18–19

PREFACE

This book has something of a rich history. My interest in literary and narrative criticism goes back to the period between 1979 and 1982 when I studied English Literature for my first degree at Cambridge University. During the three years of the course, I attempted to construct a Christian approach to literature. These three years were instrumental in providing me with a foundational understanding of literary theory, and in helping me to gain experience in the whole area of interdisciplinary studies. I am particularly grateful to my Roman Catholic friend and supervisor, Dr Eric Griffiths, for the acuteness of his expert tuition.

After a spell of teaching English and RE, I started my training for the ordained ministry in the Church of England at St John's College, Nottingham. There I did a shortened second degree in biblical studies. It was here that I started working on a new angle of my interdisciplinary methodology. Having studied literature from a biblical perspective at Cambridge University, I now started studying the Bible from a literary perspective at Nottingham University. I am deeply indebted to my dear friend Dr Andrew Lincoln for his teaching and support through these three years. Dr Lincoln was one of the very few biblical scholars in Great Britain interested in looking at the New Testament from a literary-critical perspective. Studying under him at this stage was indeed providential.

After being ordained deacon, I started a challenging job as a curate in Nottingham. It was during this four-year curacy that I completed my part-time doctoral dissertation entitled 'The Artistry of John'. I am thankful to a number of people who supported me as I burnt the candle at both ends during this difficult time. First of all, I owe a debt of thanks to Dr John Muddimann, who supervised me for my Ph.D. with exemplary erudition and sensitivity. Secondly, I am grateful to the Rev. Charles Hall, my vicar, who encouraged me in my biblical studies. Thirdly, I am for ever in the debt of my wife

Alie, and our children Philip and Hannah, who had to put up with me working on 'The Artistry of John' on rare days off and holidays.

Since the completion of the thesis, I have received warm and perceptive comments from Professor Graham Stanton, my external examiner, and Robert Morgan. Both have helped me considerably in preparing the thesis for publication, very aptly, with the Cambridge University Press.

This book, finally, is dedicated to my father, Philip Stibbe. It was he who introduced me to literature as something to love. I cannot put into words the debt I owe to him.

ACKNOWLEDGEMENTS

Throughout this book, I have used Raymond Brown's excellent translation of the fourth gospel, which the reader can find in Brown's Anchor Bible Commentary on *The Gospel According to John*. I have also referred throughout my book to *The Greek New Testament* edited by Kurt Eland et al. (third edition, 1975). References to Euripides' *Bacchae* are made using the Penguin Classics translation of the play by Philip Vellacott (1975 version).

Finally, I am grateful to the SCM for allowing me to reproduce some of the material I used for their *Dictionary of Biblical Interpretation* (London, 1990). Some of the material in chapter 2 appeared in my section on Structuralism in that volume (650−5).

INTRODUCTION

One of the aims of this book is to show that the gospel of John is a *multi-story* phenomenon calling for a multi-disciplinary narrative methodology. We cannot properly appreciate John's storytelling art unless we are prepared to expose his story to a comprehensive exegetical approach which has room for historical as well as literary questions. In looking at narrative criticism in part I, I will expose the weaknesses in two current extremes in biblical criticism: first of all, the recent anti-historical bias of text-immanent, literary analysis of biblical texts; secondly, the largely anti-aesthetic bias of traditional, historical-critical methods. In the first half I proceed to construct a method which looks at Johannine narrative at the level of *text, context and pre-text*; that is to say, the surface level of the narrative, the social context of the narrative, and the historical reference, sources and tradition of the narrative. My rationale for joining these disciplines is not merely the desire to reconcile what have hitherto been estranged bed-fellows. The narrative form itself cries out for such a quasi-metaphorical conjunction. As I will show throughout this work, questions surrounding the narrative form are not asked in literary faculties alone: they are also asked by philosophers of history such as W. B. Gallie, and social ethicists such as S. Hauerwas. What this means is that a narrative criticism which is only concerned with the literary issues of characterization, plot and structure seriously restricts the functions of narrative. Narratives are crucial not only for aesthetic purposes but also for the social reconstruction of history. One of the contributions of this book is that it highlights the philosophical grounds for integrating the synchronic and diachronic aspects of biblical criticism.

Perhaps the one adjective which I would use to describe this book is 'integrative'. First, in chapter 1 I integrate literary and theological questions. By insisting that narrative devices are used for rhetorical and Christological purposes, my method of narrative criticism will open up the possibility of assessing Johannine theology from a literary-critical perspective. Secondly, in chapter 2 I integrate structuralism and historical criticism. By radically adapting structuralist narratology, I will show how narrative critics can identify the deep, generic structures which are part of the grammar of the gospel writer's culture. Thirdly, in chapter 3, I integrate literary and sociological areas of enquiry by showing how the narrative form is used by social groups in the construction of communal identity. By integrating socio-redaction criticism with narrative criticism, I will open up the possibility of examining the story of John as a code determining community values. Fourthly, in chapter 4 I integrate literary and historical methods by pointing out the importance of the narrative form for the social reconstruction of history. For too long, German Johannine scholars have presupposed that the fourth gospel cannot be both poetic and historical. F. C. Baur (1847), Bruno Bauer (1846), J. Wellhausen (1908), E. Schwartz (1907), E. Hirsch (1936) and H. Windisch (1923) all insisted that John's gospel could not be history because John was a creative poet. In this book I will expose the fallacy of this presupposition. The gospel of John is poetic history: it is a creative redescription of historical tradition in which the concrete reality of Jesus' life is by no means destroyed. By integrating aesthetic and historical criticism, I will open up the possibility of travelling from the narrative of Jesus' experience, through the narrative sources, to the narrative-shaped gospel.

In the final analysis, it is by the fruits of a new method that we can know its usefulness. In this book, the application of this new form of narrative criticism to John's gospel and its passion narrative yields some interesting results. Some of the innovative discoveries in part II are the following: the discovery in John 18.1−27 of the narrative echo effects with the Good Shepherd παροιμία (10.1−18); the discovery of Dionysiac echoes in John's story as a whole, and particularly in the binding of Jesus (John 18.12ff.), the dialogue with Pilate (18.28ff.) and the pathos of Jesus' crucifixion (19.16ff.); the discovery of the sociological significance of John's passion narrative, specifically the adoption scenario in 19.25−7; the discovery, finally, of the importance of time-shapes in John's reconstruction of Jesus' history in John 18−19. I hope it will now be seen, especially by British scholars (who have been slow to embrace the new literary approaches to the Bible), that narrative criticism provides a potentially rich resource for those who wish to approach the fourth gospel as both literature and history.

PART I

THE METHOD OF NARRATIVE CRITICISM
AND THE GOSPEL OF JOHN

1

THE PRACTICAL CRITICISM OF JOHN'S NARRATIVE

The emergence of narrative criticism

Until the late 1970s, the traditional methods for the study of the gospels and Acts were form criticism, source criticism, historical criticism, tradition history, redaction criticism, and textual criticism. Broadly speaking, these methods were concerned to answer the following questions: (1) What forms of material were available to the evangelists, and how were they used in the earliest church? (form criticism). (2) What sources were available to the evangelists when they wrote their gospels? (source criticism). (3) How much do the gospels tell us about Jesus and about the churches for which they were written? (historical criticism). (4) How much did the words and works of Jesus change during the years before the gospels were composed? (tradition history). (5) What theological and sociological purposes lie behind the evangelist's selection and expression of Jesus material in the gospels? (redaction criticism), and (6) What variations exist in the manuscripts of the gospel texts, and which has the greatest claim to be correct? (textual criticism). In other words, traditional methods of interpretation were more concerned with what lay behind NT narratives than with their form and their literary, artistic features. Although most of these methods comprised meticulous exegesis of NT narrative, none of them sought to answer the question, 'What artistry is there in these NT stories?'

A change began to occur most noticeably in the 1980s, when two books were published on *Mark as Story* (Rhoads and Michie, 1982; Best, 1983); one on *Matthew as Story* (Kingsbury, 1986), one on *The Narrative Unity of Luke – Acts* (Tannehill, 1986), and one on the *Anatomy of the Fourth Gospel* (Culpepper, 1983). Each of these works, and a number of lesser-known books and articles (see references), took up the challenge of looking at the final form of the gospels and Acts in order to highlight those narrative dynamics which traditional methods had neglected. The history behind this paradigm shift has been well documented, especially in Stephen Moore's

Literary Criticism and the Gospels (1989). It is now clear that the groundwork for NT narrative criticism was begun by Eric Auerbach, who, in 1953, published an influential book on realism in narrative called *Mimesis*. His second chapter, in which he praised the extraordinary realism of the narrative in Mark, caused something of an awakening in biblical studies. In 1964, Amos Wilder published his book *Early Christian Rhetoric*, and included an important chapter on the gospels as story. In 1970, William Beardslee also highlighted the narrative form of the gospels in his *Literary Criticism of the New Testament*. In 1972, Norman Perrin advocated a greater interest in the narrative dynamics of the NT in a widely read paper entitled 'The Evangelist as Author'. In 1978, Norman Petersen published his *Literary Criticism for New Testament Critics* and Edgar McKnight his *Meaning in Texts*, both concerned with narrative hermeneutics in connection with the gospels and Acts. In 1979, Frank Kermode published a book on narrative hermeneutics called *The Genesis of Secrecy* which used Mark as its principal sample-text. With these works published, the stage was well and truly set for the ferment of narrative approaches to the NT. A brief summary of the major contributions now follows.

The gospel of Mark

The gospel which attracted nearly all of the initial attention of emerging narrative critics was Mark, and the first book to devote itself to a full-length study of its narrative was Rhoads and Michie's *Mark as Story* (1982), subtitled *An Introduction to the Narrative of a Gospel*. In this work, two American scholars combined to focus on the final form of the text as narrative rather than on its hypothesized prehistory. The two authors stated that their aim was a literary rather than an historical one. On its own, such a comment might have been confusing for two reasons: first because the phrase 'literary criticism' had been a synonym for source criticism in NT studies (the very opposite of what Rhoads and Michie intended); secondly, because the very idea that the gospels and Acts might in some sense be literature had been questioned by form critics such as Martin Dibelius from the 1920s. However, it is clear from an article published in the same year entitled 'Narrative Criticism and the Gospel of Mark' that the authors preferred their method to be called narrative rather than literary criticism (Rhoads, 1982: 411–12). This was a sensible move, because literary criticism implies that the authors regard the gospels as literature (which is by no means obvious), whilst narrative criticism is a much safer term (no one doubts that the gospels are narratives). The authors brought out the narrative qualities of Mark by providing a new translation of the gospel and by analysing narrative qualities, such as the narrator, narrative settings, plot and characterization. In conclusion, both Rhoads and Michie stated that 'the author of Mark's Gospel tells a dynamic story and has woven the tale so as to create powerful effects on the reader' (p. 108).

In 1983, the British scholar Ernest Best published his *Mark: The Gospel as Story*. Best pointed out in his first chapter that traditional scholarship had used Mark as a quarry for information about a Christian community. Now, however, scholars had begun to recognize that books have an existence of their own once they are written. Consequently, 'discussion on Mark has turned around once again and the Gospel is now viewed as a whole' (p. 2). Best's argument throughout his book is that the pre-Marcan material which was eventually incorporated into the second gospel possessed no overall coherence. Miracle stories, parables, sayings all came to the author from independent streams of tradition. They were not already episodes in a larger narrative totality. What the author achieved when he transformed oral traditions into a written gospel was the creation of a plot. As Best puts it, 'it is the "plot" which holds Mark together' (p. 108). The plot forms the cement which links together all the material selected by the author (p. 100). The items of traditions are like pearls, but the plot which Mark establishes is the connecting thread of purpose which links these pearls into a unified, narrative Christology (p. 112). Mark is therefore best described as narrative, 'though the narrative is not put forward as fiction' (p. 141). It is not fictional narrative, because the author did not feel free to alter or create as he liked. 'There is positive evidence that he had a real respect for the tradition and preserved much of its detail faithfully' (p. 118).

The gospel of Matthew

The year 1986 saw the publication of *Matthew as Story* by the American scholar Jack Dean Kingsbury. Kingsbury began by stating that his book was 'a study in literary, or narrative criticism' and that it was 'one of the first such books on Matthew to be written' (p. vii). His aim was 'to explore the world of Matthew's thought with an eye to the flow (plot) of the gospel-story that is being told' (p. vii). His method is a 'product of literary criticism', and he carries out his investigation 'in terms of categories that literary-theorists employ in their investigation of works such as the novel' (p. vii). Thus Kingsbury uses Seymour Chatman's communicational theory of narrative and E.M. Forster's *Aspects of the Novel* and applies their terminology to the gospel of Matthew (p. 10). Consequently, we have sections on events, characters, settings, the implied author, the narrator, the point of view, the implied reader, and structure. All these qualities are analysed as aspects of Matthew's unified narrative. There is little attention to historical questions, because 'when one reads the Matthean narrative, one temporarily takes leave of one's familiar world of reality and enters into another world that is autonomous in its own right' (p. 2). Some attention is given to the community for which the gospel was written, and this is done by taking the implied reader in Matthew's story as an index of the real readers (p. 120). In his dependence on Seymour Chatman and modern theorists of the novel (such as E.M. Forster), Kingsbury was following Alan Culpepper's *Anatomy of the Fourth Gospel* (1983), as we shall see in a moment. The same criticisms which we shall make of Culpepper's literary approach to John (that it treats the gospel as an a-historical novel) can also be directed against Kingsbury's work.

Luke–Acts

Luke–Acts had already been exposed to a number of literary studies before 1986, which saw the publication of the first volume of Robert Tannehill's *Narrative Unity of Luke–Acts*. Robert Tannehill's narrative-critical articles on the Synoptic gospels and Acts had been consistently perceptive before the publication of this work. Particularly interesting had been his 'Disciples in Mark' (1977) and his 'Gospel of Mark as Narrative Christology' (1979). Now, after a preparatory article entitled 'The Composition of Acts 3–5: Narrative Development and Echo Effect' (1984), Tannehill turned his attention to the narrative of Luke–Acts. He began with the remark that 'Luke–Acts ... was written by an author of literary skill and rich imagination who had a complex vision of the significance of Jesus Christ and of the mission in which he is the central figure' (p. 1). Luke–Acts is therefore a 'unified literary work of two volumes' (p. 1). Tannehill's claim is that traditional methods of biblical criticism lack the leading concepts which enable scholars to see how a narrative like Luke–Acts achieves unity. However, 'the recent development of narrative criticism ... opens new opportunities' (p. 1), and helps us to identify the author's disclosures of his overarching purpose. The key concept Tannehill uses is that of narrative 'echo effects'. These are the internal connections between different parts of the narrative. As Tannehill puts it, 'Themes will be developed, dropped, then presented again. Characters and actions may echo characters and actions in another part of the story, as well as characters and actions of the scriptural story which preceded Luke−Acts' (p. 3). Although Tannehill calls his method literary criticism without arguing for the literary status of Luke−Acts, his work is an interesting example of how to examine the gospels as story, and we shall be employing some of his leading concepts in our narrative criticism of John.

The gospel of John

What examples do we have of narrative studies of the fourth gospel? There have been a number of attempts to open up the literary qualities of the fourth gospel throughout this century. Hitchcock looked at the dramatic qualities of John in 1923, as did Bowen (1930), Connick (1948), Martyn (first edition, 1968), Smalley (1978), Flanagan (1981), Domeris (1983) and others (such as Strachan and Charnwood). Other scholars have highlighted some of the literary features of the gospel, such as Windisch (1923 − see introduction), Muilenburg (1932), Deeks (1968), Wead (1970), Talbert (1970), Newman (1975) and de Jonge (1977). The 1980s have seen a blossoming of such approaches to John by South African scholars such as Domeris (1983), Du Rand (1985) and Kotzé (1985), and by American scholars such as Giblin (1980), Crossan (1980), Cahill (1982), Webster (1982), Phillips (1983), Nicholson (1983), Hartman (1984), Duke (1985), O'Day (1986), Malina (1985) and Staley (1988).

By far the most influential of these has been Alan Culpepper's *Anatomy of the Fourth Gospel* (1983). Culpepper's best-known work of Johannine scholarship before this was his *Johannine School* (1975), which was an attempt to reconstruct through the Johannine literature the school of writers responsible for the composition of John. Culpepper's *Anatomy* could not have been more different. Instead of a work of historical reconstruction, *Anatomy* was a study in the narrative world of the fourth gospel. Indeed, Culpepper almost seemed to reject his earlier work when he criticized Johannine scholars in general for treating John as a window on to the history of the Johannine community as opposed to 'the literary creation of the evangelist' (p. 4). John, in Culpepper's eyes, is 'novelistic, realistic narrative' (p. 8), and it should be read primarily as story and not as history. Thus, questions concerning sources and origins are set aside because 'the experience of reading the text is more important than understanding the process of its composition' (p. 5). What is required instead is a method for appreciating the fourth gospel as a unified narrative. As in the case of Kingsbury's later book on Matthew, Culpepper uses Seymour Chatman's communicational model of narrative as his starting-point (p. 6).

One understands the model as follows: a narrative presupposes a storyteller, a story and an audience. Between the author and the reader stands the text of this story. An important distinction must then be made between the real author and the real reader, on the one hand, and then between these two entities and their counterparts in the narrative itself (the implied author and the implied reader). The implied author is the author suggested by the choice and the arrangement of material, the author who is inferred from the internal narrative dynamics. This implied author may well be different in character from the actual author, just as the inferred or implied reader may be different from the real reader. Altogether, the reader's response is shaped and directed by characterization (the way in which the characters in the story are depicted), by narrative settings, plot (the selection and organization of material into a chronological unity), and implicit commentary (the means used by the narrator to communicate indirectly with the reader, including irony and symbolism). It is these narrative elements which establish the communication between author and reader: that is why Culpepper's book focusses on point of view, narrative time, plot, characters, implicit commentary and the implied reader in John's story (categories hitherto neglected in Johannine studies). It is precisely through these narrative elements that the gospel communicates its confessed aim of moving the reader to new insights and to faith in Jesus as the Son of God (John 20.31).

Culpepper's study is a significant methodological experiment and an extremely valuable contribution to Johannine studies. Above all, it has helped scholars to rediscover the unified story of a gospel whose narrative unity had suffered greatly at the hands of displacement theorists like Rudolf Bultmann. However, the value judgement Culpepper passes on John's story, that it is 'magnificent but flawed' (p. 231), could really be passed on his own book. For example, Culpepper takes it too much for granted that a gospel can be studied as if it were a novel. The major theorists on whom he (and Kingsbury later) depends are all students of modern fiction (E.M. Forster, Gerard Genette and Seymour Chatman in particular), but it is a moot point whether their novel-based models are applicable in the context of first-century narratives. Eric Auerbach's *Mimesis* is partly responsible here: by showing how 'realistic' or novel-like Mark was, he unwittingly encouraged a number of biblical scholars to treat the gospels as novels. Also to blame is what Scholes and Kellog have described as the modern idolatry of the novel form (1966, p. 8). So, whilst Culpepper is not guilty of calling gospel narratives primitive literature, it needs to be stated that the sophistications of gospel narrative are quite different from the subtleties of modern novels. Gospel narratives share in the subtleties of ancient Hebrew and Graeco-Roman narratives, not in the more self-conscious subtleties of modern novels. Put simply, they are closer to Homer's *Odyssey* than they are to Joyce's *Ulysses*. It is against the background of the Old Testament and Graeco-Roman narrative that Johannine narrative should be judged, and not against the background of the modern novel. As it stands, Culpepper's method is fundamentally anachronistic.

A related problem with Culpepper's work centres on his neglect of the historical dimension of John's story. He begins his book by stressing that he is not against historical criticism, and yet the emphasis is on John as fiction and on the plea for John not to be used as a window on to the Johannine community (pp. 3–5). However, the recent so-called 'new look' at John's gospel has re-emphasized the value of its historical traditions, and scholarship from J.L. Martyn's *History and Theology* (first edition, 1968) onwards has mainly devoted itself to identifying community history within the fourth gospel. Even though Culpepper may not be using the word fiction to connote invention and falsehood, the general approach of his book does tend to obscure the value of the gospel as narrative history and as community narrative. As far as historicity is concerned, the reason for this lies in his dependence on Frank Kermode's 1979 narrative analysis of Mark, which began the trend of regarding the gospels as fictional novels. As for Culpepper's neglect of the community dimension, this may derive from the allegorizing tendencies of various community reconstructionists, but it probably also derives from Culpepper's New critical bias. Like New criticism, his method is text-immanent; that is, it bypasses extrinsic, historical and sociological factors in the task of literary interpretation. The problem here is that biblical narrative is a functional structure; it is social discourse orientated to an historical audience (Sternberg, 1985, p. 1). It is also a report in story-form of past history. One cannot ignore the question of the historical audience or the historical Jesus of John's story without reducing and restricting the functions of narrative.

Conclusions

In this section I have very briefly traced the emergence of narrative criticism from the time of Eric Auerbach. I have demonstrated how NT narrative criticism has encouraged scholars to look at the artistry of gospel story, and yet at the same time I have exposed the weaknesses of regarding the gospels as fictional novels, and of neglecting the original milieu in which these narratives were composed. In this book, it is my aim to introduce a form of narrative criticism which does full justice to John as a first-century narrative by taking into account historical questions concerning sources and community. A brief description of the new, integrated method that I have devised can be seen in the introduction above. An important contribution made in this study is in the area of theology and Christology. One of the things which has been omitted by narrative critics is a careful consideration of the relationship between theological purpose and the narrative form. Sometimes narrative critics have been guilty of implying an art-for-art's-sake mentality on the part of the evangelists.

In *John as Storyteller*, I am particularly eager to avoid this impression. Throughout the study I am indebted to Robert Tannehill's ground-breaking article 'The Gospel of Mark as Narrative Christology', which had two fundamental aims: first, to identify and evaluate the narrative composition of Mark, especially those aspects of composition which make it a continuous, developing story; secondly, to show that these narrative qualities are used by the author to persuade the reader of the truthfulness of his Christological credo. This led Tannehill to a close scrutiny of plot, characterization, role relationships, commissions, conflicts, developments, themes, narrative patterns, irony, paradox, and the ways in which these narrative dynamics function in the communication between author and reader. Tannehill's article is important because it shows how NT narrative is a rhetorical phenomenon carefully engineered to reinforce a particular theological understanding of Jesus in the minds of its readers.

My description of John's story as *narrative Christology* in this book owes much to Tannehill's approach outlined above. In this chapter, I shall be looking at the Christological purpose behind

John's distinctive narrative composition. Where I will later be going beyond him is in the three areas of narrative genre, social discourse and narrative history. In the case of narrative genre, I shall be employing the categories of structuralism in order to show how the fourth evangelist chooses a narrative genre which is particularly suited to his Christology. Tannehill himself seems dubious about the value of structuralism as a constructive interpretative tool (p. 58), but I hope in this study to illustrate something of its importance for a discussion of narrative genre and its relationship to Christology. In the case of social discourse, I shall be employing categories from the sociology of knowledge and the sociology of religion in order to show how John's narrative Christology must not be read as a closed world but as an index of its community's value-system and as *a functional discourse*. In the case of narrative history, I shall be employing categories from the narrative history debate in the 1960s and 1970s (a debate conducted mainly by philosophers of history) to ask what status John's narrative Christology possesses as historiography. In diagrammatical form, my integrated narrative hermeneutic looks like this:

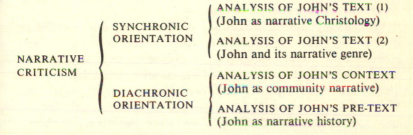

It is my hope that this method will show future Johannine scholars how to appreciate John not only as story but also as community narrative, and as narrative history.

The narrative artistry and unity of John

The emphasis of this chapter so far makes a value judgement about the final form of John's gospel because it implies that the gospel is an understanding of Jesus artistically expressed in the language of story. This much has been recognized for many decades. E. F. Scott wrote in 1906 that 'John did not set himself to write a complete history, but only to enforce a given view of the Christian revelation in the light of selected facts. He is thus left free to shape his narrative on a deliberate artistic plan, and it unfolds itself with something of the ordered majesty and simplicity of a Greek tragedy' (1906, p. 16). In 1932, P. C. Sands emphasized Johannine craftsmanship when he wrote of 'the book's unity, its appearance of being "woven without seam", as Strauss said, in spite of certain dislocations of sections in our present text' (1932, p. 49). Twenty years later, C. H. Dodd made this statement:

> what he [John the storyteller] gives us is no ordinary narrative, where one thing follows another in a simple succession. The links that connect one episode with another are extremely subtle. It is rather like a musical fugue. A theme is announced, and developed up to a point; then a second theme is introduced and interwoven with the first, then perhaps a third, with fresh interweaving, until an intricate pattern is evolved, which yet has the unity of a consummate work of art. The Fourth Gospel is more than any of the others an artistic and imaginative whole. (1950, p. 40)

In 1970 David Wead crystallized many of these thoughts in his book on the fourth gospel as literature.

From these comments we can see that there have been times during this century when John's story has been praised as a unified and artistic narrative Christology (though no one has explicitly used this description of it). However, just as form criticism delayed widespread literary appreciation of the final form of the Synoptic gospels and Acts, so source criticism had a destructive influence upon the literary appreciation of John's final form. There are few literary studies of the fourth gospel between the 1930s and 1960s, the period when source criticism was dominant in Johannine studies. That is because source criticism questioned Strauss's belief that the gospel was like the seamless robe mentioned in John 19.23. As the source critic Robert Fortna wrote in 1970: 'the interpreter of John's Gospel is confronted from the outset by a fundamental literary phenomenon, and one which, in degree at least, distinguishes that Gospel from the other three, namely the presence of the so-called aporias — the many inconsistencies, disjunctures, and hard connections, even contradictions — which the text shows, notably in the narrative portions, and which cannot be accounted for by textual criticism' (p. 2). These aporias, which Fortna interprets as interruptions in the flow of the narrative, are editorial seams. They are clues which tell us that there has been substantial redaction or editing of an original *Vorlage* (narrative source). This leads Fortna to propose that the gospel is the work of one principal author, but that this same person edited and altered his earlier narrative in such a way that the beauty and the smoothness of the original narrative was lost.

More detailed appreciation of Johannine narrative had to wait until the presuppositions and discoveries of such source criticism had been called into question. Barnabas Lindars was one of the first scholars to outline the problems with Robert Fortna's approach. He questioned Fortna's working hypothesis that John had 'incorporated virtually the whole source in his gospel (so that it can be reconstructed simply by stripping off the non-Johannine elements)' (1971, pp. 32–3), and complained that it ignored a unity of style in John's style argued by Eduard Schweizer (1939) and E. Ruckstuhl (1951). Time and again, argues Lindars, Fortna ascribes to John's source features which are characteristic of John's creative writing style. Time and again Fortna describes as aporias what can be explained in terms of narrative logic. The picture of the author which is consequently developed is one of a 'scissors-and-paste' man, and not the more accurate one of 'a highly creative writer' (p. 33). The picture of the text which is evoked is one of a clumsy patchwork quilt, and not the unified narrative symphony Dodd so clearly perceived. As John Robinson saw, the problem is that some of the aporias are arguably more in Fortna's mind than they are in the text. As he cynically remarked, 'Fortna's analysis is inevitably interspersed with frequent examples of "may", "probably" and "apparently" (with "obviously" and "clearly" thrown in to lend an air of confidence ...)' (1985, p. 16). Roughnesses there might be, Robinson conceded, but there needs to be less subjectivity in identifying where exactly these can be found.

In spite of this valid critique, it is possible to go too far in dismissing source criticism. When Marinus de Jonge strengthened the momentum towards synchronic, literary analyses of John in the late 1970s, he was too quick to dismiss source-critical considerations from his programme (as most narrative critics have) (1977, p. viii), and the result was that subsequent scholars like G. C. Nicholson began uncritically to assume that this rejection of the method was unimpeachable (1983, p. 13–15). In reality, however, cautious agnosticism is preferable to outright rejection. The widespread use of sources in NT documents should persuade us 'that we must not shy away from the possibility that the fourth evangelist too availed himself of written materials in the tradition known to him' (Kysar, 1975, p. 33). That there are occasional roughnesses in the narrative is evidence for the existence of sources, since they look more like editorial interruptions than authorial oversights. Editorial activity, of course, suggests that the gospel was composed at different stages, and, indeed, this is the view of John's composition which has remained the most plausible throughout this century. In this developmental picture, the gospel is seen principally as the work of an evangelist in the Johannine community (Jii), whose work draws on oral and written traditions deriving from the beloved disciple (Ji), but whose material has been supplemented and even altered by a later redactor (Jiii) — hence some of the aporias.

One question needs to be asked at this stage concerning the implications of this developmental theory for the literary unity of the gospel. Does this compositional hypothesis not confirm the argument concerning narrative disunity in the fourth gospel? Do not the breaks and inconsistencies, coupled with the idea that the fourth gospel was composed by different hands, deny its claim to unity? Raymond Brown has persuasively answered this question in his commentary (1966, pp. lxxxvii–viii). He argues that the gospel is principally the work of a single hand, even though it derives from an earlier eyewitness and has been edited later. This single hand belonged to a distinctive figure in the primitive church who used the raw material of an eye-witness tradition of Jesus' words and works and turned it into a story with distinctive theological and artistic characteristics. This material he eventually gathered into a continuous gospel narrative, which closely followed the traditional pattern of the baptism, the ministry and the passion, death and resurrection of Jesus. Even though a later redactor rearranged the narrative at points (for example, placing the discourses after 14.31), and even though he added more traditional material (chapter 21, for instance), the gospel is still principally the work of a single creative mind — that of the evangelist who preached and taught in the primitive church. As Brown concludes, the beloved disciple is the authority behind the gospel, whilst the evangelist is the author (p. lxxxviii). It is the evangelist's imagination which provides the narrative unity and artistry of the gospel. He is the gifted storyteller alluded to in the title of this book.

Added to this, the evidence for narrative and stylistic unity in John is more compelling and conclusive than the evidence against adduced by Fortna. I shall now outline some of the literary strategies which help to give the gospel its unity and which indicate a single, artistic imagination behind the narrative:

Christology

When Robert Tannehill wrote his article on 'The Gospel of Mark as Narrative Christology', he wrote that 'Jesus is the central figure in the gospel of Mark, and the author is centrally concerned to present (or re-present) Jesus to his readers so that his significance for their lives becomes clear. He does this in the form of a story' (p. 57). Tannehill saw Mark as a unified narrative because, in spite of clear division into episodes, there are connecting Christological threads which bind the story together. This led him to commend the phrase narrative Christology as a fitting description of the gospel genre. In truth, there could be no more apt description of John's story. The aim expressed by the author in John 20.31 is as follows: 'these have been recorded so that you may have faith that Jesus is the Messiah, the Son of God'. In terms of our narrative categories, we might retranslate this as follows: 'every detail of this narrative has been selected and expressed in such a way that you might accept its fundamental Christological belief, that Jesus is the Christ'. That Jesus is the centre of everything in John is an obvious truism which is borne out simply by looking at the number of times 'Ιησοῦς occurs in the fourth gospel. This fact alone shows how Christology functions as the primary unifying thread in the fourth gospel.

Number patterns

Another unifying narrative strategy is the author's marked preference for structuring material into units of seven and/or three. Some examples of seven are: the seven discourses (3.16−21/4.5−27/5.19−47/6.27−58/7−8/10.1ff./14−17), the seven signs/miracles in chapters 1−12 (2.1−11/4.46−54/5.1−15/6.1−15/6.16−21/9.1−7/11.1−44), and the seven ἐγὼ εἰμί sayings with predicative nominatives (6.35/8.12/10.7/10.11/11.25/14.6/15.1). Some examples of threes are: the three passovers (2.13/6.4/13.1), Pilate's threefold protestation of Jesus' innocence (18.38/19.4/19.6), and the three equal sections of the passion narrative (18.1−27/18.28−19.16a/19.16b−42).

Narration and dialogue

John often has a narrative in the context of discourse material which deepens the reader's interpretation of details in the narrative sequences. So, for example, the lengthy discourse on the Bread of

Life in 6.27−58 follows almost immediately the multiplication of the loaves in 6.1−15. This relationship between the narration and dialogue is a feature of the gospel as a whole, though the exact nature of the relationship between the two is used with variety.

Themes

John has themes or unifying concepts which unite the different parts of his narrative. Brown has done a thorough study of most of these in appendix I of the first volume of his Anchor Bible Commentary. Principal amongst the Johannine themes identified by Brown are: love, truth, sight, glory, commands, life, the world, remaining, believing, knowing, light, darkness, hour, signs and works (pp. 497−518).

Narrative progression

John has a pattern of developing conflict and tension. The conflict derives from the hostility of the Jews to Jesus. The tension arises through the attempts made upon Jesus' life by the Jews. Until chapter 5, there is really no significant conflict between Jesus and the Jews. After the healing at Bethesda, however, things change dramatically. The first mention of the Jews' desire to kill Jesus occurs in John 5.18. Jesus, however, escapes every time the Jews make an attempt on his life (7.30/8.20/8.59/10.31/10.39/11.53/11.57/12.10) until his appointed hour arrives. This growing conflict, along with the escape stories in the fourth gospel, gives unity, dramatic tension and pace to the story.

Irony and dualism

John often employs irony in his gospel. He frequently presents characters saying and doing something which they do not fully understand, but which the reader (from his enlightened vantage-point) fully grasps. This ties in with the device of dualism. Particularly useful to the Johannine use of irony is the dualism between misunderstanding and understanding, and between darkness and light.

Double entendre

'A literary device used by the author of the fourth gospel follows a dual pattern. The author uses words with two meanings both of which may be applicable' (Wead, 1970, p. 30). The classic example of double entendre is the use of the verb ὑψόω. The lifting up of the Son of Man is mentioned explicitly at 3.14/8.28 and 12.32−4. The phrase at one level denotes the physical elevation of Jesus upon the cross. At a deeper level it connotes the spiritual exaltation of Jesus to the glory of his Father.

Symbolism

Symbols are connecting links between two levels of meaning in a story. For example, the fourth evangelist throughout the gospel connects concrete images with abstract meanings. As we shall see in part II, the evangelist uses concrete images in his passion narrative (the innocence of Jesus, the day of Preparation, the hyssop branch, the immediate effusion of blood and water, and the fact that Jesus' bones were not broken) to establish an abstract level of meaning: that the death of Jesus is the atoning sacrifice of the supreme passover lamb.

The trial motif

'The whole gospel develops a courtroom scene in which the Son of God, who has come to earth, is on trial for his Sonship. Thus, as we might expect, John's vocabulary is full of legal terminology. In particular, the words krisis/krinein and marturia/marturein play a prominent role as the courtroom drama unfolds' (Pfitzner, 1976, p. 2). This forensic language is clearly used as a unifying, structuring device in the first half of the gospel. The background for this literary device lies in the trial speeches of Deutero Isaiah, where Yahweh is also shown defending who he is (ἐγὼ εἰμί in LXX) in a quasi-courtroom setting.

Ring composition (*inclusio*)

'John will often mention a detail or make an allusion at the end of a passage to recall something recorded at the beginning of the passage, so tying the unit together. Three examples are: the references to the two Cana miracles (2.11 and 4.46,54); the references to the Transjordan (1.28 and 10.40); and the two implied references to the Passover lamb (1.29 and 19.36)' (Newman, 1975, p. 238).

Chiasmus (inverted parallelism)

John sometimes has this sophisticated literary device in his gospel, though a chiasmus is often in the eye of the beholder rather than in the text itself. Raymond Brown gives the following example of a chiasmus in the structure of the passion narrative (1966, vol. II, p. 911):

a. 19.16b−18.   Crucifixion.
b. 19.18−22.   Pilate refuses Jews' request.
c. 19.23−24.   The soldiers divide Jesus' garments.
d. 19.25−27.   Jesus, his mother and the beloved disciple.
c. 19.28−30.   Soldiers offer Jesus wine.
b. 19.31−37.   Pilate grants Jews' request.
a. 19.38−42.   The Burial.

Brown also sees a chiasmus in John 18.28−40 (Vol. II, p. 859), a narrative constructed again of seven scenes alternating between the interior and exterior of the praetorium (18.28−32, 33−8a, 38b−40, 19.1−3, 4−8, 9−11, 12−16a) and focussing on the scourging (19.1−3) as the centre-piece.

Narrator's asides

In John's gospel one often finds explanatory asides from the narrator. These explain names (1.38,42), and symbols (2.21/12.33/18.9), they correct possible misunderstandings (4.2/6.6), they remind the reader of related events (3.24/11.2), and reidentify the characters of the story (7.50/21.20). There are approximately sixty of these asides, and they are further evidence of a uniform literary style.

Narrator's point of view

The same narrator and the same voice speaks throughout the gospel. His voice is always in the third person. He stands outside the action, and has a privileged view and understanding of the words and works of Jesus. As Culpepper has shown, the narrator sees inside Jesus' mind (4.1/5.6/6.6/6.15/6.61/6.64/11.5/11.33/11.38/13.1/13.11/13.21/16.19/18.4/19.28) and he serves as the authoritative interpreter of Jesus' words (2.21/6.6/6.71/7.39/8.27/12.33/13.11/18.32/21.19/21.23) (p. 22). He sees matters from an enlightened, post-resurrection stance (2.22/12.16) which has clearly been influenced by Old Testament Scripture and by the Spirit-Paraclete (14.26).

Suggestion, negative response and positive action

C. H. Giblin (1980) has pointed out that a similar pattern is used by the fourth evangelist in his structuring of a number of episodes. In 2.1−11 (the wedding at Cana), 4.46−54 (the healing of the nobleman's son) and 11.1−44 (the raising of Lazarus), a pattern of what he calls 'suggestion, negative response, and positive action' emerges. A petitioner brings a problem, lack or misfortune to Jesus' attention. Jesus' initial response to the petition appears to be negative, but it is then followed by a positive course of action to remedy the situation. Adele Reinhartz has developed Giblin's insight and argued that this same pattern is present in the gospel narrative as a whole: 'The gospel story itself can be described in terms of positive suggestion on the part or on behalf of those who look to Jesus for salvation, an apparently negative response, in the form of the crucifixion, and a positive action, namely the resurrection and related events' (1989a, p. 70). Thus the sign-stories contain implicitly within them the gospel as a whole.

The elusive Christ

In chapter 4, one of the new insights I shall be offering is the thesis that John's leading theme is the theme of the elusive Christ. Throughout the gospel we find the motif of 'hide-and-seek'. Constantly people seek Jesus. When that seeking takes a negative direction, Jesus is said on a number of occasions to hide from his opponents. He proves elusive, just as the Spirit (3.8) and the Father prove elusive. Like the Scarlet Pimpernel, the Jews seek him here, they seek him there, they seek him everywhere, but it is only at the appointed time when Jesus chooses to be caught that he is found (18.1ff.). This theme of the elusive Christ pervades the entire gospel and accounts for the excitement and suspense of the story.

Style

Eduard Schweizer argued in 1939 that there is a uniformity of style throughout the fourth gospel. He based his conclusions on a list of 33 stylistic features characteristic of John, but uncommon in the rest of the NT. Eugen Ruckstuhl expanded this list to 50 in 1951 but grouped them in three categories: 19 most important features, 12 semi-important features, and 19 less important features. As Schweizer pointed out, these observations suggest that 'the style is essentially a unity throughout. So the unity of the gospel cannot be sought in a "basic document" but only in a compilation at the end of the process of development or in a unitary composition' (p. 108).

To summarize, this sample list of narrative strategies supports the argument for an overall narrative artistry and unity in the gospel, even though the reader must concede that Fortna is right when he says that some of this has been spoilt by a later redaction. For example, there are repetitions in the discourses, and there are occasions where the material seems to fit very uneasily into its context; there are the occasional aporias. All these disruptions to the narrative flow mean that the unity of John's narrative style may not be quite as polished as Schweizer and Ruckstuhl maintained. However, the argument of this chapter is that a number of narrative strategies are used consistently enough throughout the gospel to suggest that we can speak of an overall unity to the story. Furthermore, these narrative strategies are consistently employed for the same purpose: Christological persuasion. If John raises and develops a theme, it is because it says something about Jesus. If John uses double entendre, dualism, irony or symbolism, it is again to direct the reader to a significance about Jesus of Nazareth that he wants the enlightened reader to perceive. Quite clearly, the author is writing narrative Christology, and it is his Christology which unites the concepts, images and episodes of the gospel into a coherent whole. John may contain moments where the narrative appears flawed, but the overall picture is one of a gospel which has been artistically conceived so that its readers might have a true faith in Jesus of Nazareth.

The practical criticism of the fourth gospel

How, then, do we analyse the gospel of John as narrative Christology? In this book, the procedure begins with something called practical criticism, and not, as traditionally, with source criticism. This is because the final form of the text (once the correct manuscript readings have been established) 'remains determinate and stable under wide terminological, even conceptual variations' (Sternberg, 1985, p. 15). By 'practical' I mean 'realistic' in this context. Already in the first section I have drawn attention to the anachronistic tendency of novelizing the gospels, a tendency which Alter describes as 'the pitfall of gratuitously modernizing the ancient through the subtle pressure of interpretative ingenuity' (1981, p. 131). I choose instead to assess NT narrative against its natural background, which is primarily OT narrative, and secondarily those Greek narrative forms whose presence can be clearly felt. By 'criticism' I mean something more than just scientific exegesis. Robert Fowler distinguishes between reading and criticizing in reader-response theory (1986, pp. 1–2). For Fowler, reading involves an openness to the story, whilst criticism requires detachment. The former requires participation, the latter distance. In my use of the word criticism I want to include both poles of this reading/criticism continuum. Practical criticism begins with a reading of the narrative as it is. It begins with an imaginative openness to the text's narrative world. It then proceeds to a detailed analysis of the narrative dynamics which elicit the responses we experience.

Practical criticism of NT narrative aims to uncover the basic ingredients of its stories and the ways in which they serve the rhetorical purpose of persuading an audience about the significance of Jesus. What are these basic ingredients? In part II, I shall be analysing John's passion narrative by looking at the following strategies, most of which Culpepper describes in his *Anatomy*: summaries, characters, plot, structure, implicit commentary, narrator, point of view, echo effects, and so on. I shall be interested in the way in which these strategies are used Christologically (i.e. to achieve the aim expressed by the narrator in 20.31).

Narrative summaries

Practical criticism of Johannine narrative begins with the exercise of discovering and redescribing the story under discussion. When I expose the Johannine passion account to the narrative-critical method in part II, I shall call these redescriptions narrative summaries. Such summaries are not arbitrary acts of renaming. They are carefully modulated evocations of the events and setting whose purpose is to enable the reader to recognize the significant items of the narrative under discussion. In the case of the setting of each narrative, we shall want to discern the narrative space depicted in the story, whether it is geographical, topographical or architectural. For instance, in the trial narrative (John 18.28–19.16a), we need to recognize the two-stage setting inside and outside the praetorium if we are properly to appreciate the dramatic quality of the narrative. In the case of events (actions or happenings which can be described by a verb), these can be identified at a number of different levels. There are physical events, speech events and mental events in narratives. A physical event is what Chatman calls a 'process statement' (1978, p. 19), such as 'at daybreak, they took Jesus from Caiaphas to the praetorium' (John 18.28). A speech event is simply a statement made in direct speech, such as Pilate's, 'What accusation are you bringing against this man?' (John 18.29). A mental event is the description of a thought, feeling, perception or sensation, such as the statement, 'when Pilate heard this kind of talk, he was more afraid than ever' (John 19.8). Out of all these, only the 'kernel' events (Chatman, 1978, p. 19) (i.e. the ones which cannot be deleted without destroying the narrative) will be named in my summaries.

Characterization

Another major object of investigation in our practical criticism of Johannine narrative is the characters in the story and how they are depicted. In recent narrative criticism of the NT it has been customary to use Forster's classic distinction between flat (or one-dimensional) and round (or developed) characters as the yardstick for evaluating gospel characterization. Culpepper believes that the implications of this observation for the study of the gospels is powerful (1983, pp. 102–3). However, even though the value of Forster's study cannot be ignored, its precise application to gospel narratives is much more questionable than Culpepper, Kingsbury and others appear to recognize. There are two things in particular which make Forster's terminology impractical. First, his criteria are aspects of the novel and not aspects of first-century narrative. Characters in the gospels need to be analysed with reference to history, and not according to the laws of fiction. Secondly, it needs to be recognized in any case that very few narrative theorists use Forster's terminology without criticism. Rimmon-Kenan has argued that Forster draws too stark a dichotomy between flat and round characters (1983, pp. 40–1). Forster's categories would consequently fail to explain the vitality and depth in John's minor characters such as Pilate. Joseph Ewen proposes instead a system of classification in which characters are seen as points along a continuum (Rimmon-Kenan, 1983, p. 41). I would argue that Rimmon-Kenan and Ewen, because they are Hebrew narrative theorists, are better guides than Forster for interpreting so markedly Jewish a gospel.

A more useful model for evaluating gospel characters is as follows: first of all one should aim to evaluate what 'kind' of characterization a figure in the gospel exemplifies. Daiches (1968, p. 351) argues that there are three ways of creating a character, and even though this probably represents an over-simplification, his model is a helpful starting-point. One can provide a 'complete initial portrait' as the character enters the narrative world, 'followed by events which confirm the portrait'. Or one can introduce a character as 'a shadowy and indeterminate creature' who only becomes a living, definable personality after responding to various events — 'the emergence of the complete character from the action'. Or finally, one can have 'the character changing or developing', so that while the initial portrait is valid with reference to the situation presented at the beginning, it ceases to be valid by the time we reach the conclusion. Characterization in John tends to be of the second type: 'the emergence of the complete character from the action'.

Secondly, one should aim to assess the nature of the characters depicted. To this end, Robert Alter has shown that there is, in biblical narrative, a 'scale of means, in ascending order of explicitness and certainty, for conveying information about the motives, the attitudes, the moral nature of characters' (p. 116). At the lowest end of the scale, we infer character from actions or appearances. This is particularly true of Johannine characterization. At the middle of the scale, we weigh different claims that arise from a character's actual words. This will prove to be crucial when we look at John's characterization of Pilate. Higher up the scale, we have the report of inward speech, where we enter relative certainty — of which there are some examples in John's characterization of Jesus. At the top, we have the narrator's explicit statement of what the character feels, intends and desires, and here we move into the realm of certainty. In any discussion of gospel characters we must bear in mind Alter's insistence that biblical narrative displays an artful reticence where modern fiction gives us psychological precision. Above all, it needs to be stressed that Johannine characterization is inseparable from Christology. Throughout the fourth gospel, and particularly in the passion narrative, characters act as foils: that is to say, they speak and behave in such a way that our understanding of who Jesus really is is enhanced. Characters are therefore not generally introduced and developed for their own sakes as they are in the modern novel.

Plot and structure

A useful discussion of plot in gospel studies can be found in Frank Matera's 'The Plot of Matthew's Gospel'. Matera points out that an author creates a plot when he or she arranges incidents into a coherent narrative whole with a beginning, a middle and an end. Plot therefore has to do with time and causality, 'because actions occurring after the beginning result as the natural consequence of what has preceded, and the end is the inevitable or natural result of what has taken place' (1987, p. 235). Paul Ricoeur talks of 'emplotment' as a configurational act which creates a meaningful 'ensemble of interrelationships' (1984, p. ix), a synthesis of disparate material into a beginning, a middle and an end. He compares it with metaphor. In a metaphor, heterogeneous facts of life are brought together into an unlikely and surprising accord. Thus (to take an example of our own), when Ted Hughes describes a thistle as 'a grasped fistful of splintered weapons', he achieves a surprising unity between a fist, splinters, weapons and thistles (note also the approximate unity of sound between thistle and fistful). Ricoeur argues that plots do this work of synthesis as well, for they bring together goals, causes and chance into the temporal unity of a whole and complete action.

Plot, like characterization, is used Christologically in John. This is especially true in the passion narrative, where the evangelist consciously synchronizes the death of Jesus with the slaughter of the passover lambs in the temple. Plot here is employed in order indirectly to suggest the Christological idea that Jesus is the true paschal lamb. John therefore uses narrative chronology to highlight narrative Christology.

What, then, is structure in narrative theory? It is important that we are clear about the meaning of 'structure', because narratologists seem to have their own definitions of the term. The major difference between plot and structure is this: whilst plot is the organizing principle which gives order and meaning to separate events, structure is the architectural end-product of this arrangement of parts into a whole. For example, the fourth evangelist organizes episodes in his gospel so that the death of Jesus coincides with the slaughter of the passover lambs in the temple. This process is called emplotment since the evangelist has yoked two different events into one poignant and complete temporal unity. However, this coincidence of events is merely one aspect of a larger body of material which has been given a final shape by the evangelist. As I shall point out in part II, the evangelist has imposed a particular structure on his passion account. It is made up of three equal sections in turn comprising groups of either three or seven episodes. Such a structure is an architectural unity which is clearly visible. Structure is therefore the end-product of emplotment, and again it is used often for Christological purposes. A good example of this would be the section from 18.15 to 18.27. Here Jesus' informal interrogation before Annas, in which Jesus appeals to his disciples as witnesses, is framed by two episodes in which Peter proves his total unreliability as a witness to Jesus.

Implicit commentary

One cannot speak of the emplotment and structure of a narrative without speaking of its implicit commentary, since it is often by recurrent themes, symbols and irony that John's Christology is indirectly communicated. Themes are the basic ideas of narratives, and their function is to give internal shape and completeness to a sequence of episodes. In other words, themes are organizing narrative concepts. In John 18.1–27, for example, the organizing concept seems to be the theme of Jesus as the Good Shepherd who lays down his life for the sheep. In John 18.28–19.16a, the organizing concept seems to be the idea that Jesus is King. In John 19.16b–42, these two themes are repeated but with the additional unifying idea of Jesus-as-paschal lamb. See again how Christology and the narrative form are inextricably linked in this thematic triptych.

Symbols are also connective conceptual devices. As many theorists have shown, the word symbol derives etymologically from a Greek verb (συμβάλλειν) meaning 'to put together'. Symbols are connecting links between two spheres, the sphere of the symbol itself (surface reality) and the sphere which the symbol represents (deep reality). For example, in John 19.23, the seamless tunic is arguably a symbol of the unity of the church. In John 19.34, the water and the blood which flow from the pierced wound inflicted by the guard's spear is arguably a symbol of the life which Jesus, in death, paradoxically gives to the world.

Irony is a complex oppositional structure in which words or happenings can be interpreted at two different levels, a superficial level and a deep level. As Paul Duke has shown, irony is used repeatedly in the fourth gospel to lead the reader into that dimension of truth about Jesus which most of the characters within the narrative world seem to miss. The narrator guides the implied reader into responding with understanding and even faith where certainly the Jews misunderstand and disbelieve. As Duke has said, 'so crucial is this irony to the Johannine message that it may fairly be said, if we do not grasp the irony we do not grasp the Gospel' (1985, p. 156). Examples of irony abound in the Johannine passion narrative. One of the most poignant is the moment when Peter chooses to warm himself beside the charcoal fire outside Annas' house, whilst Jesus, the Light of the World, is being interrogated on the inside (John 18.15–27). The irony consists of the fact that the reader can see that Jesus should be the true source of Peter's warmth and light, whilst Peter chooses to depend on the charcoal fire and to side himself with the servants and soldiers. Again narrative mode and Christological claim are inseparable.

Narrator and point of view

Paul Duke, like Alan Culpepper and David Wead before him, speaks of the narrator of John 'winking' at the reader (1985, p. 156). Jeff Staley speaks of the narrator *victimizing* the reader (1988, pp. 95ff.). What this implies is that Johannine narrative is a quasi-secretive act of communication between narrator and reader, and that the narrator figure is important in any appreciation of narrative. In John's gospel we are aware of being told a story – we are aware of a narrating voice. The source of this transmission is the narrator, and the narrator is the voice of the author within the universe which the gospel depicts. Though it may be too strong to say that he is omniscient (he is, after all, not a divine figure), the narrator is a character who is both transcendent and immanent to the narrative world. Within that world, it is the narrator who provides temporal and spatial coordinates, who introduces characters, who indicates who is speaking, who interprets words and works, who describes, explains, addresses, announces, and so on. He makes no effort to hide his voice. Everywhere the narrator works obviously – though not clumsily – to coax the reader round to the point of view or ideological stance which he embraces. That point of view is the enlightened post-resurrectional understanding of Jesus as the Messiah, the Son of God, and it is this understanding which undergirds the narrator's rhetorical strategy expressed in John 20.31. Any true analysis of Johannine narrative must therefore include narrator and point of view in its programme, and must evaluate the extent to which the aim of 20.31 is achieved (i.e. the persuasiveness of the gospel's narrative Christology).

Narrative echo effects

Another aspect of Johannine narrative which is worthy of mention is the technique of repetition. Robert Alter describes biblical narrative as 'an elaborately integrated system of repetitions, some dependent on the actual recurrence of phonemes, words or short phrases, others linked instead to the actions, images and ideas that are part of the world of the narrative' (1981, p. 95). As Alter explains, this habit of constantly restating material is hard for us to naturalize because we are so accustomed to modes of narration in which elements of repetition are made to seem far less obtrusive. Yet it is an important aspect of biblical narrative discourse and, in particular, of the gospel of John. In his study of Luke—Acts, Robert Tannehill describes such unifying repetitions of images, actions and themes as 'narrative echo effects'. These echo effects are patterns of recurrence in parts of a narrative which require an active reader-response. This reader-response consists of connecting the recurrent images, actions or themes into a whole. When we come to our narrative reading of John 18.1—27, we shall be employing Tannehill's categories in order to show how the evangelist has expressed his story in such a way that echo effects are set up with the Good Shepherd discourse in John 10.

Concluding remarks

I have, in this last section, provided an outline of the first synchronic orientation of narrative criticism. This first synchronic approach is practical criticism. There are no binding rules about how to approach a gospel narrative in this perspective, but at least part of my aim in part II will be to respond to the final form of John 18—19 as a story, and to seek to identify those narrative dynamics which evoke the reader-responses we experience. This will inevitably lead to a discussion of content (summaries), characterization, plot and structure, and additionally to a consideration (where relevant) of other items in John's narrative repertoire, such as implicit commentary and narrative echo effects. The advantage of such a narrative appreciation is that it reclaims the final form of the text as a narrative unity, it helps us to see how John's portrait of Jesus is communicated to the reader, and it enables us to examine the significance and persuasiveness of John's narrative Christology.

2

GENRE CRITICISM OF JOHN'S NARRATIVE

The question of genre

At the end of the last chapter, our attention turned to the second synchronic orientation of narrative criticism, that of genre criticism. There I intimated how I considered the description 'narrative Christology' to be an appropriate term for the gospel genre. In giving this impression, I may have implied that attempts by genre critics to identify comparisons between the gospels and known genres, such as Graeco-Roman or Jewish biographies, should now cease. Was I really suggesting that the description 'narrative Christology' means no further work is needed in the area of genre criticism? Certainly not. Even though the gospels as a whole do not fit neatly into the categories of known genres, they are not brand new literary creations. The gospels, like all literary texts, have affinities and literary relationships with other works of literature. They are not isolated phenomena in the streams of literary tradition running through the cultures of the four evangelists. Mark and John, who seem to me to resemble each other more closely than any other combination of the gospels, certainly have analogies with Graeco-Roman literature. Bultmann was therefore overstating the case when he posed himself the question, 'what analogies can be suggested between the gospels and other literature?' and responded with the comment, 'There are none in the Greek tradition!' (1921, p. 227). Similarly, he was certainly guilty of exaggeration when he argued that the gospel type is 'an original creation of Christianity' (p. 228).

As far as John's gospel is concerned, the question of genre is important if we are to appreciate the gospel as narrative Christology. I take it as axiomatic that the fourth evangelist received a number of disparate items of both oral and written traditions: a Galilean miracles source, a Samaritan tradition, a dialogue source, a collection of Jesus sayings, and a primitive ur-gospel deriving from the orally communicated reminiscences of the beloved disciple, a Judaean follower of Jesus. As I shall argue in chapter 4, I also regard it as probable that the evangelist knew and presupposed some of the Marcan tradition; he may well have known Mark's story of Jesus. Out of these materials, the fourth evangelist constructed a literary whole. He assembled his material into a meaningful structure whose form reflects his theology. In short, John the storyteller created a point of view and a plot which were his own contribution. The overall plot will have been dictated at the most general level by the traditional sequence embraced by the beloved disciple's reminiscences: baptism, calling of disciples, ministry of teaching and of miracles, conflict with the Jewish authorities, arrest, trial, crucifixion and resurrection. But John's contribution did not consist purely in repeating this general outline. He also redescribed Jesus-history using aspects of a particular *mythos* or plot-structure used by storytellers in the literary tradition of his culture. Consequently, John did not construct a narrative plot in isolation from his cultural setting. His story, like all stories, contains a relationship to conventions within his culture. It is the job of genre criticism to identify the story-shape which the evangelist regarded as suitable.

From what has been said in these opening paragraphs, it is clear that genre criticism is important for the reading and criticism of narratives. As E. D. Hirsch has said, 'an interpreter's preliminary generic conception of a text is constitutive of everything that he subsequently understands' (1967, p. 74). Put more simply, as soon as the reader consciously or unconsciously discerns what kind of story he is reading, his expectations are influenced by what he has experienced in other stories of the same type. Of course, today the discerning of story-types is considerably helped by cover titles. For example, a modern best-seller may have the following words printed on the cover: 'the new best-selling romantic novel from the author of …'. The words romantic and novel immediately create a set of anticipations in the reader's mind which governs his subsequent reading experience. As Marcelin Pleynet puts it: 'It is indeed this word (novel, poem) placed on the cover of the book which (by convention) generically produces, programmes, or "originates" our reading. We have here (with the genre "novel", "poem") a *master word* which from the outset reduces complexity, reduces the textual encounter, by making it a function of the type of reading already implicit in the law of this word' (Culler, 1975, p. 136). With texts like the fourth gospel, however, the *master word* is unfortunately missing. The present texts just have ΚΑΤΑ ΙΩΑΝΝΗΝ, and it is difficult to argue that John's use of the word βιβλίον as a description of his work in

20.30 is referring to a genre of writing. It merely reflects John's awareness that he was composing a work of literature. As far as the genre is concerned, we shall need to look at John's plot-structure (the intrinsic approach in genre criticism) and then see if we can find any family resemblances between that and other literary works (the extrinsic approach).

Genre criticism is important both for our interpretation of the author's contribution and for our own reading experience and responsible interpretation. At the level of the author, the following question has to be asked in narrative criticism: what plot genre has most influenced John's storytelling? At the level of the reader: what expectations does our knowledge of generic dynamics within the fourth gospel create? How are those expectations met/frustrated? It is the argument of this chapter that the approach to genre provided by structuralist literary theory has a considerable amount to offer in our genre analysis of John's story of Jesus. Dan Via has paved the way for such an approach to the gospels in his *Kerygma and Comedy in the New Testament* (1975), which establishes a dialectical theory of genre criticism in the context of Mark's gospel. For Via, establishing the genre of a story consists of the following processes: first, the reader begins with a narrative that is clearly a unit. Then the reader seeks gradually to establish intelligible relations between this text and other texts, noting common elements or family resemblances. From these related texts, the genre critic constructs an infrastructure of relatively fixed sequences which characterize the genre. Finally, the reader looks to other texts which both participate in and depart from it. So the dialectical process goes on. As Via puts it, 'structural analysis is concerned about the relationship of a text to a (relative) superstructure or genre' (p. 12). The writer (for example, John) may well be unconscious of the superstructure or genre he is drawing upon. 'Gattungen or genres are inherent structures of the human mind' (p. 25) which must be conceptually articulated by analysis. This is where the structuralist version of genre analysis can prove so useful.

It needs to be admitted, however, that structuralism has not been a widely adopted ideology in biblical criticism in Great Britain. It is because of this conservative neglect of the rather radical, innovative approach which structuralism offers that we must spend some time at the beginning of this chapter engaged in a description and evaluation of structuralist literary theory and criticism. General structural analysis of narrative derives ultimately from Ferdinand de Saussure's pioneering work in the area of linguistics at the turn of this century.

The countless popular summaries of both Saussure and the development of structuralism all agree that Saussurian linguistics was pioneering because it questioned the presuppositions behind previous linguistic philosophies. The general philosophical perspective which Saussure inherited was one in which the world was seen to consist of independently existing objects which are both clearly visible and easily classifiable. Saussure saw, however, (a) that it is impossible to perceive individual entities with complete objectivity, (b) that there is a relationship and not a detachment between the observer and the observed, and (c) that the world is made up of relationships rather than things. As Terence Hawkes has pointed out, this emphasis on relationships represents the great change in perception at the beginning of the century and forms the basis of all structuralist thinking. The new perception recognized that 'the full significance of any entity or experience cannot be perceived unless and until it is integrated into the *structure* of which it forms a part' (1977, p. 18). What is now of interest is the permanent structures into which all things fit.

Fredric Jameson has rightly described structuralism as 'an explicit search for the permanent structures of the mind itself, the organisational categories and forms through which the mind is able to experience the world' (1972, p. 109). This emphasis upon permanent structures is first evident in Saussure's complex linguistic theory. His *Course in General Linguistics* (first edition, 1915) presents the argument that language should be studied not only in terms of its individual parts, and not only diachronically, but also in terms of the relationship between those parts, and synchronically. In short, he proposed that a language should be studied as a unified, self-sufficient system, as we experience it now. Previous linguistic philosophies had been too preoccupied with the historical, evolutionary development of language (the diachronic emphasis). Saussure, on the other hand, insisted that language is a system which is complete at every moment, no matter what developments take place. This system he called *langue*, a concept which he distinguished from *parole*. *Langue* signifies the abstract set of rules, the permanent structures, the grammar of language. *Parole* is the individual, concrete speech-utterance which we make in obedience to that grammar. The former is a closed field of interrelationships which can be perceived synchronically. The latter is an individual manifestation of that code or structure. *Langue* is to *parole* what the rules of chess are to an individual move (Hawkes, 1977, p. 20).

Structuralism began with Saussure's attempt to discover and describe the permanent, deep structures of language. Subsequent structuralist narratologists (narrative theorists) took Saussure's theory of language and applied it to narratives. They basically went in three directions. First of all, there was what I shall call the *functional* approach. The Russian folklorist Vladimir Propp first used the functional approach to narrative. In his *Morphology of the Folktale* (first edition, 1928), he endeavoured to establish a scientific explanation of the way Russian fairy-tales are composed. For Propp, the highest goal of any science is to discover laws, and this was precisely his aim in the more limited area of the fairy-tale genre. The very word morphology connoted this, since it referred to a branch of the natural sciences whose abiding aim had been to provide a holistic description of the overarching scheme that embraces all nature. On the basis that 'the realms of nature and of man are not isolated from one another', that 'they share some common laws' (1978, p. 59), Propp tried to find the overarching scheme that embraces all fairy-tales. After close inspection of 100 such tales, Propp began to notice that there were significant constants or 'significant interchangeable variables' (1978, p. 60) in them. Underneath the multiplicity, there seemed to be a unity which could be determined logically. For example, in one story, a king gives an eagle to a hero and the eagle carries the hero away to another kingdom. In another story, a princess gives Ivan a ring from which some men magically appear in order to whisk him away to another place. In both stories, though the characters have different names, the same action is performed — namely, a gift causing a transfer (1978, p. 69).

What is the permanent structure behind the narrative genre known as the Russian fairy-tale? Propp reckoned that he had found a deep structure or grammar of possible relationships which all fairy-tales obey. This structure was composed of a limited number of possible actions which the characters of the stories perform (for example, the giving of a gift effecting a transfer of the protagonist). These actions Propp called 'functions', and their principal characteristic was simply that they did not change. Whilst the names of the characters in the above illustration seem variable (a king and a hero/a princess and Ivan), the actual function is essentially the same. As Claude Brémond has put it, 'the invariant is the function that a particular event, by its very happening, fulfills in the course of the narrative. The variable is the concrete manifestation chosen for the production and circumstances of this event. What counts therefore is to know what a character does and what function it fulfills' (1978, p. 9). Propp chose to determine each narrative function through a specific comparative analysis of the material. He discerned each through a painstaking process of 'comparison, of correlation, of abstraction of a logical structure from thousands of cases' (p. 70). His method was neither arbitrary nor subjective, but meticulously empiricist, and the permanent or 'monotypical' structure which he inferred from his research turned out to be a kind of Russian alphabet of thirty-one possible functions which involved seven types of characters.

If the first direction of structuralist narratology was the *functional* approach, the second was the *binary* approach. The binary approach derives from Claude Lévi-Strauss, who used Saussure's linguistic system in his study of myths (1968). Lévi-Strauss believed that the rules which govern myths and the rules which govern language emerge from identical unconscious structures. For Lévi-Strauss, the unconscious structure behind myth is the tendency to think in oppositions and the tendency to resolve such oppositions — a mental operation analogous to the one described by Saussure, in which the mind grasps meaning through the recognition of differences. This stress on unconscious structures means that Lévi-Strauss's analyses are not characterized by a careful concern for surface stories, however interesting these may be in themselves. Nor do they exhibit any central interest in the characters and their actions in terms of their psychological depth and verisimilitude. Lévi-Strauss is interested in the permanent structure, the *langue*, if you like, behind mythical stories. This *langue* is established through the discovery of recurrent combinations of constant features or 'mythemes' (1969, p. 211). These combinations obey the rules of a kind of transcendental grammar, a universal 'mythologic' which is manifested in the resolution of things existing in binary opposition (p. 230). When reading Lévi-Strauss, one therefore finds a concentrated preoccupation with the degree of mediation between certain universal contrasts, such as Immortal/Mortal, Male/Female, Parent/Child, and so on.

If the first and second directions taken by structuralist narratologists were these functional and binary approaches, the third major direction was the *actantial* approach, associated with A. J. Greimas. Greimas's approach is an ambitious development of Propp's, for whilst Propp confined himself to one particular narrative genre (the Russian folk-tale), Greimas came up with the following model, which he regarded as the permanent structure behind all narratives:

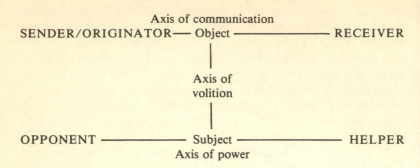

This diagram reveals six different character poles of narrative (subject, object, sender, receiver, helper and opponent) and three functional axes (communication, power and volition). A story is usually begun when a sender tells a receiver to undertake some task. The volitional axis represents this quest; the power axis, the struggle involved in its execution. Thus, a story in which a king sends a prince to find his daughter, and in which the prince is waylaid by bandits before being helped by a magic horse to his prize, would be schematized by Greimas as follows:

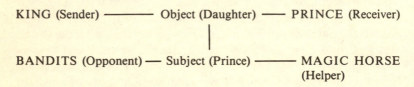

The first experiments in biblical structural exegesis were practised on Genesis, perhaps because it was felt that this, of all the books of the Bible, most closely resembles the genres of fairy-tale and myth. The noted French structuralist Roland Barthes employed a functional and an actantial approach to Genesis. His article entitled, 'The Struggle with the Angel: A Structural Analysis of Genesis 32:22–32' (1971: in Barthes, 1977) was to become one of the most celebrated examples of structuralist literary criticism. In an earlier article, 'An Introduction to the Structural Analysis of Narratives' (1966: in Barthes, 1977), Barthes had proposed both the universality of narrative and the universality of the permanent structures behind narratives. 'The narratives of the world are numberless' (p. 79), he wrote. They can be spoken or written, they can be found in myth, legend, fable, tale, novella, epic, history, tragedy, drama, comedy, and so on. There appears to be an 'almost infinite diversity of forms' (p. 79). 'Nowhere is nor has there been a people without narrative. All classes, all human groups, have their narratives'; 'narrative is international, transhistorical, transcultural; it is simply there, like life itself' (p. 79). Furthermore, all narratives obey a fundamental narrative grammar. Just as sentences obey a system of rules, so do narratives, because 'a narrative is a long sentence' (p. 84). Behind and within the great variety of narratives in the world, there is 'an atemporal logic lying behind the temporality of narrative' (p. 98).

In his article 'The Struggle with the Angel', Barthes attempts to test the implications of this grammatical approach to narrative. He begins with a sequential analysis of the narrative itself. In this part of his article he simply names the indices of the narrative, and to these he gives the metalinguistic terms 'The Crossing', 'The Struggle' and 'The Namings' (p. 128). In the second part of his article, Barthes subjects the narrative to the kinds of approach established by Propp and Greimas. The story itself is about Jacob's struggle with a man or an angel who turns out, at the moment of the denouement, to be God. Barthes begins by defining the actants (characters) in the tale in terms of their functions. As far as Barthes is concerned, they are stock items from the world of folk-tale plots. Jacob is the hero who is on a quest, one of the commonest of all folk-tale plots. God stands behind the events of the story as the sender or originator of this quest. The man with whom Jacob wrestles is his opponent, since he is the one who waylays the hero and tries to prevent him from accomplishing his mission.

Barthes argues that, at the moment of the struggle, a number of narrative developments are possible. The Originator/Sender (God) could step in and help the hero defeat his Opponent. A magical Helper could appear to whisk Jacob away. But what actually occurs is in effect quite peculiar and unexpected. At the moment of discovery, Jacob recognizes that his Opponent is none other than God himself! In narratological terms, the Receiver realizes that the Sender and the Opponent and the Helper are all one and the same! It is God who sends Jacob down the axis of volition, and it is God who meets Jacob on the axis of power. In Greimas's diagrammatical terms, the story looks like this:

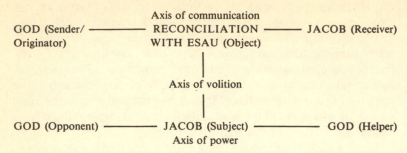

The diagram accentuates the surprise factor here. As Barthes suggests, 'that the sender be the opponent is very rare' (p. 138); it is bound to surprise. In fact, there is only one kind of narrative which can present this paradoxical form: 'narratives relating an act of blackmail' (p. 138), and it is this that makes the reader recognize how audacious the tale is, both structurally and theologically. Structurally, it seems to break a rule of folk-tale grammar. Theologically, it seems to imply the kind of radical monotheism which will not permit the existence of an opposing spiritual power. Barthes's structural analysis reveals how and why Genesis 32:22−32 is a tale of the unexpected.

Whilst Roland Barthes was the first to use the functional and actantial approaches in biblical studies, Edmund Leach was one of the first to apply the binary approach to biblical narrative. In his article 'Genesis as Myth' (1969), Leach used Lévi-Strauss's structural analysis of myth in order to highlight the permanent mythical structures behind Genesis. Leach agreed with Lévi-Strauss that 'myth is constantly setting up opposing categories' (p. 8). Myth has a binary structure; it 'first discriminates between gods and men, and then becomes preoccupied with the relations and intermediaries which link men and gods together' (p. 10). 'In every myth system', Leach continues, 'we will find a persistent sequence of binary discrimination as between human/superhuman, mortal/immortal, male/female, legitimate/illegitimate, good/bad ... followed by a "mediation" of the paired categories thus distinguished' (p. 11). Right the way through Genesis, Leach claims that we are presented with common opposites: Heaven/Earth, Light/Darkness, Man/Garden, Tree of Life/Tree of Death, Unity (Eden)/Duality (outside Eden), Gardener (Cain)/Herdsman (Abel), and so on. As Leach concludes, 'every myth is one of a complex', and 'any pattern which occurs in one myth will recur, in the same or other variations, in other parts of the complex' (p. 22). There is a structure which is common to all variations, and that structure lies behind and within Genesis. Genesis, like all other myths, is an observable phenomenon expressive of unobservable realities – namely, the permanent structures of myth.

I cannot claim to have been exhaustive either in my account of structuralism or in my summaries of the work of Propp, Greimas, Lévi-Strauss, Barthes and Leach. A brief evaluation of the methodological soundness and practical usefulness of the structural analysis of narrative will follow in the next section, when I discuss its use in recent NT studies. As a conclusion to this section, I want to emphasize some important principles: (1) that structuralism in general and structural exegesis in particular are both concerned with the discovery and description of transindividual, permanent structures; (2) that the permanent structure according to Lévi-Strauss is revealed in the mediation of binary opposites (binary approach); (3) that the permanent narrative structure according to Propp and Greimas is a grammar of limited actants and functions (functional and actantial approaches); (4) that structural analysis of narrative will most commonly follow either Lévi-Strauss's concentration upon deep mental structures, or Propp's and Greimas's concentration upon deep plot structures; (5) that structural exegesis alone can elicit the kinds of insights about which Barthes and Leach have written; (6) that structural approaches to biblical narrative are fundamental to genre criticism because they identify the story-structures which the evangelists had in mind as they composed their gospels; (7) finally, that it is the *functional* approach to narrative which has most to offer the NT narrative critic who wants to establish the genre of the gospel stories.

Structuralist genre criticism and the gospels

I want in this section to qualify the judgement I made in the last section that it is the *functional* approach to narrative which has most to offer the NT genre critic. Let us look at two case-studies, the first resembling the approach of Lévi-Strauss and Leach (the binary approach), and the second resembling that of Propp (the functional approach). It should become clear from these two studies that the functional approach to narrative is better suited to the establishing of genres. Much of the structural exegesis which has so far been attempted in NT studies has focussed on the gospel of Mark. Our first case-study supports this general statement. Elizabeth Malbon's *Narrative Space and Mythic Meaning in Mark* (1986) is a structural exegesis of the second gospel based on Lévi-Strauss's principles.

Malbon begins by outlining the nature of her investigation. 'The present study is marked by a concern for the Markan Gospel as a literary and theological whole, and for its narrative space as a system of relationships' (p. 2). The methodology she uses is 'an adaptation of the methodology of the French structural anthropologist Claude Lévi-Strauss for analyzing myth' (p. 2). Lévi-Straussian analysis understands myth as a narrative which operates to mediate irreconcilable differences. Though Mark 'is not, strictly speaking, a myth', Malbon argues that 'a mythic structure may also be operative in a text like Mark' (p. 2). As she continues, 'the unique contribution the present study seeks to make is twofold: to broaden understanding of Markan narrative space by considering *all spatial references* and to deepen understanding of Markan space by considering the *system of interrelations* of these references' (p. 13).

Malbon proposes that there are three types of relations that constitute the Marcan spatial order: 'geopolitical (named regions, cities, towns), topographical (physical features of the earth, such as the sea, wilderness, mountains), and architectural (human-made structures, such as houses, synagogues, the Temple' (p. 8). The first step in her analysis consists of a detailed description of all the narrative facts which relate to space, and of isolating their relations. This leads her to compose elaborate tables listing references to place names like Galilee and Judaea, references to land and sea, heaven and earth, wilderness and towns, and finally references to tombs and buildings, houses and palaces, synagogues and temple, interior and exterior. Her second step is to analyse the sequence in which these references occur, so that we see, for example, that Galilee is the dominant geopolitical location in the opening portion of Mark, whilst Jerusalem is the stage for the closing third. The third step involves an investigation into the latent structure by which all these relations are organized. That latent, mental structure is the mythic process of opposition and mediation. We have sea opposed to land, foreign land opposed to Jewish homeland, Judaea opposed to Galilee, and so on. As far as mythic meaning is concerned, these correspond to the universal contrast of chaos/order or unfamiliar/familiar in myths. What is interesting in Mark is the degree to which these binary oppositions are mediated.

A good example of the fruits of Malbon's method can be seen if we look at one aspect of her structural exegesis of *architectural* space (pp. 106f.). She finds twelve categories in this architectural suborder: synagogue, house, door, roof, tomb, temple, buildings, housetop, guest room, courtyard, forecourt, and praetorium. Particularly interesting is the dynamic relating to house and synagogue. Malbon begins by discovering that there are nineteen references to οἰκία, οἶκος and eight references to συναγωγή in Mark. She then discerns that, even though 'the initial architectural mode of the gospel of Mark is "in the synagogue", the fact is that the dominant architectural marker of the Gospel of Mark is *house*' (p. 131). Throughout the gospel, 'Jesus is often reported to be in his home or in a house teaching or healing' (p. 131). For Malbon, there is a contrast between house and synagogue: 'a synagogue, of course, is a religious space, a sacred space; in relation to it a house, a residential space, is profane' (p. 131). The two architectural terms stand in a binary opposition which, in mythical terms, should be understood as an antithesis between sacred and profane. The mediation between house and synagogue is manifest in 'the takeover of the functions of one by the other' (p. 133). From chapter 6 onwards, the house becomes the centre of sacred teaching, replacing the synagogue as it were. As Malbon concludes: 'In terms of the fundamental opposition underlying the architectural schema, the sacred realm is inadequate to contain Jesus' "new teaching" (1.27), and it overflows into the profane realm' (p. 133).

Our second case-study of structural criticism of NT narrative also takes Mark as its text. However, it is structural criticism after the fashion of Propp (functional approach), not Lévi-Strauss and Leach (binary approach). George Nickelsburg's 'Genre and Function of the Markan Passion Narrative' (1980) approaches Mark 15−16 from a holistic perspective. Nickelsburg is not primarily interested in theological motivation, or in literary themes, but in the genre of the passion narrative, in the 'question of generic influences in the formation of the passion narrative' (p. 155). His view is that Mark 15−16 is based on a particular generic model, 'the stories of Persecution and Vindication in Jewish Literature' (p. 155). These stories are to be found in the Joseph narratives in Genesis 37ff., the story of Ahikar, the book of Esther, Daniel 3 and 6, Susanna, and Wisdom of Solomon 2, 4−5. 'All the aforementioned stories are characterised by a common theme: the rescue and vindication of a persecuted innocent person or persons' (p. 156). As Nickelsburg continues, 'this theme is emplotted by means of a limited number of narrative elements or components, most of them describing "actions", a few of them, motivations or emotions' (p. 156). These components perform specific functions in the flow and logic of the narrative. They are named as introduction, provocation, conspiracy, decision, trust, obedience, accusation, trial, condemnation, protest, prayer, assistance, ordeal, reactions, rescue, vindication, exaltation, investiture, acclamation, reactions and punishment.

Having established the basic structure of all stories concerning the rescue and vindication of persecuted innocents, Nickelsburg proceeds to analyse Mark 15–16 as a story of persecution and vindication. As far as Nickelsburg is concerned, there is a formal consistency in the stories he studies, and most of the formal components of the genre are present in the Marcan passion narrative. Though some of the components are more explicit than others (choice, trust and obedience are only suggested), there is clearly provocation in Jesus' cleansing of the temple and the anointing in Bethany, there is conspiracy in the behaviour of the chief priests, scribes and Judas, there are two trials and accusations, there are plenty of reactions (though this label is large enough to cover almost any narrative action), there is assistance (Pilate's attempt to release Jesus), there is condemnation, investiture, acclamation, ordeal, prayer and death (all in Jesus' final hours), there is vindication (in the rending of the temple curtain) and acclamation (the centurion's confession). The investigation reveals that almost all the components of the genre are present in the Marcan passion narrative (p. 162). Indeed, many of these components are doubled. Thus, just as Propp had discovered a morphology of Russian fairytales, Nickelsburg discovers a morphology of Jewish persecution/vindication stories. The resemblances between the methods of Nickelsburg and Propp are noticeable.

What are the limitations and strengths in these structural approaches to NT narratives? On the positive side, we may point to the usefulness of the functional approach for genre criticism of NT narratives. I have suggested throughout this chapter that the functional approach of Propp is better suited to genre criticism than the binary approach of Lévi-Strauss. This ought to have become clear from the two case-studies just examined. Malbon's book is a penetrating study of the oppositions in Mark's gospel. Using Lévi-Strauss's terminology, she looks at all the major contrasts in the gospel and argues that this is an example of mythical thinking by Mark. Whilst mention of myth may seem to imply some argument concerning the narrative genre in Mark on Malbon's part, she nowhere seeks to argue that Mark's gospel is in fact a myth. On the other hand, Nickelsburg's functional approach is quite evidently one that can be used successfully by the genre critic. His approach is to identify the basic plot functions and story shape of the Marcan passion narrative and then relate it to stories with a similar deep structure. In chapter 6, when I come to look at the genre of John's passion story, my approach will resemble Nickelsburg's more than Malbon's. It will be a functional rather than a binary approach.

As far as the weaknesses of structuralist narrative criticism are concerned, the following points need to be made:

(1) Structural exegesis of the NT has a very ambiguous and sometimes even antagonistic attitude towards historical criticism. Propp is adamant that one cannot separate structural from historical research, 'nor can one place them in opposition'. For him, 'the comparative study of plots opens up broad historical perspectives', since one is interested in 'the historical interconnections between the plots' (1978, p. 66). However, in spite of Propp's insistence, structural exegesis of biblical narratives has tended to ignore the historical or diachronic aspect of these texts. In its emphasis upon the final form, it suppresses all consideration of pre-textual transmission. In its post-structuralist suspicions concerning the relationship between signifier and signified, it has neglected the referential dimension of historical narratives. In its heavy preoccupation with the deep structures of the mind, it has tended not to ask whether structure or narrativity is a characteristic of temporality, of experience, of history. Alfred Johnson may well be right when he claims that 'structuralism does not attack history per se but a particular kind of history – the Hegelian evolutionary scheme of history which makes Western culture the norm against which other cultures are to be judged' (1979, p. 4) – but the fact is that in practice, the emphasis upon synchrony nearly always suppresses diachrony. Leach treats Genesis as myth; Barthes treats Genesis 32:22–32 as a fairy-tale. Malbon claims that she has no antipathy towards historical criticism and yet omits historical considerations. Only Nickelsburg wants to ask questions about the sources behind Mark 15–16.

(2) There is an arbitrariness and subjectivity about some structural classifications. Part of the structural exegete's procedure involves the identification and naming of binary oppositions and/or basic genre components. Yet it is precisely in this very act of labelling that structural exegesis sometimes falls apart. For example, when Edmund Leach proposes that Orpheus rescues Eurydice from Hades by means of music, but loses her because of silence, it seems that the desire for a binary opposition has suppressed the obvious explanation. Orpheus quite plainly loses Eurydice because he turns round (Ruthven, 1976, p. 41). Similarly, it is very easy to be subjective when moving

from the narrative under scrutiny to the proposed generic structure of which it forms a part. Consider the two following definitions, one of epic plots, the other of romance plots: (a) 'These (epic) plots are episodic, and present the deeds (or *gestes*) of a hero in some chronological sequence, possibly beginning with his birth, probably ending with his death' (Scholes and Kellog, 1968, p. 278). (b) A romance presents a successful quest with three main stages: 'the preliminary minor adventures; the crucial struggle, usually some kind of battle in which either the hero or his foe, or both, must die; and the exaltation of the hero' (Culpepper, 1983, p. 83). If one were taking a holistic view of John's plot sequence, one could infer that John was a performance either of the epic or the romance generic paradigms. The process of labelling in structural exegesis therefore requires methodological rigour and integrity. Even in Nickelsburg's article, the event labels are so general that one feels that, like horoscope predictions, they could cover just about any eventuality.

(3) Structural exegetes have not recognized the limitations of the interpretative models which they employ. For example, Greimas's actantial model for the interpretation of all narratives is quite clearly not as versatile as its discoverer wished. Whilst it works very well in the context of smaller and simpler narrative units, such as folk-tales or myths, its usefulness in longer and more complex narratives is highly questionable. For example, when Daniel and Aline Patte try to use it in their structural exegesis of the Marcan passion narrative, they find it impossible to fit the whole of Mark 15–16 on to the one semiotic square. Instead, they are reduced to applying it to much smaller narrative units with the result that their book is really just an almost indecipherable plethora of actantial diagrams (1976). If this is what happens in the context of two chapters of the gospel, it is almost unthinkable what might happen in the context of a long and sophisticated modern novel. Structural exegetes need to remember Corina Galland's remark about Greimas's model, that 'it is difficult or artificial to apply this schema systematically to all texts' (Johnson, 1979, p. 194). Perhaps a more fruitful way forward is suggested by Propp and Nickelsburg. One should seek to penetrate the generic structure of which individual narratives (such as John 18–19) are manifestations, instead of adhering to some improbable notion of one universal narrative grammar.

(4) Terry Eagleton has demonstrated that structural analysis undermines the details of narrative, especially characters. He invents a story about a boy who runs away from home and falls into a pit. The father

comes after him, peers into the pit but cannot see him. At that moment, the sun rises to a point directly overhead and illuminates the pit's depths with its rays, allowing the father to rescue his boy and effect a joyous reconciliation. Eagleton points out that a structural analysis of a story like this is bound to change it into a series of binary oppositions (low versus high, for example). The problem with such a procedure is that one 'could replace father and son, pit and sun, with entirely different elements − mother and daughter, bird and mole − and still have the same story. As long as the structure of relations between the units is preserved, it does not matter which items you select' (1983, p. 95). Structural exegesis of biblical narrative needs to begin with a thorough appreciation of details and characters within the text, and not to obscure their importance by reducing them to abstract items on a quasi-mathematical grid. That is why, in part II, I shall only include a structuralist interpretation of John 18−19 *after* I have exposed the same text to a rigorous narrative analysis in chapter 5.

(5) The structural analysis of narrative at best obscures and at worst obliterates the figure of the author. Roland Barthes's celebrated article 'The Death of the Author' (1968: in Barthes, 1977) typifies this anti-authorial stance within structuralism (p. 142). It needs to be recognized that the whole structural approach to narrative really depends on the notion that it is deep structures and not we ourselves that generate meaning. And yet, is this not after all a form of linguistic total-itarianism? Jean-Marie Domenach writes that this sort of philosophy ends up with the following scenario: 'I don't think, I am thought; I don't speak, I am spoken; I don't deal with something, I am dealt with.' This is unacceptable because 'The system, a thinking that is cold, impersonal, erected at the expense of all subjectivity, individual or collective, negates at last the very possibility of a subject capable of expression and independent action' (Palmer, 1969, p. 216). However, one cannot avoid questions of theological motivation and authorial intentionality (the concerns of redaction criticism) in the narrative criticism of the NT. This does not mean that we shall fall foul of the celebrated intentional fallacy. The intentional fallacy rightly exposed the dangers of judging the merit of a literary work on the basis of its author's definable intention for it. It was never supposed to be an indictment against any discussion of authorial intention. If authorial intention were to be excluded from the pro-gramme of literary and biblical hermeneutics, then we should have to drop redaction criticism altogether.

In spite of these methodological weaknesses, structuralism is capable of providing insights about biblical narrative which no other method could supply. This is evident especially in works like Roland Barthes's 'Struggle with the Angel' which, more than any other critical analysis, helps to explain how and why we experience a kind of 'surrealistic sense of disorientation' in reading the tale – a disorientation that is not unlike discovering that the detective is really the murderer (Barton, 1984, p. 105). In this book I shall be using the functional approach deriving from Vladimir Propp on John's story in a way which, I hope, will help us to see this familiar text in a fresh light and from a fresh vantage-point. In part II, my aim is to establish the genre of John 18–19 using (as Nickelsburg does with the Marcan passion narrative) the functional analysis of narrative as my model.

The narrative genre of John's story

What might a structural approach to the fourth gospel look like, and what might it contribute to our understanding of the gospel's genre?

At the outset of this final section of the chapter we need to make an important distinction between structural exegesis and critical studies on the proposed narrative structure of John's gospel. Birger Olsson's *Structure and Meaning in the Fourth Gospel* (1974) is one example of a Johannine study which is concerned about structure and yet which is not structural exegesis. Olsson's method is text-linguistic; that is to say, it proceeds with the help of 'linguistics dealing with semantic structures, analysis of discourse and textual problems' (p. 2). Olsson is not concerned about sources or historicity, but with the message and the nature of the text in its final form: 'from an analysis of the constitutive elements in the text I shall try to determine its message and then describe its linguistic and literary form (text type)' (p. 3). Olsson chooses linguistic units which have definite beginnings and endings: the first, John 2.1–11 (a narrative text), and the second, John 4.1–42 (a dialogue text). He then describes the linguistic principles by which the minute information units in each text are linked together to form a total literary structure. This involves analysis of phrases, clauses, terminal features, tenses, prepositions, and so on. As Olsson rightly remarks, 'my investigation is but little influenced by the French structuralist method', for the emphasis is not on abstract translinguistic structures but upon linguistic, semantic structures (p. 9).

Another sort of structure-analysis on John which is not structural exegesis is exemplified in David Deeks's article 'The Structure of the Fourth Gospel' (1968). Again, as in Olsson's title, the word structure may lead the reader to expect an example of structural exegesis, but this is not provided. Deeks is interested in the surface structure of John's narrative, that is, in the visible organization of material into definable narrative sections. For Deeks, John's gospel is composed of four sections: (A)1.1−18, (B)1.19−4.54, (C)5.1−12.31 and (D) 13.1−20.31, with John 21 regarded as a later appendix. The prologue of the gospel is seen as the crucial key to the gospel's structure. It too is composed of four subsections which provide a summary of the contents of the four main sections of the gospel. These four sub-sections Deeks labels cosmological (1.1−5), the witness of John (1.6−8), the coming of the light (1.9−13) and the economy of salva-tion (1.14−18). He proposes that this pattern has been deliberately constructed and that this complex structure reveals John as a skilful artist. The skill is further visible in the way in which the latter two sections (C and D) repeat in reverse order the themes of the first two (A and B), so that the gospel is seen as a huge chiasmus: A,B;B' (= C),A' (= D) (p. 122). Clearly such an approach is not structural exegesis. As practised on John by the likes of Deeks, Talbert, Webster and Staley, it is neither structural exegesis nor narrative criticism, but an exercise better described as architectural analysis.

One of the few genuine examples of structural exegesis in Johan-nine studies is J. D. Crossan's 'Structuralist Analysis of John 6' (1979) − which uses the binary approach. In this study, Crossan assumed the literary unity of John 6 and openly excused himself from historical-critical issues. He began with a detailed analysis of each segment of the text, separating narrative from discourse (deeds from words) and actants from action (personae from effects). The first half of his analysis deals with narrative, since 'the simplest reading of the text reveals how the predominance of narrative in 6.1−21 gives way to the predominance of discourse in 6.22−71' (p. 239). In the narrative material, the actants are Jesus, the disciples and the crowds (who become the Jews from 6.41 onwards). The two principal actions are 'moving' and 'feeding'. In the discourse, the actants are God (mentioned by Jesus with various titles), the Son of Man, the One Sent, Moses, the prophets, and so on. The discourse actions are 'transcendental Moving and transcendental Feeding' (p. 244), for we have in direct speech a descending−reascending scheme, and an identification between the I of Jesus and The Bread, which did not appear in the narrative. Thus, Crossan's structural exegesis cleverly shows how things existing at different levels at the beginning of the text are mediated by the end of it. Though Jesus is different from the bread he offers at the start, he is metaphorically one with it at the end. There is a gradual focussing of crowds into Jews, disciples into the twelve, literal moving and feeding into transcendental moving and feeding. Things existing as binary opposites at the start of the narrative have been mediated by its conclusion.

If Crossan's analysis of John 6 owes much to Lévi-Strauss's binary approach to myth, P. J. Cahill's 'Narrative Art in John IV' (1982) shows similarities to Vladimir Propp's functional approach to Russian fairy-tales. For Cahill, John 4 is a 'sustained artistic accomplishment', 'a masterpiece of narrative design' in its own right (p. 41). However, it is also 'a story reflecting literary characteristics manifested in OT narratives of great antiquity' (p. 41). In order to establish the OT generic structure of which John 4 forms a part, Cahill uses a method which combines recent OT analysis of type scenes with the structural approach deriving from Propp. In true structuralist style, Cahill begins with a description of the surface features of the text, concentrating particularly on structure, repetitive devices, motifs and themes. Even though the story of the Samaritan woman appears to be about marriage, Cahill argues that 'the theme of the narrative is true worship' and that 'the controlling metaphor, skillfully contrived by the writer, is not that of marriage but of betrothal' (p. 41). Many of the narrative characteristics of John 4 fit into the pattern of the OT betrothal scene, especially the mention of Jacob's well, which is a reminiscence of the well in the betrothal scene of Genesis 29.1–20. However, the marital symbolism and betrothal echoes are figurative devices. 'False worship, of which the Samaritan woman is but a symbol, is infidelity or adultery' (p. 44). John 4 is an ironic betrothal scene in which infidelity is false worship and marriage true worship.

From these two papers we can see again that functional analyses (such as Cahill's) are more profitable for genre criticism than the binary approach of Crossan. It is important to note that the method of genre analysis I have chosen in chapter 6 resembles Propp more than it resembles Lévi-Strauss. Edgar McKnight has shown that the structural analysis of narrative which derives from Vladimir Propp is interested in plot whilst the structural analysis which derives from Lévi-Strauss is interested in structures unrelated to plot (1978, pp. 256–66). We have seen this in the preceding section of this chapter. George Nickelsburg's article was interested in discovering the underlying narrative genre of Mark's passion account. From a syntagmatic labelling of each part of the passion narrative he was able to see that Mark 15–16 is based on a particular generic model, stories of persecution and vindication in Jewish literature. Plainly this is an approach to the deep structures of a gospel which assesses the nature of its plot, and then seeks to discover the underlying generic plot-grammar of which it is a performance text. This emphasis upon plot is noticeably absent from Elizabeth Malbon's structural analysis. She does not provide a syntagmatic appreciation of Mark's plot. In fact, Malbon shows no real interest in plot at all. Just as Lévi-Strauss is primarily interested in the mental structure which has produced mythic texts, so Malbon is primarily interested in examples of the mind's innate tendency to mediate opposites. So, whilst Nickelsburg explores deep structures related to plot, Malbon explores deep structures unrelated to plot. It is because Nickelsburg's method is plot-related that it is more interested in genre than Malbon's work.

My own structural approach to John 18–19 is one which explores structures related to plot. It is derived from Propp and follows Nickelsburg and Cahill rather than Malbon and Crossan. What I want to explore in chapter 6 is the narrative grammar which lies behind the evangelist's construction of his passion-plot. Northrop Frye has shown how, when an author sets about composing a story, he cannot create a completely original story-form because he is subject to 'some kind of controlling or coordinating power' (1971, p. 245) in his mind. This power asserts itself very early on in the process of composition and 'gradually assimilates everything to itself, and finally reveals itself to be the containing form of the work' (p. 246). Frye sees this power as originating in four 'pre-generic elements of literature', 'generic plots', or 'mythoi' (p. 162): comedy (the *mythos* of spring), romance (the *mythos* of summer), tragedy (the *mythos* of autumn), and irony and satire (the *mythos* of winter) (pp. 163f.). The *mythos* which dictates the plot-structure of John's passion is tragedy. As Frye has written, '*Pathos* or catastrophe, whether in triumph or defeat, is the archetypal theme of tragedy' (McKnight, 1978; p. 261). As he continues, 'Anyone accustomed to think archetypally of literature will recognize in tragedy a mimesis of sacrifice. Tragedy is a paradoxical combination of a fearful sense of rightness (the hero must fall) and a pitying sense of wrongness (it is too bad that he falls)' (Frye, 1971, p. 214). In chapter 6 I shall be proposing that the tragic *mythos* dictated the narrative composition of John's story of the death of Jesus. It is hoped that this experimental, structuralist contribution will enhance greatly our appreciation of the genre of John 18–19.

3

THE SOCIAL FUNCTION OF JOHN'S NARRATIVE

Narrative and social identity

In chapter 2, we looked at the importance of the genre approach for narrative criticism, and in doing so mentioned on several occasions how genres function as social conventions for both the writer and the reader. Narrative criticism as it has been practised so far has, however, shown little concern for the culture and social communication implicit within NT narratives (the province of redaction criticism). Indeed, Culpepper's *Anatomy* begins with a critique of redaction criticism which one often finds in introductions to NT narrative criticism. He criticizes redaction-critical approaches to John because they use the gospel as 'a "window" through which the critic can catch "glimpses" of the history of the Johannine community' (1983, p. 3). They assert that 'the meaning of the gospel derives from the way it was related to that history' (p. 3). Culpepper is following Norman Petersen here. In his *Literary Criticism for New Testament Critics* (1978), Petersen had criticized redaction critics for construing texts 'as *windows* opening on the preliterary history of their parts rather than as *mirrors* on whose surfaces we find a self-contained world' (p. 24). Both scholars offer an alternative method in which the text is seen as a mirror, and in which meaning evolves out of the interaction between mirror and observer, text and reader. In this paradigm, the narrative world of each gospel is seen neither as a window on to the history of a community, nor as a window on to the ministry of Jesus. Biblical narratives are no longer analysed in historical and sociological perspective, as in form and redaction criticism, but rather in the kind of text-centred perspective which we are now in a position to associate with the New criticism.

More recently, voices have been raised against this somewhat narcissistic approach to interpretation. Meir Sternberg begins his thorough investigation into the *Poetics of Biblical Narrative* (1985) with the reminder that narrative critics must take note of social functions as well as literary forms. For Sternberg, biblical narratives are functional structures: they are 'a means to a communicative end, a transaction between the narrator and the audience on whom he wishes to produce a certain effect by way of certain strategies' (p. 1). As Sternberg continues, 'like all social discourse, biblical narrative is oriented to an addressee and regulated by a purpose or set of purposes involving the addressee' (p. 1). There is therefore a danger in reading biblical texts out of communicative context, in separating forms from functions. To concentrate on forms, devices and configurations instead of communicative design is not enough, because 'a sense of coherence entails a sense of purpose' (p. 2). By failing to consider the relationship between narrator and audience, many narrative critics have degenerated into precisely the kind of atomism they despised in their historical-critical forebears. The fact that recent narrative critics of the Bible have indulged in a purely synchronic, often subjective analysis of patterns or surface structures is a source of regret for Sternberg. Such people 'advocate the methods and rehearse the manifestoes of the New Criticism, but without duly adjusting them to the theoretical revaluations made since or to the conditions of biblical study' (p. 7).

To Sternberg's cautionary reminder we should also add William Riley's thesis in 'Situating Biblical Narrative' (1985), which examines the relationship between poetics (for example, the strategies used for composing a narrative) and the transmission of community values. Riley begins with a criticism of the recent narrative approaches to Scripture because they eschew rigorous consideration of context. As Riley puts it, 'the concern of the scholar has always been to locate the scripture under consideration within its context, be it the context of the written text itself or the historical context from which it arises. If the narrative approach is to be critically grounded and avoid the subjectivity to which it is sometimes prey, context may provide the key to the process' (p. 38). Riley's point is that one cannot avoid 'the community dynamic of which the text is the tangible evidence' (p. 38). One cannot avoid the fact that 'traditional narrative communicates the values of the traditional community in which it functions' (p. 38). These stories perpetuate insights and values which are durable and special in the life of their authors' communities. When one reads a biblical narrative, one must therefore be alert to the value-system which is either explicit or implicit in the narrative, and to the sociological significance of these value-signs. For both Sternberg and Riley, therefore, narrative criticism does not imply a purely text-immanent approach but rather a more eclectic procedure in which social function and context are important ingredients.

A way through the current anti-sociological bias of NT narrative criticism may lie in an understanding of the relationship that exists between narrative and social identity. At a personal level, narrative is the indispensable and inevitable medium for expressing my own sense of identity. As Stephen Crites has written, 'a man's sense of identity seems largely determined by the kind of story which he understands himself to have been enacting through the events of his career, the story of his life' (1971, pp. 302f.). The actual process of constructing this sense of identity is exceedingly complex. It involves an identification of the kernel events within the mass of all our past experiences. This primary activity is the activity of remembering or recollecting key images from the womb of memory. The second activity involves imagination, the synthetic faculty in the human mind. At this second stage, the imagination fuses the kernel events into a coherent plot, with the result that a sense of order, meaning and narrativity begins to emerge. The final activity, that of story-telling, involves incarnating this sense of purposeful personhood in an oral or a written medium. The medium nearly always chosen is narrative, because the narrative form is a cognitive instrument; it is 'an irreducible form of understanding' (Mink, 1978, p. 132). In summary, then, our sense of identity is the result of a complex and often lifelong process in which key memories are identified (remembering) and fused (imagination) into an identity-enhancing narrative (storytelling). The nearer we get to the conclusion of our lives, the clearer the sense of narrative may become in our past. The temptation to construct a narrative autobiography with a coherent plot therefore becomes enticing indeed, especially as the need to reaffirm our individual identity and life's meaning increases.

Personal identity is not, however, discovered and constructed in solitary confinement. As Peter Berger has cogently argued, 'identity is a key element of subjective reality and, like all subjective reality, stands in a dialectical relationship with society' (Berger and Luckmann, 1984, p. 194). As Berger continues, 'identity is formed by social processes. Once crystallized, it is maintained, modified or even reshaped by social relations. The social processes involved in both the formation and the maintenance of identity are determined by the social structure. Conversely, the identities produced by the interplay of organism, individual consciousness and social structure react upon the given social structure, maintaining it, modifying it, or even reshaping it' (p. 194). In other words, a person's identity not only influences social structure, but is also influenced by that structure. This implies that 'communities, like persons, have identities' (Stroup, 1984, p. 132), and that the two construct identity in an analogous way. This is indeed what Berger contends. The individual discovers a sense of identity when the experiences of life have congealed in recollection 'as recognizable and memorable entities' (p. 85) – a process Berger calls 'sedimentation' (p. 85) – and when these kernel entities are expressed in (auto)biographical form. Community identity is established as a result of 'intersubjective sedimentation' (p. 85), a process in which common experiences are incorporated into a common stock of knowledge which is then objectivated in a shared sign-system (p. 85). In Berger's system, remembering/imagining/storytelling is replaced by sedimentation/objectivation, yet the two processes are analogous. Just as the individual constructs his identity through story, so a social group can discover individuality, meaning and cohesion through the process of storytelling.

For Berger, the decisive sign-system is linguistic (i.e. articulated in a spoken or written form) because 'language objectivates the shared experiences and makes them available to all within the linguistic community, thus becoming both the basis and instrument of the collective stock of knowledge' (p. 85). In a community's linguistic sign-system, the symbolic universe of that community is established, described and maintained. The symbolic universe is 'an overarching universe of meaning' (p. 115) which is socially constructed. It is the 'matrix of all socially objectivated and subjectively real meanings' (p. 114), a matrix which helps the individual to recognize that 'the entire society now makes sense' (p. 121). Moving back to our narrative-centred argument, we can see that narrative is a crucial medium in this objectivation of shared knowledge and this maintenance of the symbolic universe. Berger does not mention narrative as such. The nearest he gets to it is in his discussion of mythology as one of the conceptual means by which the universe is maintained (p. 129). However, narrative is important for his discussion because it is narrative which collects events into a meaningful temporal unity including past, present and future. Communities live in what Brian Wicker has called a 'story-shaped world' (1975) and, as Stephen Crites has written, 'such stories, and the symbolic worlds they project, are not like monuments that men behold but like dwelling-places. People live in them ... they are moving forms, at once musical and narrative, which inform people's sense of the story of which their own lives are a part' (1971, p. 295). We might put it this way: once a community has established a sense of tradition and a sense of corporate identity, the most common way of articulating those things is through narrative forms such as myth, legend, saga, history.

In my programme of narrative criticism, I consider it crucial to adapt and incorporate the sociological bias of form and redaction criticism. I want to consider the way in which narrative poetics are made to serve the sociological function of transmitting community values. Put another way, I want to discover those communicative strategies by which the original addressee is encouraged to incorporate his own biography into the overarching narrative world of the gospel. In the paradigm offered here, gospel narratives are seen as the result of a complex procedure comprising remembering, imagining and storytelling. Through particular social pressures, the evangelist takes on the role of spokesman in the community. He gathers together kernel facts from the community's traditions about the historical Jesus, facts which will enable him to meet the needs of the community in which he writes. In this process of recollection, the evangelist seeks to combine his stock of heterogeneous social knowledge into a meaningful and instructive totality. This yoking together of material is the imaginative part of his procedure. It is a synthesis of disparate events into a new temporal and causal unity which we call a plot. Once a coherent plot has been established, the process of storytelling can begin, and what the evangelist produces is an overarching narrative world or symbolic universe which makes sense of the real world in which his community lives. In other words, all four evangelists use the narrative form not only as the most appropriate medium for relating the history of Jesus, but also as the most appropriate medium for communicating community values. In this sense, a gospel is not unlike a letter: it is a form of address as well as a means of description.

Redaction criticism has always emphasized this community dimension to NT narrative, and in this regard it is surprising that narrative critics have divorced themselves from the method with which they arguably have most in common. However, redaction criticism itself is an insufficient ally for narrative criticism so long as the former remains distinct from the social sciences. Early redaction criticism of the gospels was distinctly non-sociological. For example, in his *Mark: Traditions in Conflict* (1971), Theodore Weeden attempted to discover the origin of the gospel and the situation in the life of the church which inspired its creation. Weeden frankly confessed the difficulties of trying to read Mark with the analytical eyes of a first-century reader, but he argued that the key to appropriating the proper stance lay in the characters and the characterization of the second gospel. The disciples are prominent in Mark, and Weeden detects three stages in their relationship to Jesus. In 1.16−8.26 their relationship is characterized by unperceptiveness about the true nature of Jesus' identity and mission. In the second stage, from 8.27 to 14.9, they are characterized by misconception. In the final stage, they are characterized by rejection. Weeden's conclusion is that 'Mark is assiduously involved in a vendetta against the disciples' (p. 50), that 'he is intent on totally discrediting them. He paints them as obtuse, obdurate, recalcitrant men who at first are unperceptive of Jesus' messiahship, then oppose its style and character, and then finally totally reject it. As the coup de grace, Mark closes his Gospel without rehabilitating the disciples' (pp. 50−1).

The conflict between Jesus and the disciples is a Christological one. Whilst the disciples understand Jesus as a powerful *theios aner* (divine man), Jesus expresses himself as a suffering 'Son of Man'. It is at this point that Weeden interprets the narrative in terms of its possible social function. He argues that the reason why this conflict is of consuming interest in Mark is that there was a similar debate taking place within his own community (p. 81). From Mark 13, Weeden concludes that false prophets had infiltrated the church, proclaiming a *theios aner* Christology at a time when it was experiencing intense confusion over its own and Jesus' apparent powerlessness. As Weeden puts it, Mark 'stages the christological debate of his community in a "historical" drama in which Jesus serves as a surrogate for Mark and the disciples serve as surrogates for Mark's opponents. Jesus preaches and acts out the Markan suffering-servant theology. The disciples promulgate and act out theios-aner theology' (p. 163).

There are a number of problems with Weeden's book. It is not immediately evident that the disciples are portrayed in the clear-cut way Weeden describes, nor is it obvious how extensive and definable was the *theios aner* mythology at the time of Mark's gospel. However, on the positive side, Weeden does at least attempt to show how form is inseparable from function in Mark's narrative. In other words, he does try to identify the social functions of certain narrative forms. However, as in much early redaction criticism, there is no terminology from the social sciences to give greater precision to his argument. There are no categories from the sociology of religion/knowledge in his description of the social significance of the second gospel. But Mark's gospel is, in a sense, a social construction of reality.

Howard Kee makes this point in his 1977 study of Mark entitled *Community of the New Age*. Kee's form of redaction criticism supersedes Weeden's because it adds models from the realm of social history to the normal literary and conceptual models with which biblical scholars have worked. Kee's argument is that 'without due attention to the *social dynamics* that were operative in the community by and for whom Mark was produced, we cannot reach conclusions about the cultural setting and therefore about the author's intention' (p. 3). As Kee went on, '*sociological models* must be examined in order to try to reconstruct how such a community would have emerged' (p. 3). 'The horizon must include attention to the *life-world* or "sacred canopy" in which the community that lies behind this work displays its own attempt to impose a meaningful order' (p. 3).

Kee's redaction-critical study represents the logical outcome of a development in which redaction criticism in general has become more sociologically scientific, especially in Marcan research. I shall be using some of these insights from redaction criticism in my narrative criticism of John 18–19. My method owes something to Riley's emphasis on the relationship between gospel narrative and social values, and to Sternberg's reminder that biblical narratives are acts of communication and persuasion between an author and a community. It also owes something to Kee's analysis of Mark, which begins with a rigorous literary analysis of images in the second gospel, and then proceeds to a hypothetical investigation of their sociological significance in the lifeworld of the Marcan community. In this work, I shall follow these three scholars by examining Johannine images which have ecclesiological connotations and then deducing their probable social function.

Reconstructing the Johannine community

The community dimension of John's story has been explored with perceptive results by a number of redaction critics. The two seminal studies in this area are J. L. Martyn's *History and Theology in the Fourth Gospel* (first edition, 1968), and Raymond Brown's elaboration of it entitled *The Community of the Beloved Disciple* (1979). In both cases, the writers express their intention to probe into the community for which John's gospel was written. Both believe that the fourth evangelist was writing in response to particular social crises. Martyn's claim is that the student of the fourth gospel can detect 'even in its exalted cadences the voice of a Christian theologian

who writes *in response to contemporary events and issues'* (p. 18).
Brown's claim is that the fourth gospel can be read almost auto-
biographically, as the history of the Johannine community (pp. 22–3).
This being the case, both Martyn and Brown concur that 'it becomes
imperative to take up temporary residence in the Johannine community. We must see with the eyes and hear with the ears of that
community. We must sense at last some of the crises that helped to
shape the lives of its members. And we must listen carefully to the
kind of conversations in which all of its members found themselves
engaged' (Martyn, p. 18). It is this community dimension to fourth-
gospel research that marks what David Rensberger calls the new era
in Johannine interpretation. As he puts it, 'recent developments in
the study of the Fourth Gospel have the potential of bringing about
a revolutionary change ... By revealing as never before the social and
historical setting in which this gospel was written, and the conflicts
in which the Johannine community was involved, they have opened
up new possibilities in the interpretation of John' (1989, p. 15).

Martyn's book is mainly a redactional study of John 9 (the healing
of the man born blind). Martyn regards this narrative as a subtle
blend of tradition and unique interpretation, as a composite work
of dramatic art composed by the evangelist. Though the narrative is
based on a traditional healing miracle, Martyn's contention is that
we can detect in the composition 'specific reflections of some definite
situation in the life of the church' (p. 27). The key to understanding
the community dimension of John 9 is in verse 22, where the blind
man's parents are said to refuse to testify before the Jews because
they are afraid of being expelled from the synagogue. Martyn argues
that this verse is anachronistic. In Jesus' lifetime there was no such
threat of excommunication from the Jewish synagogues. The statement therefore reflects the milieu of the Johannine community late
in the first century, when we know from other historical sources that
Jewish Christians were excommunicated for believing that Jesus was
the Messiah. Indeed, Martyn believes that the wording of John 9.22
resembles the reformulated twelfth benediction issued from Jamnia
sometime after AD85: 'For the apostates let there be no hope, and
let the arrogant government be speedily uprooted in our days. Let
the Nazarenes [Christians] and the Minim [heretics] be destroyed in
a moment, and let them be blotted out of the Book of Life and not
be inscribed together with the righteous!' Martyn reads John 9.22 as
follows: 'The parents feared the Jewish authorities, for the latter had
already enacted a means whereby followers of Jesus could be detected

among synagogue worshippers. From Jamnia had come the official wording of the Shemoneh Esre including the reworded Benediction Against the Heretics. Henceforth anyone arousing suspicion could be put to a public test' (p. 58).

In this light, John 9 becomes what Martyn describes as a two-level drama (p. 60), for the narrative relates not only a traditional healing miracle, but also an incident or incidents within the history of the Johannine community. As far as Martyn is concerned, Jesus in John 9 represents a Christian preacher in the Johannine community who, in the name of Jesus, heals a Jew in the local synagogue. This Christian preacher hears that the man has been expelled from the fellowship of the synagogue — 'not an uncommon event in the experience of this preacher' (p. 62). The preacher therefore takes the initiative to find the man again. 'They stand face to face in the street. The preacher knows that the man is just at the point of readiness for a genuine Christian confession, and so puts to him the decision of faith. The beggar responds readily with words addressed to his true healer: "Lord, I believe"' (p. 35). As Martyn concludes, 'the Fourth Gospel affords us a picture of a Jewish community at a point not far removed from the end of the first century' (p. 35).

In Martyn's eyes, the fourth gospel is therefore not just a narrative about the historical Jesus, but is also a window on to the Johannine community for which it was written. This insight has been taken up by more recent Johannine scholars. As Rensberger has rightly stated: 'Subsequent studies have fully confirmed the rightness of this basic insight. While few have accepted Martyn's delineation of the action behind the Fourth Gospel in all its details, the fundamental conception that he outlined has been elaborated in a variety of directions and has become the cornerstone of much current Johannine research' (1989, p. 22). Brown's *Community* confirms this. Brown reconstructs each phase of the Johannine community history from each chapter in the gospel, in the belief that the chronology of John's narrative mirrors the history of its community. It concentrates most confidently on those passages in the gospel where Johannine theological interests come to the fore. It only argues from silence when John's silence could scarcely be accidental (as in John's omission of Jesus' eucharistic words, which Brown claims he must have known) (1979, pp. 20–1). The development of Johannine community history which Brown ends up with looks like this: in the mid 50s to late 80s, some Jews including followers of John the Baptist become disciples of Jesus (John 1–3). A second group of Jews with an anti-temple bias become disciples and make converts in Samaria (John 4). The acceptance of this second group causes the emergence of a high, pre-existence Christology. This causes hostility with non-believing Jews (John 5–8) and finally excommunication some time in the late 80s (John 9). After AD 90, the acceptance of Greek believers into the community is seen to be God's plan of fulfilment (John 12). John 14–17 suggests that the community then develops a hostile attitude not only towards other Jews but to the world in general. Founded on the beloved disciple, it becomes a tightly knit family which regards itself as the true church over and against the apostolic churches founded on Peter and James. By the time the epistles are written, this family has begun to break up because of a gnosticism which was always inherent within the community's understanding of Jesus but which became acute when a very high Christology was forged in controversy with Jewish antagonists.

How sound are these redaction-critical methods which I have associated with Martyn and Brown? On the positive side, Martyn and Brown have given Johannine scholarship a picture of the Johannine community and its history with which most people are in broad agreement. On the negative side arguments have taken place over the precise details concerning this crisis with the synagogue. The mechanism for the supposed expulsion of Jewish Christians from the synagogue is, according to Martyn and Brown, the twelfth of the eighteen benedictions read out in the synagogue's liturgy. Some scholars have, however, challenged the proposition that the twelfth benediction was an anti-Christian ban. Lawrence Shiffman has contended that the *birkat ha-minim* was only meant to exclude Jewish Christians of a particular kind; that is, those who took an active leadership role in the synagogue services (as precentors, for example). It did not imply universal expulsion for all Christian believers from the Jewish people (1981, p. 152). Reuven Kimelman has added that the 'birkat ha-minim does not reflect a watershed in the history of the relationship between Jews and Christians in the first centuries of our era' and that there was never a single edict which caused an irreparable separation (1981, p. 244). He states that the exact wording of this benediction was not fixed in the first century, that the term heretics might include Christians but not necessarily so, and that the authority of the rabbis at Jamnia may in any case not have been sufficient at this stage to have had such a critical effect on the Johannine Christian group. Given this uncertainty about the twelfth benediction, some of the details of Martyn's and Brown's community reconstructions need re-examination.

Another problematic detail arises out of the identification of what is supposed to have happened to Johannine Christians with the post-AD 85 milieu of the supposed expulsions. Both Martyn and Brown regard it as certain that the ἀποσυνάγωγος references in 9.22, 12.41 and 16.2 reflect the situation after AD 85 because there would have been no excommunications of Christians from the synagogues prior to that. This also has recently been questioned. Martin Hengel has described this interpretation of the three passages as 'one-sided' (1989, p. 114). He writes that the 'expulsion of Christians from the synagogue took place, rather, in a lengthy and painful process which began even before Paul with the martyrdom of Stephen' (p. 115). Indeed, Hengel argues that the Hellenists in Acts 6–8 were driven out of Jerusalem as ἀποσυνάγωγοι by the members of the Greek-speaking synagogues there (p. 115). He maintains that the foundation of the Pauline mission communities was often associated with an actual expulsion from the synagogue community, and points to the fivefold flogging by the Jewish authorities mentioned in II Cor. 11.24, which demonstrates the violence of these controversies. He reminds us that Stephen and James the son of Zebedee were certainly not the only martyrs (see Acts 12.1). The reference to the suffering of the 'communities of God in Judaea' in I Thess. 2.14 shows that these were not isolated but repeated events (p. 115). As Hengel concludes, the *birkat ha-minim* (the twelfth benediction) should be seen as 'the ultimate consequence of a development full of combat and suffering' (p. 115), not as a watershed experience.

Returning to the fourth gospel, we can see something of the radical effect of Hengel's critique of contemporary Johannine redaction criticism. Hengel has shown that the three ἀποσυνάγωγος references in John's gospel need not be anachronistic at all; they need not be regarded as a late first-century problem imposed on an early first-century situation (the ministry of Jesus). Indeed, when Hengel comes to John 16.2, he has some far-reaching things to say about the historicity of the verse. In 16.2, Jesus says: 'They will put you out of the synagogue (ἀποσυναγώγους); in fact, a time is coming when anyone who kills you will think he is offering a service to God.' Concerning this prophecy, Hengel makes the following statement: 'John 16.2 need not refer to an acute bloody persecution by Jewish authorities in the time of the evangelist and his school, but is meant to describe the situation of the post-Easter community generally: in the view of the evangelist it was persecuted by the Jews "from the beginning"' (p. 117). As Hengel continues, 'the abrupt controversy between Jesus and the Jews in the Fourth Gospel is in no way simply a reflection of the attacks of Jewish opponents on Johannine Christians alone. We have to be more subtle than that here. That Jesus was involved in critical controversy with the religious and political leaders of his own people and was handed over to Pilate by them was a firm and basic ingredient of the Jesus tradition prior to John, which John develops in an idiosyncratic way' (p. 117).

The fact that the late John Robinson has made similar claims (1985, p. 80) should alert us to the importance of this point. What is, I believe, certain about John's story of Jesus is this: that in general terms it reflects a severe controversy with Judaism. The social function of John's narrative form is to bring encouragement, vindication and purpose to Johannine Christians in the wake of the traumatic associalization which, no doubt, this controversy produced. As for the exact date of the controversy, and the exact mechanism for its obvious destabilizing consequences, such details cannot be described with complete confidence. All we can say is that John's story of Jesus is at the same time a story of a community in crisis, and that John the storyteller uses the narrative and literary devices at his disposal to address the pressing social needs of his day.

The social function of John's narrative

The future of redaction criticism of John's gospel depends upon its moving away from the hypothetical reconstructions of Martyn and Brown and moving towards the more sociological approaches of Wayne Meeks and Bruce Malina, Wayne Meeks's justly celebrated article, 'The Man from Heaven in Johannine Sectarianism' (1972), and Bruce Malina's lesser-known 'The Gospel of John in Sociolinguistic Perspective' (1985) both combine literary analysis of the text with technical consideration of the social function of John's language. In his study, Meeks set out to explain that special pattern of Johannine language which describes Jesus 'as the one who has descended from heaven and, at the end of his mission which constitutes a *krisis* for the whole world, reascends to the Father' (p. 141). Meeks's belief is that this picture of the descending/ascending redeemer had been treated too one-sidedly as a problem in the history of ideas. Johannine scholarship from Bultmann onwards had been too concerned with the possible mythical background for this picture in known gnostic sources. Meeks, on the other hand, is not concerned with the function of this myth in theological categories, but first and foremost with 'the function of the mythical pattern within the Johannine literature' (p. 143). As Meeks continues, 'we have not yet learned to let the symbolic language of Johannine literature speak in its own way' (p. 143). Secondly, he is interested in exploring 'the question of what social function the myths may have had' (p. 145), using Edmund Leach's anthropological theory of myths as structured signals of communication, and the sociology of knowledge deriving from Peter Berger and Thomas Luckmann. Meeks asks, in what situation did this motif provide an appropriate means of communication?

Meeks's method therefore starts with literary analysis before it proceeds to sociological explanation or community reconstruction. It does not depend upon allegorizing John's story of Jesus into a history of John's community. Meeks himself writes that his aim is 'to discern the function which the motif "ascent and descent" serves, first, within the literary structure of the Fourth Gospel, then, by analogy, within the structure of the Johannine community and its relationships to its environment' (p. 145). The first half of Meeks's article is consequently taken up with an analysis of those passages in which the motif is prominent. He discovers that 'the motif belongs exclusively to discourse, not to narrative' (p. 146); that is, it occurs in direct speech rather than in narration. He discovers that the first half of the gospel presents, through its dialogues, the descent of the Son of Man into this world as a *krisis* or judgement on the world. In the second half of the book, from 13.1−5 onwards, this judgement is identified with his ascent, culminating with his summary debriefing in chapter 17 and with his being lifted up on to the cross in chapters 18−19. Meeks also discovers that 'in every instance the motif points to contrast, foreignness, division, judgement' (p. 160). The motif has a dualistic tendency in that it stresses how Jesus is from above whilst his listeners are from below. This finding is brought out in the Nicodemus narrative in chapter 3 (on which Meeks focusses most of his analytical attention). Here, the fact that Nicodemus totally misunderstands Jesus' esoteric, heavenly secrets emphasizes the truth that he is from below whilst Jesus is from above.

From this literary investigation based in the final form of the gospel, Meeks proceeds to the following question: 'What functions did this particular system of metaphors have for the group that developed it?' (p. 161). He argues that we already know certain things about the Johannine community from direct allusions in the Johannine literature. We know that the group had to distinguish itself against the sect of John the Baptist and even more passionately against a rather strong Jewish community. We know that this community suffered defections, conflicts of leadership and schisms. Any more detail than this Meeks is not prepared, rightly, to provide. However, that is not to say that he is indifferent to the Johannine community. Far from it: his contention is that the descent–ascent schema in John forms part of the symbolic universe of the Johannine community, and that its purpose was to make sense of certain aspects of the group's historical experience. 'In telling the story of the Son of Man who came down from heaven and then re-ascended after choosing a few of his own out of the world, the book defines and vindicates the existence of the community that evidently sees itself as unique, alien from its world, under attack, misunderstood, but living in unity with Christ and through him with God' (p. 163). The descent–ascent schema is a closed system of metaphors which can only be understood by those who have been born from above (3.3). As Meeks concludes, 'One of the primary functions of the book, therefore, must have been to provide a reinforcement for the community's social identity, which appears to have been largely negative. It provided a symbolic universe which gave religious legitimacy, a theodicy, to the group's actual isolation from the larger society' (p. 163).

Meeks did Johannine scholarship a great service by describing more scientifically the implications of Johannine language for Johannine community life. In this respect it is a surprising fact that such sociological approaches to John's gospel have not been pursued between 1972 and Malina's article in 1985. Malina's study involves combining a narrative approach based on Hayden White's *Metahistory* with a socio-linguistic perspective deriving from Michael Halliday. Malina believes that the meanings encoded in John's gospel derive ultimately from the social system which has produced the gospel. As a result, his work seeks to 'look into the social system revealed in and presupposed by Jn to generate insight into the distinctive features of this text' (p. 1). He argues that language is essentially a form of social interaction. Thus he asks, 'Given the information communicated in Jn, can one infer the type of situation in which that sort of information could have been imparted?' (p. 1). He begins to answer this question by analysing the kind of story John tells. He bases his classification on Hayden White, who believes that all historians are faced with the task of creating a coherent and justifiable story out of their sources. When constructing a plot for such stories, White proposes (following Northrop Frye) that the historian is faced with four modes of emplotment: comedy, tragedy, satire and romance.

According to Malina, the fourth evangelist chose to construct a 'romantic tragedy' out of his historical material (p. 3). In other words, he chose to compose a plot which is influenced by stories in which 'the hero (individualistic) struggles unsuccessfully against opposing psychological, physical or social constraints, yet the struggle reveals how success can be found beyond the constraints or by acquiescing to them' (p. 4).

Malina is concerned not only to identify what kind/genre of story the fourth evangelist tells, but to discover what kind of social inter-action between author and audience is taking place in the language of this story. His point is that the evangelist writes as he does 'because of constraints on perception deriving from his social location' (p. 11). Malina believes that John's language (with its self-conscious distan-cing of itself from the Jews and from the world) implies a social group which has recently broken away from existing Jewish institutions and which now finds itself 'beyond ordinary limits' (p. 11). Using Mary Douglas's grid and group model, Malina argues that John's language reflects a 'weak group/low grid quadrant' (p. 8), that is to say, it stands against the social group from which it has emerged, it stresses the importance of the individual, and it upholds love as a key social value. He then claims, using Michael Halliday's socio-linguistic categories, that John's language is really an anti-language; it is the language of an anti-social group, 'a counter-society with a counter-language typical of competing groups' (p. 11). It arises from 'a social collectivity that is set up within a larger society as a conscious alter-native to it' (p. 11). He argues that this anti-language reflects a social group which upholds 'an alternative social reality that runs counter to the social reality of society at large' (pp. 13–14). He contends that it is designed to maintain inner solidarity under pressure and to assist in 'the resocialization of newcomers into that reality' (p. 14).

It is my proposal in this book that Meeks and Malina are the only Johannine scholars at present working with a method that examines the social function of John's storytelling with any precision. The problem with redaction criticism of the fourth gospel, as I have stated throughout this chapter, is that it has inferred far too much from very little evidence. The evidence which we have for the so-called Johannine community (itself a rather vague description) is *internal* to the gospel. Unlike the branch of literary criticism known as literary detection, redaction criticism works exclusively within the confines of the gospel narrative itself. Literary detectives such as Leslie Hotson have, however, worked with evidence *external* to their texts. For example, when Hotson tried to reconstruct the first performance of Shakespeare's *Twelfth Night*, he not only had the play but also many other manuscripts to work with. He argued that *Twelfth Night*, with its Duke Orsino, was in fact a command performance at Whitehall, a new comedy requested by Queen Elizabeth to entertain her guest the Duke, Don Virginio Orsino, on Twelfth Night, 1600−1. In reconstructing the motives and circumstances for the play, Hotson had manuscripts of the Queen's orders for the preparations for the ceremony, official reports of the festivities, and a detailed account of the occasion from Duke Orsino to his wife. From this evidence *external to the play*, Hotson was able to go back to *Twelfth Night* and explain many of the difficult passages in the play as topical. He was able to demonstrate how many of the obscure passages in the play have a social function or nuance related to the *Sitz im Leben* of Queen Elizabeth's court.

It is obvious that Hotson's method is always going to be more rigorous and plausible than Martyn's. Hotson begins with a close examination of the text, then unearths and inspects related contemporary evidence external to the text, before finally returning to the text in order to highlight the social significance of its language for the first audience. Such an approach is impossible in the case of the redaction criticism of the fourth gospel because of the paucity of relevant historical data external to the gospel. The answer for redaction criticism is therefore not to become more speculative about the historical details of the Johannine community, but rather to start using the sociological methods of Meeks and Malina. These two scholars begin with a literary analysis, then employ categories of explanation from the sociology of knowledge in an attempt to appreciate the social function of Johannine language. This is the approach which I shall be using in my examination of the social function of John's narrative. My initial procedure involves the analysis of narrative images which are sociological and ecclesiological in connotation. This approach derives from Kenneth Burke's model of interpretation in the realm of social anthropology. For Burke, the literary work is supremely an act of communication, a choice of verbal gesture for the inducement of corresponding attitudes on the part of the one addressed, a strategy for selecting enemies and allies (1941, p. 253). The technique of symbolic analysis best suited for understanding the writer's lifeworld (as expressed indirectly in the text) consists of codifying associational clusters of images in the overall work. The key images are defined by their frequency and intensity, and the three most common types are biological (to do with the body), personal (to do with the family) and abstract (to do with group identification) (pp. 254f.). Examining these kinds of images in a literary text reveals the writer's motives and uncovers the writer's social world.

In chapter 7 I shall show how the analysis of narrative images which are familistic in character provides an entrée into the Johannine community because 'there is a strong sense of family within this community, and the address as "brother" ... is common because the members are all children of God' (Brown, 1979, p. 60). It is by examining clusters of such socially significant images that I can fulfil the aim expressed in the first section of this chapter: to consider the way in which John's narrative transmits community values and enhances social identity. In other words, my aim is to discover those communicative devices by which John's first readers were enabled to incorporate their own biographies into the overarching story-world of the gospel. In my sociological analysis of Johannine narrative I shall mainly be employing concepts from the sociology of knowledge and the sociology of religion, which, as Derek Tidball has pointed out, provide a fruitful though underused resource for NT (and particularly Johannine) studies (1983, pp. 137–42). In using these categories, however, I shall try to resist the pitfall of social determinism — the pitfall of seeing a text as *necessarily* determined by social beliefs. With this caveat in mind, I shall proceed in chapter 7 (a) to identify ecclesiologically significant images in John 18–19, especially familistic ones, (b) to understand the network of which they form a part (in the final form of the gospel), and (c) to deduce their probable social function. My socio-narrative approach will attempt to reveal how the story of the cross was understood by the Johannine community. In other words, my approach will show how the death of Christ marked the birth of the community.

4

THE NARRATIVE-HISTORICAL APPROACH TO JOHN'S STORY

Narrative and history

Thus far I have described narrative criticism in a more comprehensive manner than most NT narrative specialists. In chapter 1 I highlighted how influential literary and narrative approaches to John were becoming, yet I also revealed how lacking they were in the area of literary theory. Scholars such as Alan Culpepper, though their works are ground-breaking and often perceptive, fail to see just how indebted they are to New criticism, and how vulnerable they are to post-New critical critiques. In advocating an anti-sociological form of textual analysis, narrative critics from Culpepper onwards have made a number of errors: they have neglected the social functions of the narrative form; they have consequently neglected the community orientation of gospel narratives, and they have in the process distanced themselves from redaction and sociological criticism (arguably their closest allies). This book is therefore partly an attempt to provide some timely correctives. At the level of the *text*, I have insisted that we examine the gospels as narrative Christology, and that in the process we make sure that we respect their genre. The gospels are not, after all, modern novels. They are narratives composed according to Hebrew and Graeco-Roman storytelling conventions. At the level of *context*, I have also insisted that narrative criticism recognizes the social function of community stories, and embraces a more sociologically rigorous form of redaction criticism. At the level of *pre-text*, I aim in this chapter to show that narrative criticism needs to embrace a new form of historical criticism centred upon the concept of narrative history worked out in American history faculties over the last thirty years.

We now turn to the relationship between history and narrative. To begin with, we need to address the question: in what sense can we speak of a Jesus-history at the heart of John's story of Jesus? I want to say first of all that I am taking it for granted in this chapter that we can actually speak of an historical Jesus. As Graham Stanton has recently written: 'Today nearly all historians, whether Christian or not, accept that Jesus existed and that the gospels contain plenty of valuable evidence which has to be weighed and assessed critically. There is general agreement that, with the possible exception of Paul, we know far more about Jesus of Nazareth than about any first- or second century Jewish or pagan religious teacher' (1989, p. 141). The tradition which John the storyteller draws upon is therefore about a real, flesh-and-blood human being (Jesus of Nazareth) with a life-story public and significant enough to warrant considerable historical reflection. The real issue is therefore not whether Jesus existed, but how much the gospel of John actually tells us about the historical Jesus. A prominent view since the publication of C. H. Dodd's magisterial *Historical Tradition in the Fourth Gospel* (1963) is that there are some aspects of John's Jesus-history which are more valuable than the Synoptic tradition. As Hengel has written,

> we find features in the Fourth Gospel which sometimes sound more realistic than in the Marcan-Petrine outline. In my view these include the lengthy activity by Jesus of at least two years covering three Passovers; the original connection with John the Baptist ... the numerous journeys to Jerusalem ... individual happenings in Jerusalem; the significance of Annas as the eminence grise who pulls the strings; and finally the even greater importance of the messianic question in the final arguments.   (1989, p. 132)

Perhaps no one has done more since Dodd to defend the fourth gospel as a window on to the historical Jesus than John Robinson in his *Priority of John* (1985). His book is an attempt to effect a change of presumption in NT scholarship. He writes, 'the presumption of scholars over the past one hundred and fifty years has been the posteriority of John' (p. 13). Robinson suggests that we should now argue for the priority of John. This does not mean assuming that John was the first of the gospels in time to be published. It means accepting that the gospel contains some of the most primitive eye-witness accounts of Jesus of Nazareth. Robinson goes on: 'I am convinced that the early Christian preaching both knew and cared much about the Jesus of history' (p. 32). This is particularly true of John. The fourth evangelist treasured historical facts because he saw them as the indispensable locus of revelation. As Bultmann, commenting on John 1.14, wrote: 'The doxa is not to be seen *alongside* the sarx, nor *through* the sarx as through a window; it is to be seen in the sarx, and nowhere else. If man wishes to see the doxa, then it is on the sarx that he must concentrate his attention' (1971, p.63). Thus, Robinson argues that even though John represents the *omega* of tradition in terms of theological interpretation, it also represents the *alpha* of tradition in terms of the age of its historical source. He says: 'there is no either—or between recognizing John as the *omega* of the New Testament witness, the end-term, or an end-term, of its theological reflection, and also as its *alpha*, standing as close as any to the source from which it sprang. His theology does not, I believe, take us further from the history but leads us more deeply into it' (p.33).

In the second section of this chapter, 'Narrative and source', I shall take issue with one of the main arguments of Robinson's thesis in my discussion of the identity of the beloved disciple. In the present context I want to confirm Robinson's thesis that we can speak of an historical Jesus at the heart of John's gospel, and indeed that we may have some confidence that John's Jesus-history preserves information which even corrects the Synoptic records at points. The basic outline and facts about Jesus recorded in John are a reliable account. The Jesus whom the Baptist heralded, who called disciples, who performed miracles, who taught about the Fatherhood of God and other matters in a way that was not necessarily unique but certainly innovative, who spoke in parables, who ministered to the poor, who confronted the Jewish authorities of the time over sabbath law and other matters, who taught in Jerusalem on a number of occasions, who transformed the Jewish passover meal, who got into trouble over his attitude towards the temple, who was arrested and tried, who was executed on a Roman cross and who was believed to have been raised from the dead, this Jesus is more the historical Jesus than a Johannine Jesus. That is not to deny for a moment the considerable amount of interpretation which this Jesus-history has been subjected to. But it does reinforce Robinson's beautifully made point that

> one gets the strong impression that fact is sacred ... The theology is drawing out the history rather than creating it or even moulding it. It is an exercise in 'remembering' in the pregnant Johannine sense of reliving the events 'from the end', through the mind of the interpreter Spirit, presenting what they 'really' meant, in spirit and in truth. It is a meta-history: not any the less historical the more theologically it is understood, but the depth and truth *of* the history.   (p.297)

The question we need to ask now is this: in what sense was Jesus-history story-like? Given that Jesus lived and died in broad outline as John describes, in what sense did the life of Jesus have the qualities of a story? It is at this point that we must tune into a debate whose contours were established in the 1960s and 1970s in American history faculties, and which have recently been refined by Paul Ricoeur in his three-volume work *Time and Narrative*. The debate, which has mostly concerned philosophers of history rather than of hermeneutics, is best summed up under the rubric 'narrative history'. 'History' here includes both its normal denotations; that is, it denotes the past as well as the historian's account of it (what I shall be referring to as historiography). The narrative history debate has mainly addressed itself to two major issues: (1) the significance of the narrative form in the historian's reconstruction of the past; and (2) the question whether the past itself already possesses a rudimentary narrativity (story-like form) even before the historian begins his work of reconstruction. For the principal philosophers in the narrative history debate, understanding history has been defined as the process by which the historian makes a coherent and justifiable story out of the historical evidence available to him. At this level there has been something of a consensus. Where the debate has raged most fiercely is over the question whether that story is imposed upon or discovered within the mass of past realities.

Most historians are agreed that the writer who initiated the narrative history debate was W. B. Gallie. His *Philosophy and the Historical Understanding* (1964) explored the connection between history and narrative. For Gallie, the narrative form is the vehicle for what he prefers to call the 'historical understanding' (p. 105). When we seek to understand past occurrences in real space and real time, we are attempting 'to connect, to appreciate continuities, to feel the forward movement' of our subject (p. 18). What we are therefore endeavouring to construct is what Gallie calls a 'followable' story (pp. 29f.). Historical understanding occurs when the past human actions which have special interest to a particular community are interconnected with other human actions and formed into a coherent narrative. As Gallie tersely remarks, 'historical understanding is the exercise of the capacity to follow a story' (p. 105), and the historian's aim is 'to present an acceptable, because evidenced and unified, narrative' (p. 103). Historical understanding consequently occurs when the historian sees trends or tendencies which connect a succession of events in spite of discontinuities, contingencies and unpredictabilities. These trends are not explanatory factors dragged into the narrative from outside; they are pattern-qualities in the story itself. Thus, Gallie claims that 'history is essentially a story' (p. 67), and because it is story, facts within the mass of history impose themselves insurmountably upon the historian as narratable (p. 104). Facts call out to be formed into a followable story.

Gallie's thesis is a great deal more complex than this short summary would suggest and, as subsequent commentators have pointed out, it does contain a number of difficulties (Mandelbaum, 1967, p. 419). One of the greatest difficulties arises from Gallie's insistence on using the word history to cover both past human actions and the historian's account of them. This sometimes makes it extremely hard to know what he is claiming. For example, when he says that history is essentially a story, does he mean that history-writing is basically a form of telling stories? Or does he mean that all past time and experience (and by inference, all present and future time and experience) possess an essential narrativity? Whatever Gallie's real thoughts on this issue, his ambiguity stimulated considerable discussion. A number of philosophers of hermeneutics and history, assuming that Gallie was saying that time and history are basically narrative in form, have sought to disprove this thesis. The two historians who have argued most trenchantly that time is not narrative in form are Hayden White and Louis Mink. Hayden White's argument is that historical narratives display a formal coherency that history lacks. As White puts it, 'we do not live stories' (1978, p. 43). When we retrospectively cast our lives in the form of stories, we create verbal fictions whose continuities are really 'fraudulent outlines' (1978, p. 44). The ideal form of historiography is therefore the chronicle or the annal, because these forms present mere sequences of facts without beginnings, middles and ends (1980), and that is how time and history are. Historical narratives are really verbal fictions because they encode the facts of chronicles and annals as components of specific kinds of plot-structure. They are fictions because history does not possess what White calls emplotment (1978, p. 46).

Louis Mink's contribution to the narrative history debate has been his concept of 'comprehension' (1970, p. 548) in the construction of narrative history-writing. Mink adopts the Kantian view of comprehension or 'understanding' as a process involving memory, imagination and conceptualization. We understand or com-prehend (conceptualization) when we grasp together (imagination) things which are experienced (memory) separately at a temporal, spatial or logical level. We immediately understand that a tree is a tree because our imaginations link all past experiences of tree-like forms so that we know the object offered to our perception. Mink calls this activity of 'grasping things together' 'comprehension', and he suggests three levels of this mental activity: (1) the level of recognizing objects like trees; (2) the level of grasping things together for purposes of classification; (3) the level of ordering our knowledge into a single system so that we see the world as a totality (1970, p. 549). It is this third level of comprehension to which the historian aspires. His aim is to achieve a synoptic vision in which antecedent events are presented as contributory or decisive causes of subsequent events. It is his aim to com-prehend or grasp together the disparate realities of the past into a meaningful because emplotted story. These stories are, however, imposed on the past; they are not discovered within it. As Mink puts it, 'Stories are not lived but told. Life has no beginnings, middles or ends ... We do not dream or remember in narrative, I think, but tell stories which weave together the separate images of recollection' (1970, p. 558). In short, 'narrative qualities are transferred from art to life' (1970, p. 558). Thus, whilst for Gallie understanding history involves discovering followable stories, for Mink it involves imposing such stories on the random flux of episodic time and experience.

Against these arguments of White and Mink, there have been a number of writers who have proposed that narrativity is discovered within, not imposed upon, time and history. Nathan Scott, in an article exposing the way in which modern fiction is partly about the impossibility of storytelling (metafiction), remarks: 'it is by no means so obvious as the literary vanguard of our period imagines that story as such is a necessarily fraudulent way of representing the human reality' (1986, p. 147). Stephen Crites, in his much-quoted 'The Narrative Quality of Experience', has argued that 'the formal quality of experience through time is inherently narrative', that memory, experience and time already possess a kind of incipient narrativity even before we begin our acts of narration (1971, p. 291). Paul Ricoeur, in *Time and Narrative*, has tackled this issue head on. He understands very well the temptation to argue that 'narrative puts consonance where there was only dissonance' (1984, p. 72), that it is a literary artifice which 'consoles us in the face of death' (1984, p. 72). But he also argues that the assertion that narrative falsifies reality is really a gross over-simplification of the problem. For Ricoeur, it is too simplistic to equate reality with disorder and narrative with order. As he continues, 'so long as we place the consonance on the side of narrative and the dissonance on the side of temporality in a unilateral way ... we miss the properly dialectical character of their relationship' (1984, p. 35). Experience and time possess 'an inchoate narrativity that does not proceed from projecting ... literature upon life' (1984, p. 74). As such, the historian is not the sole source of that form. He does not completely invent historical narrative; he comes to past records with an expectation that they will form a story, only to find that they readily yield to that narrative motivation.

The point of this brief overview of the narrative history debate is this: that most NT narrative critics have opted for an epistemology of historical understanding which they have not properly understood or explained. All NT narrative critics essentially follow Culpepper, who, in his *Anatomy* (1983), was following Frank Kermode. Kermode's *Genesis of Secrecy* (a study in the narrative of Mark and John) basically opted for three views which are characteristic of post-Modernism's antagonism towards referentiality:

(1) *History* (understood as the past) is not story-like in character; it is chaotic, episodic, unplotted. Therefore all historical narratives which present an ordered account of historical cause and effect, including Mark and John, must be seen for what they are: fraudulent outlines.

(2) *Historians*, conscious of the fictional character of their work, attempt to create a sense of history-likeness in their works by placing reality-effects in their narratives. Thus, Mark's picture of the naked young man fleeing from the scene of Jesus' arrest, and John's description of the crucifragium, are not facts but literary inventions intended to create the illusion of historical reality in the reader's mind. The gospels are therefore historicized fiction; they are inventions with history-like details.

(3) *Historiography* does not provide us with a window on to brute facts. Historical texts claim to have a referential dimension, but in truth texts cannot refer to facts outside of themselves. Since Ferdinand de Saussure's pioneering work on linguistics, we have become accustomed to recognizing that there is no inherent connection between signifiers and the things they signify. The implications of this structuralist principle for historical narratives are devastating. Such narratives cannot be said to refer to anything real at all. The narrative worlds of John and Mark do not *refer* to the real world of Jesus of Nazareth. The narrative or story time of John and Mark do not *refer*

to the real time of Jesus history. Mark and John are autonomous narrative worlds, not windows on to history.

I want to question all three of these post-Modernist presuppositions behind Kermode's narrative hermeneutics and offer a more integrative and credible alternative:

(1) *History* is not meaningless. There is a story-like character to it which calls for a storyteller. The philosophy of narrative history deriving from Gallie and Ricoeur must now replace the epistemology which has influenced NT studies since Wilhelm Hermann. As historians of biblical criticism well know, Leibniz, Lessing and Kant opened up a great divorce between event and meaning: Leibniz by distinguishing between truths of reason which are necessary and truths of fact which are contingent; Lessing by stressing the horrid big ditch between truths of reason and accidental truths of history; Kant by further distinguishing between a realm of unknowable things in themselves and a realm of phenomenal events. The impact of these philosophers on historical research was immense. Henceforth historians would deny to empirical events any inherent intelligibility and would transfer all order and structure to the human pole of the knowing relation. Thus Hermann made the famous distinction between two kinds of history, *Historie* and *Geschichte*, which was then used by Rudolf Bultmann and has now, I would argue, reappeared in the form of Kermode's radical and somewhat melancholy existentialism. Today, however, general relativity theory has called into question the old rationalist dichotomy between the empirical and the theoretical, between events and inherent rationality, with the result that historical research can begin at last, from a scientific basis, to speak of an inner logic of temporal relation within historical facts (Torrance, 1985, p. 12). In *John as Storyteller*, I propose that we therefore see the Jesus-history behind the fourth gospel as already, in some sense, story-like in character — as both episodic and emplotted.

(2) *Historians* such as Mark and John do not invent details in order to create a sense of factuality. I shall show in chapter 8 how the historical tradition contained within the passion narrative in John is by no means destroyed. Details such as the crucifragium need not be relegated to falsehoods designed to deceive the reader. The notion that John is historicized fiction, a kind of myth with history-like details included as aesthetic deceptions, will not stand up against the discoveries of historical critics such as Dodd, Robinson

and Hengel. However, this is not to say that Mark and John are see-through documentaries of Jesus-history. Mark and John — indeed all the gospels — are fictionalized history, not historicized fiction. They are collections of facts which have been organized into follow-able and coherent plots, using the techniques we associate with fictional narratives. In this sense, their *plots* are precisely what the word connotes: conspiracies. They are imaginative redescriptions of Jesus-history in which the true significance of Jesus, always inherent within the fabric of his life-story, is liberated for the interpreter who is prepared to read John *from* above, not *from* below.

(3) As for *Historiography*, I readily agree that works of narrative historiography are not mimetic in the sense of exact copies or represen-tations of reality. In that sense they are not like the camera lenses of modern, realistic, historical documentaries. However, this does not mean that they are not, in some sense, windows on to the historical Jesus. The level of interpretation exercised by the evangelists and their communities has doubtless coloured the glass through which we reverentially peer. But does this mean that their transparency has been completely destroyed? Is it not significant that there is a noticeable movement away from the exclusivist, post-Modernist view of texts merely as mirrors to a more integrative understanding of them as both mirrors and windows at the same time (Vorster, 1985, p. 61)? The referential dimension of texts like John, especially in the wake of Robinson's *Priority* and Hengel's *Johannine Question*, can no longer be relegated to history-like reality-effects. Historical nar-ratives like John contain both historical reference and universal mimesis (Walhout, 1985, pp. 49f.).

As far as fourth gospel research is concerned, my conclusion is as follows: first of all, the emergence of a more optimistic view of time in scientific and historical research means that we can speak of a story-like character inherent within the life-history of Jesus. In short, the ultimate source of John's story is already a narrative calling out for a storyteller. Secondly, the emergence of an intellectually rigorous apology for John's historical value means that we cannot relegate the facts of his story to the level of history-like reality-effects. Thirdly, the movement away from the structuralist ditch between signifier and signified, narrative worlds and real worlds, means that we can speak again of the historical values of John's referential dimension.

By far the most important of these for my present purposes is the first conclusion. The whole aim of this chapter is to show the reader that

John's gospel is a narrative text which has built on at least two previous narrative texts. The first level of narrativity is, as I have shown above, the life-story of Jesus' existence. Jesus-history is his-story. We must turn now to the second level of narrativity, namely, the narrative sources on which John the storyteller drew. I am aware that John probably had at his disposal a large quantity of speech sources: a collection of proverbial sayings (Dewey, 1980), a collection of discourses (Smith, 1965, pp. 22–3), a collection of authentic Jesus sayings (identified by the double Amen formula: Lindars, 1972, p. 48), and possibly a collection of controversy dialogues with the Jews (Schenke, 1988). However, in the next section I want to look only at the possible *narrative* sources at his disposal: that is, the sources which were cast in story form.

Narrative and source

The questions concerning the historical functions of the narrative form in the preceding section make it imperative for NT narrative critics to have a diachronic, historical dimension to their methodology. In the last section I argued for an epistemology which allows for structure within history and for reference within historiography. In proposing this, I suggested that John does refer to facts about Jesus, and that these facts were originally part of a life-history with its own, internal narrativity. In this section I want to propose that some of the sources behind John's story of Jesus were also cast in a narrative form. In this regard I am swimming against the tide of Johannine literary and narrative criticism. As early as 1977, Marinus de Jonge (who was influential in the emergence of literary criticism of John) wrote: 'The present author is very skeptical about the possibility of delineating the literary sources in the Fourth Gospel ... In many cases we cannot possibly know what the redactor had in front of him and, consequently, we shall have to take him seriously as author, i.e. as composer in his own right' (pp. vii–viii). My response to this is twofold: first, that the narrative history debate compels us to have an historical-critical dimension to NT narrative criticism; secondly, that 'the growing evidence of the widespread use of source (and/or traditional) materials in New Testament documents should persuade us that we must not shy away from the possibility that the fourth evangelist too availed himself of written materials in the tradition known to him' (Kysar, 1975, p. 33). In the pages which follow I provide a tentative account of the narrative sources available to the fourth evangelist.

A Bethany gospel

It is clear even from a superficial reading that the gospel of John claims to have an eye-witness at its source. This eye-witness is not named; he is given various epithets, most commonly 'the disciple whom Jesus loved' or 'the/an other disciple'. His first appearance is arguably in the region of Bethany as a follower of John the Baptist. He is one of the two disciples of John mentioned in 1.35 (the other is named as Andrew). His second appearance is at the last supper in Jerusalem (13.23), where we see him leaning on Jesus at the meal-table and where he is described as 'the disciple whom Jesus loved'. His third appearance is again in Jerusalem (18.15), where he escorts Peter into Annas' courtyard and where he is referred to as 'another disciple'. His fourth appearance is outside Jerusalem (19.25), where he stands at the foot of the cross and is commanded to look after the mother of Jesus ('the beloved disciple'). His fifth appearance is again outside Jerusalem (20.3f.), where he outruns Peter to the empty tomb ('the other disciple'). His sixth appearance is in 21.7 by the sea of Tiberias, where he recognizes the risen Jesus and shouts to Peter, 'it is the Lord!'. Here he is called 'the beloved disciple' again. His seventh and final appearance is in 21.20, where Jesus speaks of the beloved disciple's ultimate destiny. Clearly, then, this disciple has a prominent and vital place in Johannine tradition. This 'beloved disciple' (henceforth the BD) is the eye-witness of the events where he is present. This is stressed in 19.35, where the author says of him that 'the man who saw it has given testimony, and his testimony is true'. In 21.24 the author says of the BD: 'This is the disciple who testifies to these things and who wrote them down. We know that his testimony is true.'

The BD is therefore regarded as a particularly special recipient of Jesus tradition and revelation. This is supported by the fact that he lies 'on the bosom of Jesus' in 13.23: a position which reminds the reader of Jesus' special relationship with the Father in 1.18 ('in the bosom of the Father'). Just as Jesus knows the heart of the Father, so the BD knows the heart of the Son. However, the BD himself is not the actual author of the fourth gospel. It is made clear in 19.35 that he is the authority but not the writer because the narrator speaks of the BD as someone distinct, as 'he', not 'I'. The author says, 'his testimony is true' in 19.35, not 'my testimony is true'. The statement in 21.24, 'he wrote these things down', need not in any way contradict this; the word he still suggests a radical distinction between the narrator (the storyteller) and the implied author (the BD). The narrator is stressing that the gospel is based on the reliable written tradition of the BD himself. Who, then, was the BD? Tradition has it that the BD was John bar Zebedee, but that has recently been called into question by prominent Johannine scholars. Martin Hengel has highlighted two particular arguments against the John bar Zebedee tradition. First of all he argues that the fourth gospel centres upon Jerusalem, and 'in its topographical (and historical) information about Jerusalem and Judaea the Gospel is far superior to the Synoptics' (1989, p. 124). This makes it 'extremely improbable that the Gospel was written or even prompted by a Galilean disciple' like John (p. 124). Secondly, he points to 'the marked "aristocratic" character of the work, which has nothing of the "aura of poverty" surrounding Galilean peasants and fishermen' (p. 124). The luxury pervading the Cana miracle and other factors mean that the BD could not have been a man of John bar Zebedee's social class.

It is my conviction that the gospel of John makes much better sense if we see John the elder as the author of the final work, and another candidate besides John bar Zebedee as the principal authority and eyewitness source behind him. This authority called 'the beloved disciple' can only be one person if John's story is read on its own terms and without any knowledge of the somewhat unreliable second-century traditions connecting him with John (Brown, 1966, pp. lxxxviii). He *has* to be Lazarus of Bethany, as a number of scholars, who have not been taken seriously enough, have stated (Kreyenbuhl, 1900; Eisler, 1938; Garvie, n.d.; Filson, 1949; Eller, 1987). In defence of this radical thesis I would offer the following arguments:

(1) There is a strong and distinctive emphasis upon Jesus' love for Lazarus when the latter is introduced in John 11. In 11.3 Lazarus' sisters send word to Jesus that 'the one whom you love is sick'. There is no name mentioned here. Jesus and the first readers of the gospel, it is supposed, will know who is meant. The phrase in the sisters' message points to a community code-name for Lazarus, 'the one whom Jesus loved'. This is emphasized again in verse 5 ('Jesus loved Martha and her sister and Lazarus') and again in verse 36, where the Jews say, 'See how much he loved him!' It is then within a few pages that the author introduces the epithet 'the disciple whom Jesus loved' at the last supper in 13.23. After the very overt signals given in chapter 11, this can only be Lazarus. This is further suggested by the fact that the BD in 13.23 is in the same situation as Lazarus is in 12.2, 'reclining at the table with Jesus'.

(2) All the BD passages make much better sense if Lazarus is identified as the BD.

In 13.23 it is inconceivable that it is John bar Zebedee reclining on Jesus. Jesus would hardly have allowed John this place of honour so soon after the incident where John (and James, his brother) sought to sit with Jesus in the ultimate place of honour, in glory. Mark 10.41 says that the other ten apostles were indignant when they heard of John's request. Would Jesus have risked upsetting his followers so close to his death by giving John the very place which the other ten felt so touchy about? Surely not. It makes better sense to see Lazarus as the BD here. His resurrection would have marked him out as something of a celebrity guest. The fact that the Synoptics do not mention him would be due solely to their own concentration upon the Galilean Twelve, not on other disciples such as this Jerusalem follower.

In 18.15 it is highly improbable that the other disciple (the BD) is John bar Zebedee. How could a Galilean fisherman have been on friendly terms with a high priest? Robinson's thesis that John was well known because he delivered fish to Annas' house is hardly convincing (1985, pp. 116–17). It makes more sense to see this anonymous follower as Lazarus. We can presume that he was of the kind of aristocratic standing that would have made such a relationship possible. Indeed Eller calls Lazarus the 'apostle to the Jewish intelligentsia!' (p. 55).

In 19.25 it is probable that Lazarus is the BD standing at the foot of the cross. The author writes that the BD took Mary to his home from that time on. If the BD is Lazarus, that fits well: Lazarus lived in Bethany, which, as the author takes trouble to point out in 11.18, is very near to Jerusalem. The distance which Lazarus would have travelled in escorting Mary was very short and would have allowed Mary close access to Jerusalem at the time of the ascension and Pentecost (where we know from the beginning of Acts she was present). Again, this identification of the BD as Lazarus is more plausible. If the BD was John, then why do the Synoptics not mention him at the cross? (Indeed they imply that the apostles were all conspicuous for their absence.) Furthermore, if the BD was John, that presupposes an awful lot of travelling for him and Mary between the crucifixion and Pentecost: John, after all, lived in Galilee. John Robinson's attempt to argue that John had a flat in the city to which he took the mother of Jesus hardly helps the cause! (1985, p. 117).

In 20.3f., the other disciple who runs with Peter to the empty tomb is clearly the BD. That the BD is Lazarus is suggested by a number of points: if it was John, then why does Luke not mention him in Luke 24.12? Secondly, the BD outruns Peter in verse 4 because he has experienced the resurrection power of God himself (John 11.38–44). The excitement of anticipation gives John greater faith than Peter and, furthermore, greater haste. Thirdly, the author states that it was the σουδάριον, the head-cloth, which the BD sees and which inspires resurrection faith in him. This makes very good sense when we recall the only other use of σουδάριον by John is at 11.44, where it is said of the resurrected Lazarus that he came out of the tomb with a σουδάριον, a burial cloth, around his face.

Finally, the allusions to the BD in chapter 21 make good sense if the BD is Lazarus. Clearly Lazarus has died at the time of composing this chapter. The author feels it necessary in verse 23 to dispel the rumour that the BD would not die (which would only need stating in the context of bereavement). If the BD is John bar Zebedee, this makes no sense at all. Why would such a rumour have sprung up concerning the immortality of a Galilean fisherman? What of the church tradition that claims John was martyred? If the BD is Lazarus, on the other hand, everything seems much more logical. I can easily envisage a scenario in which a group of Christians centred on Lazarus, who had been raised from death, believed in the immortality of their founding father. It is entirely plausible that they came to mistake his temporary resuscitation for a permanent resurrection. When Lazarus, the BD, eventually did die, an explanation was needed, and John the elder sought to provide it in John 21.23.

In this section, I want to argue that the primary source behind John's story of Jesus is the eye-witness tradition of Lazarus. In the past, there has been a basic scepticism about Lazarus. Both the existence of Lazarus and the resurrection miracle which he experienced have been called into question (Fortna, 1989, p. 96). However, neither view can be sustained. There is no good reason for doubting the existence of Lazarus (Brown, 1966, Vol. I, p. 422); indeed, his existence is confirmed by the fact that his personal history occupies the structural centre and turning-point of the gospel. A fictional character could not have exerted such an influence on the overall narrative without the credibility of the gospel's witness (which the author wants to defend, not threaten) being seriously called into question by the author's community. Furthermore, the fact that he was raised from death is in no way to be used against the identification of the BD as Lazarus. The Synoptics contain resurrection miracles (Mark – Jairus' daughter; Luke – the son of the widow of Nain). In fact, many of the gospel's puzzles are solved if we see the BD as Lazarus. The distinctive theme of 'life' (ζωή) in John's story is but one example. If the eye-witness authority behind the fourth gospel is a man who has been raised to new life, then it is not hard to infer that his theological reflection on that experience greatly influenced the character and the emphases of the gospel.

Thus, there is a valuable historical tradition in John's story which originates in the eye-witness of Lazarus of Bethany. But what was the form of this tradition? Here I propose two tentative suggestions: first, that the main form in which Lazarus' eye-witness material was handed down was narrative; secondly, that this narrative was a primitive, written ur-gospel (21.24). The contents of this document may have been as follows:

1. Stories concerning John the Baptist's ministry around Bethany (John 1.19–42, 3.22ff.), especially if this Bethany is being identified by John as the Bethany where Lazarus lived (Parker, 1955).
2. Stories concerning encounters between Jesus and individuals from the Jerusalem area (Nathaniel in 1.43–51, Nicodemus in 3.1–15, 7.45–52, 19.38f.).
3. Stories concerning Jesus at the feasts in Jerusalem (5.1, 7.1–13, 10.22f.), in particular the passover visits (2.13, 13.1).
4. Stories concerning Lazarus himself (John 11 and 12.1–11, 12.17–19, 13.23f., 18.15–18, 19.25–37, 20.3f., ch.21).
5. Stories concerning Jerusalem-based miracles (5.1–15 at Bethesda, and 9.1–34 at Siloam) which clearly come from a different milieu from the other miracle stories.
6. Stories concerning the last supper (the basis of the narrative and discourse in chapters 13 and 14) and passion/resurrection.

From the material described above, it becomes clear that a Bethany gospel must have been composed early in the history of John's tradition. I would propose the following hypothetical reconstruction of the ur-gospel centred upon Lazarus' reminiscences:

PART 1 The Jerusalem ministry of Jesus

(a)   The preparatory ministry of John the Baptist in Bethany

(b)   The calling of the first disciples, including Lazarus

(c)   Encounters with Jerusalem-based individuals: Nathaniel and Nicodemus. Again witnessed by Lazarus

(d)   Jerusalem-based miracles (Bethesda in ch. 5, Siloam in Ch. 9, Bethany in ch. 11, though not necessarily in this order). These miracles are set within Jesus' visits to the capital and were witnessed by Lazarus

(e)   Conclusion to part 1. The controversy with the Jewish leaders in Jerusalem caused by these miracles finalized the plot to kill Jesus (material now in chapters 11 and 12). At the end of part 1, Lazarus' sister ominously anoints Jesus' feet

PART 2 The last days of Jesus in Jerusalem

(a)   The entrance into Jerusalem and the cleansing of the temple

(b)   The last supper, including institution narrative, Judas material, washing of disciples' feet and some last words of Jesus

(c)   The arrest, trial and execution of Jesus

(d)   The resurrection (the race to the empty tomb in John 20.3f.)

(e)   The conclusion to part 2.

From this outline, we can see that the major source behind John's story of Jesus may have been a primitive gospel which was already cast in narrative form. We may somewhat boldly call this source the gospel of Lazarus.

The signs gospel

What, then, of the signs gospel, which has so often been regarded as one of the principal narrative sources behind John's gospel? The last two years of the 1980s have seen the publication of Fortna's *The Fourth Gospel and its Predecessor* and von Wahlde's *Earliest Version of John's Gospel*. Fortna's position is as follows: 'The Fourth Gospel as we have it can be understood as chiefly the product of two literary stages, a pre-Johannine narrative source (or two) and an extended Johannine redaction, including the composition of the discourses' (pp. 5–6). Fortna distinguishes between the older and the younger gospels in John by examining the aporias in the gospel – those moments in the narrative where the redactor is seen to be adding something of his own and interrupting the flow of the story. Fortna uses five kinds of evidence for identifying an aporia: contextual, stylistic, theological, form and text-critical, and finally Synoptic evidence (p. 6). Having pealed off the redactional layer, Fortna identifies what he calls the signs gospel behind John's gospel. He proposes that 'the text of the source survives on the whole intact within the present Gospel' (p. 7). It is a complete gospel in itself. In the first part of Fortna's SG (signs gospel), there are four Galilean miracles followed by three Judaean miracles, and they have a logical itinerary. In the second part, the SG follows the traditional sequence of the Synoptic accounts of Jesus' last days.

Von Wahlde's SG contains noticeably more than Fortna's, but that is because their methods differ. Whilst Fortna identifies the SG by using the aporias, von Wahlde identifies his SG through linguistic differences. Von Wahlde's main argument is that SG uses two different ways of describing the religious authorities and Jesus' miracles. As far as the authorities are concerned, von Wahlde contends that the earliest stratum of the gospel uses Pharisees (19 times), chief priests (10 times) and rulers (4 times). The later stratum uses 'the Jews' in a hostile sense (37 out of the 71 uses of this phrase he describes as hostile in nuance). In the case of miracles, von Wahlde shows that John has 'works' where he has 'Jews' in the hostile sense, whilst he has 'signs' where he has 'Pharisees', 'chief priests', 'rulers' and 'Jews' in a neutral sense. Using other criteria as well, von Wahlde concludes that the passages where we find 'Pharisees'/'chief priests'/ 'rulers'/'Jews' (neutral sense) with 'signs' for Jesus' miracles are from the earliest version of John's gospel. Passages using 'the Jews' in a negative way, alongside the use of the word *works* to describe Jesus' miracles, are from a later hand (the evangelist's redaction). Using this method, von Wahlde recreates the SG and claims that it was originally an artistically structured narrative in its own right. He sees in the SG a progression in which the signs become more and more dramatic manifestations of Jesus' power. Numbers are important in this progression: 6 jars at Cana, the 5 husbands of the Samaritan woman, the 38 years of suffering in the Bethesda patient, the 5,000 fed, the man born blind, Lazarus 4 days dead, and so on. Both Fortna and von Wahlde reconstruct their SG and show how it was a narrative with a plot.

The problem with Fortna's book is that it nowhere answers the damaging critique levelled against Fortna's *Gospel of Signs* by Barnabas Lindars in his *Behind the Fourth Gospel* (1971). In the latter, Lindars showed how close to impossible it is to distinguish between tradition and redaction in John because the evangelist's style permeates every sentence of the gospel. Fortna has certainly not refined his method to take this into account. As for von Wahlde, although his basic approach distinguishing between two different understandings of the miracles and the Jewish hierarchy is innovative, the twenty other criteria he introduces for distinguishing between source and redaction are not convincing, and seriously undermine his method. Furthermore, both Fortna and von Wahlde fail to see that there are differences between the Galilean miracles and the Judaean miracles in John. In the first place, there are differences in geographical context: the Judaean miracles all occur in or around Jerusalem. In at least the case of Bethesda and Siloam, archaeology has revealed that the topography of these miracles reflects an accurate knowledge of Jerusalem before AD 70. Secondly, there are the differences in literary form: in the Judaean miracle narratives, the healing of the man at the pool of Bethesda, the healing of the man born blind at Siloam, the raising of Lazarus very near Jerusalem, all lead on to controversy with the Jewish authorities. Unlike the Galilean miracles (except for the multiplication of the loaves in John 6), they lead into heated debates with the Jewish hierarchy and into discourse material which elaborates themes from the miracles. These two major differences between the Jerusalem-based and the Galilean miracles (one geographical, the other literary) make it important to distinguish between two miracle traditions in John's gospel – a Galilean miracles source and the Judaean miracles in the Bethany gospel. I propose that there was no signs gospel, but that there was a collection of Galilean signs/miracles.

The Synoptic gospels

In the light of these brief and hypothetical comments concerning John the storyteller's source material, we are in a position to make two claims: first of all, the principal narrative source for John's story of Jesus was a written gospel originating in Lazarus' eye-witness accounts; secondly, there was no signs gospel behind John's story but a collection of Galilean miracles which John the storyteller added later to the BD's ur-gospel. This has implications concerning John's dependence upon the Synoptic gospels as narrative sources. C.K. Barrett has insisted on John's knowledge of Mark's gospel in its written form for some time (1978, pp. 42–6). His position has recently been strengthened on the Continent by the work of de Solages (1979) and Neirynck (1979). The very thorough treatment of this question by de Solages has argued on the one hand that 'Jean n'utilise pas les

Synoptiques comme source' (the title of part 1 of de Solages, 1979), but on the other hand that 'Jean connaît la tradition synoptique' (the title of part 2). De Solages, in other words, contends that John did not have the written texts of Mark, Matthew and Luke before him, but that he had either heard them read, or read them himself, or at the very least knew of their traditions. My own position is as follows: firstly, John did not use the written versions of the Synoptics as his source. Of the 868 verses of John's gospel, 153, or 17.2 per cent have Synoptic counterparts. When one remembers that 609 of Mark's 662 verses have counterparts in Matthew, it proves the point (Smith, 1987, p. 129). Secondly, however, it is possible that John may have known Mark's story of Jesus but not in a written form. As we shall see later, John's story of Jesus has affinities with the genre of tragedy. The same observation has frequently been made about Mark's story. It is at least possible therefore that John was familiar with Mark's storytelling.

Narrative and gospel

If Lazarus is the authority behind John, he is not the author. The Greek texts of the fourth gospel describe the work as 'according to John'. We should understand this John as the elder mentioned at the start of the second epistle of John (2 John 1) and not as the apostle John, one of the sons of Zebedee. John was an extremely common name in first-century Palestine (Hengel, 1989, p. 26, 109f.). Indeed, Papias distinguishes between two Johns when he writes:

> And if anyone chanced to come who had actually been a follower of the elders, I would enquire as to the discourses of the elders, what Andrew or what Peter said, or what Philip, or what Thomas or James, or what John or Matthew or any other of the Lord's disciples; and the things which Ariston and John the elder, the disciples of the Lord, say.
>
> (Hengel, 1989, p. 17)

The two Johns whom Papias is describing are John the son of Zebedee, who was one of the Twelve, and John the elder, who was also a follower of Jesus (though not necessarily a first-generation follower), but was separate from the first group of seven disciples. My proposal is that Lazarus was the principal eye-witness and authority behind John's story but that the elder John is responsible for the gospel as we now have it. Lazarus is to John what Peter (it is argued)

was to Mark. When we speak of 'John the storyteller' we are therefore not referring to John bar Zebedee but to a second-generation
follower of Jesus. He took the Bethany gospel, a signs source, and
certain discourse sources (maybe other narrative sources too, such
as a Samaritan tradition) and recast them into a carefully constructed
story designed to address social needs in his church(es). The source
material from the Bethany and signs traditions was already narrative
in form. However, it was crude compared to the story which John
creates.

There are three important points to make about this elusive John
if we are truly to appreciate him as a storyteller. To start with, John
was a preacher. A number of scholars have done valuable work on the
discourses in John which show that these passages have been modelled
on the synagogue homily or sermon (Borgen, 1985). Lindars regards
these homilies as the evangelist's own preaching and not as the
evangelist's reports of Jesus' preaching, or of the BD's preaching
(1990, pp. 36f.). He argues that the homiletic theory explains the
unique feature of the discourses. What John does is to take a saying
from the tradition which we can regard as the text of the sermon.
This saying is an authentic and historically valuable item of John's
Jesus tradition. Thus, the discourse with Nicodemus starts with a
logion (3.3,5) which Dodd and many others have shown, on the basis
of parallels with Matthew 18.3 and Mark 10.15, must be traditional.
It introduces the theme of origination from God which is the theme
of the whole discourse (cf. verses 6 and 31). The same thing happens
after John 5.19, which Dodd argued was a parable from the tradition
(the parable of the apprenticed son), in John 6 with the bread of life
discourse, after John 8.12 ('I am the Light of the World'), after
8.36 (the parable of the slave and the son) and after 10.1−5 (the
parable of sheep and shepherd). Other sayings can be found in 6.52−6
and in 8.51−2. In each case, sayings from the tradition occur at
strategic places in the discourses and appear to function as the springboard for the evangelist's profound homiletical reflections on the
sayings of Jesus. Lindars's conclusion seems to me to be right. He
states, 'it is reasonable to suppose that the ... discourses are based
on the evangelist's own homilies delivered in the Johannine church'
(p. 36).

What this suggests is that John's preaching on the sayings of Jesus
has provided him with the material for his dramatic use of discourse
in the gospel. Two things need to be said, however, before the reader
relegates these sections of the gospel to fiction. First of all, Lindars

has ably demonstrated that the discourses are based on the historical sayings of Jesus, even if they have also been the basis for interpretative elaborations. Secondly, John was not only a preacher, but also a prophet. Eugene Boring has shown that there are striking similarities between the description of what the Paraclete is to do in John, and the functions of Christian prophecy in the New Testament (1978). Boring cites eleven parallels, of which the following are most convincing:

1. The Paraclete and prophecy are post-Easter gifts of the Holy Spirit.
2. The Paraclete has a specific speech function, as does prophecy.
3. The Paraclete, like the gift of prophecy, seems to be a particularized function of the Spirit.
4. The Paraclete, like the prophet, is depicted as the link between the Exalted Christ and the church.
5. The Paraclete – like the prophet in I Cor. 14.24–5 – convicts the world of its sin (16.8–11).
6. The Paraclete, like the Christian prophet, never speaks *aph heautou* (16.13).
7. The Paraclete, like the prophet, declares 'things to come' (14.13).
8. The word Paraclete ('comforter') has prophetic connotations which make it an appropriate surrogate for 'prophet' (I Cor. 14.3,31).

Boring's conclusion is that John's story emerged from a developing community in which Christian prophets played an important role.

John was thus not only a preacher but a prophet, and his dramatic interpretations of Jesus tradition should not be seen as the inventions of his mind but rather as prophetic reflections on Jesus tradition. But if John was a preacher and a prophet, he was also finally a poet. It was R. G. Collingwood who described in his classic work *The Idea of History* (before the narrative history debate began) the resemblance between the historian and the creative writer:

> Each of them makes it his business to construct a picture which is partly a narrative of events, partly a description of situations, exhibition of motives, analysis of characters. Each aims at making his picture a coherent whole, where every character and every situation is so bound up with the rest that

this character in this situation cannot but act in this way, and we cannot imagine him as acting otherwise. The novel and the history must both of them make sense; nothing is admissible in either except what is necessary, and the judge of this necessity is in both cases the imagination.

(1953, p. 245)

Collingwood's great contribution in this area was to destroy what he called the 'common-sense' view of history. By that he meant the commonly held theory that history-writing is purely a matter of the historian faithfully redescribing ready-made authorities which the reader then has to believe. He exposes the fallacy of this theory by describing what all historians really do with their sources. 'He selects from them what he thinks important, and omits the rest; he interpolates in them things which they do not explicitly say; and he criticizes them by rejecting or amending what he regards as due to misinformation or mendacity' (p. 235). The point is that the historian uses his imagination. There is no such thing as a complete copy of historical events any more than there is, in art, a complete copy of nature. History-writing is 'a web of imaginative construction stretched between certain fixed points provided by the statements of his authorities' (p. 242).

In the context of the gospel of John, those who hold the common-sense theory of history would therefore say that John had ready-made, authoritative sources which were infallible, and that he has merely copied down what were complete copies of the Jesus-history they depicted. The narrative historian, however, would say that John's sources are already the result of the poetic imagination since they are narrative in form, and that John himself has exercised a high degree of imaginative skill in omitting, selecting and combining this varied material into his own story. This is the position taken here. Obviously we are in the realm of speculation when we propose the existence of narrative sources behind John, but such sources must have existed even if we cannot be too specific about their genre, their contents and their function. What John has done with this tradition is to recast the story, omitting some of the material in his sources, adding material which he believed to be communicated by the Exalted Jesus through the Paraclete, selecting and combining everything with certain narrative principles in mind. In chapter 1, for example, I pointed to the use of the judgement theme in the fourth gospel. The whole of John's story feels like a courtroom scene in which Jesus is in the dock. This is John's work and probably reflects his community's sense of being on trial at the hands of Pharisaic Judaism. But its literary origins are in Deutero Isaiah, which depicts the courtroom of Yahweh (41.1). Indeed, some of John's imagery may also have its literary origins here. Glory/shepherds/revelation/tents of dwelling/witness/I am sayings/light and darkness/blindness/water/the temple/truth/lifting up/the lamb of God — all these images are in Deutero Isaiah too.

What I am saying is that John the storyteller had various narrative pre-texts at his disposal. He had the actual life-history of Jesus, which was, as all human lives are, already an inchoate story. He had various sources redescribing Jesus in narrative form, in particular, the reminiscences of the BD (which may already have been a rudimentary gospel including a passion/resurrection narrative), a catena of Galilean miracle stories, a Samaritan mission tradition, and so on. He also had the pre-text of the Old Testament which, as the testimonies in the passion narrative and the references to Deutero Isaiah above amply reveal, were clearly important to him as a repertoire of narrative possibilities. The fourth gospel therefore represents a very complex journeying through various pre-texts to the final form we have today, and the principal imagination behind the creative narrative reworking of these pre-texts is that of John the storyteller — preacher, prophet and poet. The poetic and imaginative aspect of John's work can really only be appreciated if the reader is prepared to read or to listen to the whole story of the fourth gospel at one go. Too often we have been guilty not only of treating the gospels as archaeological mounds (as Culpepper rightly shows: 1983, p. 3). We have also been guilty of atomizing them, of isolating individual pericopes and in the process forgetting that each pericope has a relationship with other pericopes which, altogether, create a carefully designed whole. Looking at the whole gospel as story can be a refreshing experience for those only used to seeing this text as an untidy montage of displaced and rearranged episodes, or as a clumsy patchwork of tradition and redaction in which the seams are all too visible. The poetic aspects of fourth-gospel narrative require a holistic reader response for their true appreciation.

We shall be looking in detail at the narrative-poetic qualities of John 18–19 in part II. In conclusion to part I I want to identify the leading theme in John's story — one which has received no attention from scholars. This is an example of the poetic contribution of John the storyteller. The theme in question is *the theme of the elusive*

Christ. Throughout John's gospel there is a kind of hide-and-seek dynamic in the narrative which creates suspense and excitement. In many parts of John the storyteller depicts men and women seeking Jesus. Some of this seeking is positive. In other words, some of the characters in the story seek Jesus for help or healing. In chapter 1, the disciples seek him to know where he is staying (1.38). In chapter 2, Jesus' mother seeks him for help at the wedding feast (2.3). In chapter 3, Nicodemus seeks Jesus to find out more about him. In chapter 4 the Samaritans seek him for confirmation of the woman's story, and the official seeks him for the healing of his son. The only other examples of positive seeking of Jesus are in 11.9 after the raising of Lazarus, in 12.18f., where the Greeks seek him, and in 20.1f. (the resurrection) − arguably the climax of this theme. However, there is negative as well as positive seeking of Jesus. The negative seeking of Jesus emerges at the point where positive seeking breaks off, i.e. at the end of chapter 4. After the Bethesda miracle, the Jews seek him to persecute and kill him (5.12, 16, 18). In chapter 6, the crowds seek him to make him king (6.15, 24). In chapters 7−11, this negative quest for Jesus intensifies with the Jews' attempts to capture and kill him (7.30, 7.44, 8.20, 8.59, 10.31, 10.39, 11.53, 11.56). The climax of the theme is in 18.4f., when seeking at last becomes finding.

Alongside this theme of seeking there is the theme of hiding. The suspense in John's story consists almost entirely of the negative seeking of Jesus and the concomitant hiding and elusiveness of Jesus. He is elusive, first of all, in his whereabouts. The remark in 6.25, 'Rabbi, when did you get here?' expresses this elusiveness perfectly. At a number of points in the fourth gospel Jesus moves about in secret, or withdraws and hides from those who seek him (4.3, 5.13, 6.15, 7.1, 7.10, 8.59, 10.39, 11.54). Sometimes his elusiveness is due to the fact that his hour has not yet come (7.30, 8.21). What is interesting about Jesus is the way in which his elusiveness is extended to the Father whom he looks to (5.37, 14.8) and the Spirit whom he gives (3.8).

Secondly, Jesus can be elusive in his speech as well as in his whereabouts. The problem of misunderstanding dogs disciples, enquirers and unbelievers alike. The disciples rejoice in 16.29 that at last Jesus is opting for plain speaking rather than the elusive language of figures and metaphors. The enquiring Nicodemus in chapter 3 seems incapable of understanding Jesus' metaphor of rebirth. Unbelieving Pilate, in chapters 18 and 19, is absolutely perplexed by the evasiveness of Jesus in the face of his questionings.

Thirdly, it is not only the whereabouts and the speech of Jesus that proves elusive: there is also the matter of his past and his future. The question of his origins proves elusive throughout (for example, in 6.42, 19.9–10) and, in the farewell discourses, Jesus constantly promises his disciples that he is about to become even more elusive ('where I am about to go, you will not be able to come!', 13.33, 14.19, 6.16).

Throughout the story, the reader is conscious of this dialectic of seeking and hiding. People seek Jesus with very different motives, but he hides himself from those who would do him harm until the appointed hour arrives. People try to understand Jesus, but his language constantly evades them. People seek to penetrate the mystery of his origins, but that eludes them too. In the past (his origins), in the present (his moments of withdrawal) and the future (going the way men cannot follow) Jesus proves elusive. He is as much Jesus the Concealer as Jesus the Revealer. This interpretation is an example of the storyteller's poetic handling of tradition throughout the gospel. Indeed, plot, characterization and vocabulary seem to have been designed carefully to evoke this sense of elusiveness, mystery, excitement and suspense. I would even venture to suggest that some of the so-called aporias and mistakes are part of this strategy. For example, at one notorious point the storyteller seems to make Jesus' movements almost impossible to follow. I am referring, of course, to the itinerary of chapters 5 and 6. H. E. Edwards remarks: 'It is as if you were reading a letter from a friend in which he was telling you about salmon fishing in Scotland, and then, as you turn the page, the letter went on, "After this I went over London Bridge" (1953, p. 53). It is not impossible that the author intended this sequence in order to heighten the sense of Jesus' ability to move about so quickly and so elusively.

Where, finally, did this theme of the elusiveness of the Stranger from heaven come from? In part, the theme would have been implied by certain features in John's traditions, for we know that the historical Jesus moved and spoke evasively at times from the other gospels. In part the theme may have been prompted by echoes between the story of Dionysus (the archetype of the elusive god) and the story of Jesus, as we shall see in chapter 6. But the degree to which this theme surfaces in John suggests that the community for which the book was written was undergoing the kind of social crisis which made strategies of evasion absolutely crucial. The anonymity of the founding father (the BD) suggests that the community needed to be secretive. The references to Jesus withdrawing from the Jews seem to connote some sort of emigration of Jewish Christians from areas of vulnerability (a city area?). Indeed, the statement in 11.54, 'therefore Jesus no longer moved about publicly among the Jews. Instead he withdrew to a region near the desert, to a village called Ephraim, where he stayed with his disciples', may be more significant than anyone has realized. Could it be that here we have, in code form, an indication of the hidden life adopted by John's readers? It is impossible to be certain. Whatever the case, this one example of the theme of Jesus' elusiveness, so brilliantly achieved and sustained throughout John, should be sufficient to show that the author was indeed a masterful storyteller; that he was not only a preacher and a prophet, but also a poet. The narrative qualities in John's story of Jesus Christ are ones worthy of attention and of praise. In part II, I shall endeavour to show in much greater detail from chapters 18–19 how artfully John the storyteller redescribes his historical tradition in story-form.

PART II

AN APPLICATION OF THE METHOD OF NARRATIVE CRITICISM TO JOHN 18 – 19

INTRODUCTION

We now come to the application of the method of narrative criticism to the text of the Johannine passion narrative (chapters 18−19). In what follows, the chapters correspond to their equivalents in part I. So in chapter 5 I expose John 18−19 to practical criticism, with particular emphasis upon structure, characterization, themes, symbolism and narrative echo effects. In chapter 6, I shall look at the genre of John 18−19 using categories drawn from the functional analysis of narrative (structuralism). In chapter 7, I look at the social function of these chapters for John's original addressees. In chapter 8, I look at the narrativity of the history of Jesus' passion, the narrativity of John's source for that history, and the artistic contribution of the storyteller in the final major stage of the composition of these chapters. In choosing chapters 18−19 of John's story, I have been particularly conscious of the lack of literary and narrative criticism of this carefully constructed and well-rounded narrative text. Apart from two somewhat disappointing articles by C. H. Giblin (1984; 1986), an interesting essay on the dramatic qualities of John 18−19 by Ehrman (1983), and some literary insights in the commentaries of Brown, Ellis and Sloyan, the main trends for the analysis of these chapters have emphasized sources (Goguel, 1910; Buse, 1957; Borgen, 1959; Dauer, 1972; von Wahlde, 1989; Fortna, 1989), historical tradition (Haenchen, 1970; Bruce, 1980; Robinson, 1985), theology (Pfitzner, 1976; Lindars, 1977; Thompson, 1988) and symbolism (Schwank, 1964; Dauer, 1967; de la Potterie, 1969). *John as Storyteller* is a first on two accounts: it is the first scholarly, book-length study of John 18−19 in English (Fenton, 1961, and Bligh, 1975, wrote popular studies), and the first comprehensive narrative-critical study of these chapters.

5

A PRACTICAL CRITICISM OF JOHN 18–19

The arrest of the shepherd. John 18.1–27

Narrative structure and summary

After the lengthy discourses of chapters 14–17, we come to the climactic moment in the gospel, namely, the moment of Christ's passion, death and burial (John 18–19). I have elected to examine 18.1–27 as the first of three sections because it represents the first division of John's passion account. Some scholars have divided 18.1–27 into two separate units, the first dealing with the arrest of Jesus and the second with the denials of Peter (and the concomitant initial interrogation of Jesus by Annas). Most notable amongst these has been Peter Ellis, who, in an experimental, composition-critical commentary, divides 18.1–27 into two separate acts (1–12, 13–27), both containing a chiastic structure involving five scenes (p. 247). However, it is quite plain that 18.1–27 is meant to be regarded as a single structural unit, with 1–11 emphasizing Jesus against Peter, 12–14 as a transitional pericope, and 15–27 (of equal length with 1–11) emphasizing Peter against Jesus. Three arguments support these structural divisions: (i) both scenes are rounded off with a reference to the high priest's servant Malchus; (ii) the preservation of 18.1–27 as a single unit results in a narrative triptych of three equal parts (A = 18.1–27, B = 18.28–19.16a, C = 19.16b–42, each part approximately twenty-seven verses long); (iii) the evangelist presents a consistent character contrast between Jesus and Peter which runs through the whole of 18.1–27 and which clearly ends at verse 27. These three lines of evidence support my contention that John the storyteller intended 18.1–27 to be regarded as a single act of the passion drama.

The kernel events of 18.1–27 are as follows:

(a) In vv. 1–11, Jesus crosses a valley to a garden with his disciples. It is night-time. Judas arrives at the garden with a detachment of Roman soldiers with the purpose of arresting Jesus. Jesus, outside the garden walls, identifies himself as the one whom they are seeking,

and asks that the disciples should be left to go in safety. Peter cuts
the ear of the high priest's servant with his sword. Jesus, finally,
rebukes Peter.

(b) Verses 12—14 form a narrative bridge in which the narrator
provides three important pieces of information: first, that Jesus is
bound and taken to Annas; secondly, that Annas was high priest
and father-in-law to Caiaphas; thirdly, that Caiaphas was the man
who claimed that it was expedient for one man to die for all the
people.

(c) In vv. 15—27, Peter and another disciple follow Jesus. The
anonymous disciple goes with Jesus into Annas' courtyard because
he is known here. Peter remains outside and has to have the help of
this disciple in order to get past the portress. The portress suggests
that Peter is a disciple of Jesus. Peter denies it, and goes over to a
fire to warm himself. Inside Annas' house, Jesus is questioned about
his disciples and his teaching. Jesus tells Annas to ask one of his
disciples. Jesus is slapped by an official, whom he rebukes, and sent
bound to Caiaphas. Peter, outside the house, denies Jesus two more
times and a cock crows.

Character contrasts

A number of antitheses are presented in 18.1—27 between the characters who appear on stage. The main character contrast is between
Jesus and Peter. As I have already indicated, scene one (1—11) depicts
Jesus in the foreground and Peter in the background, whilst scene
three (15—27) depicts Peter in the foreground and Jesus in the background. That the evangelist intends this contrast to be the main focus
is obvious from a number of factors. First, he sets up a deliberate
opposition between the twofold response of Jesus to an interrogation
(ἐγώ εἰμι, in vv. 5 and 8) and the twofold response of Peter to an
interrogation (οὐκ εἰμί, in vv. 17 and 25). Secondly, the evangelist
depicts Peter assaulting a servant of the high priest in v. 10, whilst
Jesus is presented as being assaulted by an official of the same high
priest in v. 22. Thirdly, the evangelist designs his narrative of Peter's
denials so that they are separated by Jesus' response to interrogation
in the high priest's house. This creates a highly ironic scene in which
Jesus calls forth his disciples as witnesses at the same time as Peter
is denying any knowledge of him. Two trials consequently appear to
be taking place: an informal trial of Jesus inside the house, and an
informal trial of Peter outside the house.

At every opportunity it seems as if the evangelist has underlined the differences between Jesus and Peter. Whilst Peter is a somewhat spontaneous hostage to fortune, Jesus exhibits a sovereign control over events. Whilst Peter's conduct smacks of human timidity, Jesus' speaks of divine composure. A number of significant narrative details highlight this sovereign domination of events by Jesus: first, Jesus goes to a place which Judas knew (v. 2), suggesting that Jesus made no attempt to escape arrest, but went as usual to the place where he rested with his disciples. Secondly, the narrator informs us that Jesus knew everything that was going to befall him (v. 4), and yet he still allowed it to take place. This stresses the voluntary nature of Jesus' acceptance of arrest. Thirdly, in John's arrest narrative, Jesus goes out to Judas instead of Judas coming to Jesus and kissing him, showing that the initiative belongs to Jesus, not to Judas (as in the Synoptics). Fourthly, Jesus' use of ἐγώ εἰμι in v. 5, the divine name, causes the arresting party to recoil in fear before the moral supremacy of Jesus. Fifthly, Jesus manipulates the situation so that he is taken, but not his disciples (vv. 8–9). Sixthly, Jesus' question, 'am I not to drink the cup the Father has given me?' (v. 11) manifests confident resignation to suffering, rather than shrinking fear (as in Matthew 26.42). How vividly this sovereign control contrasts with Peter, who is everywhere a victim of circumstances!

Two further character contrasts are visible in the narrative of 18.1–27, the first between the anonymous disciple and Peter, the second between the anonymous disciple and Judas. The second of these is very minor, but there is some irony in the fact that both characters fulfil the narrative function of guide (Judas to the arresting party, the anonymous disciple to Peter), though with very different motives. Judas' incentive to be guide is treachery; the anonymous disciple's is loyalty.

By far the more significant contrast is between the anonymous disciple and Peter. The anonymous believer here is undoubtedly the BD of 13.23ff., since (i) he always appears in close proximity to Peter, (ii) he is consistently faithful as a disciple, as he is here (in following Jesus into the courtyard of Annas' house), (iii) he provides access to Jesus for Peter in 13.23ff. (as he does here), (iv) he is called ἄλλον μαθητήν in 20.2 (where it clearly refers to the BD), just as he is called ἄλλος μαθητής in 18.15. The reasons why the BD is not referred to explicitly as the disciple whom Jesus loved are not easy to understand, but two possibilities suggest themselves. First, the anonymity of the BD contrasts emphatically with the complete designation 'Simon Peter' (not just 'Peter') in 18.15. This creates the ironical suggestion that an apparently unknown disciple behaved more faithfully than Peter. Secondly, if it is correct that the fourth gospel was forged in the heat of an ardent hostility to Judaism, then the fact of the BD's intimacy with the high priest Annas may well have been a cause of embarrassment – especially, as seems likely, if the BD was the founding father of the Johannine community.

The contrast between the BD and Peter centres principally on the idea of discipleship. In 18.15, the narrator makes the apparently innocuous remark that both Simon Peter and another disciple 'followed' Jesus. The verb ἀκολουθέω is, at one level, nothing more than a verb of motion explaining how the two disciples managed to be present in the vicinity of Annas' house. At a deeper level, however, the verb – especially when it has Jesus as its direct object – connotes discipleship, as the noun follower indicates. The difference between the anonymous disciple and Peter is visible in the fact that the former has easy access in and out of the courtyard, whilst Peter is stuck at the gate, refused entry by a woman gatekeeper. Paul Duke, who has written a seminal study of the irony in John's story, makes the important point that Peter's timid behaviour is in striking opposition to his rather irrational bravado with the high priest's servant. As Duke puts it, 'the sword-slinging defender melts before the word of a servant girl' (1985, p. 97). What we have in the two major subsections of John 18.1–27 is therefore an antithesis between Jesus and Peter at a primary level, and an antithesis between the BD and Peter at a secondary level. In both instances, the conduct of Jesus and the BD is paradigmatic and exemplary, whilst that of Peter is clearly misguided and coloured by pathos.

Implicit commentary

In chapter 1, we adopted Tannehill's 'narrative Christology' as an apt description of John's gospel, on the grounds that the different parts of the gospel appear to be unified by Christological themes. By 'themes' here we mean the main, recurrent ideas which give internal coherence to the narrative, and the sorts of unifying Christological ideas which we highlighted there were, for example, the notion of Jesus as Judge, the notion of Jesus' divinity (the 'I am' sayings), and so on. In chapter 4 I showed how the theme of the elusive Christ dominated the whole of John's presentation. In all these examples, we see how Christological themes recur, appearing and disappearing with enough regularity for us to discern a coherent narrative Christology.

These themes are either explicitly or implicitly stated; there appears to be a kind of sliding scale from the overt to the allusive — as can be seen in the evangelist's subtle contrasts between light and darkness, and between warmth and coldness in 18.1—27. When, in v. 1, we are told that Jesus and his disciples crossed the Kidron valley, the two notions of darkness and coldness resonate from the etymological meanings of the phrase χειμάρρου τοῦ Κεδρών (Brown, 1966, Vol. II, p. 806). When the arresting party arrive with lanterns and torches to capture Jesus in v. 3, the reader may feel that some irony is intended here, with Jesus having already been described as the Light of the World in chapter 8. When Peter warms himself by the charcoal fire in 18.18, the reader may feel that, again, the evangelist is playing on the irony of Peter's dependence on a man-made ἀνθρακιά rather than on the Light of the World. In other words, the details connotative of light and darkness, and of warmth and coldness, may lead the reader to see an implicit commentary in 18.1—27 deriving from the Christology of Jesus as light and as the true source of human vitality and warmth. Yet again we see how John's narrative details possess a symbolic resonance.

It is possible for the reader to understand 18.1—27 as an implicit commentary on the truth enunciated in 1.5 that 'the light shines on in the darkness, for the darkness did not overcome it'. But is this theme of Jesus-as-light the only Christological thought controlling the emplotment of the arrest? Whilst the commentaries are confident about the central Christological themes in the rest of the passion narrative (i.e. in 18.28f., and 19.16f.), they are less certain about the Christological emphasis in 18.1—27. This is largely because its delineations are allusive rather than explicit. However, two of the best-known Johannine commentators have made isolated and undeveloped remarks which indicate a direction which we could go in. First, C.K. Barrett has written of Jesus' desire for his disciples' safety in 18.7 that 'it seems to be John's primary intention to show, in *an acted parable*, that the "Good Shepherd lays down his life for the sheep" (10.11)' (1978, p. 435). Secondly, Barnabas Lindars, commenting on the text in 18.9 ('This was to fulfil what he had said, "I have not lost even one of those whom you have given me" '), suggests that its most logical background is 10.29, where Jesus says of his sheep, 'My Father, as to what He has given me, is greater than all, and from the Father's hand no one can snatch them away' (1972,

p. 542). He makes much of the fact that there is no flight of the disciples in John 18, arguing that such a desertion, understood via Zechariah 13.7 as a scattering of the sheep, would have undermined Jesus' status as a 'good shepherd' (p. 542).

Barrett and Lindars have started on an avenue of investigation which is promising, for there is no doubt in my mind that the evangelist intended a number of narrative echo effects with the pastoral discourse in John 10.1–21. However, John 10.1–21 is by no means unproblematic, since there are a number of difficulties with its form. For instance, it is not easy to say what literary background lies behind this pastoral imagery, or what sources have been used, or what relationship the text has to its enveloping narratives. In this context, however, we are interested in the final form of the discourse rather than its complex textual prehistory. Four things should be said about it:

(1) The structure of John 10.1–21 falls – as so often in the fourth gospel – into a tripartite pattern. Section one, vv. 1–6, forms a general picture of shepherds and their relationship to their sheep and the sheep-pen. Section two, vv. 7–18, constitutes an allegorical elaboration of this picture in which Jesus identifies himself with two elements from vv. 1–5. This second section is further divided into two subsections, with vv. 7–10 dealing with Jesus as the door of the fold, and vv. 11–18 with Jesus as the Good Shepherd. Both these subsections contain two ἐγώ εἰμί sayings, at verses 7 and 9, and 11 and 14 respectively. A recurrent theme in the second subsection is 'laying down his life for the sheep', at vv. 11, 15, 17, 18. The third subsection, vv. 19–21, describes the division amongst the people which this teaching caused, verse 20 depicting the negative response, and verse 21 the positive response.

(2) the genre of vv. 1–5 is explicitly described by the narrator as παροιμία (v. 6). As has often been pointed out, the Synoptic gospels use παραβολή, whilst John uses παροιμία. Nothing exceptional is seen in this, because the two words are used as synonymous translations of *mashal* in the LXX and other sources. However, some commentators have suggested that the nuances of παροιμία are slightly different from those of παραβολή. Lightfoot describes a παροιμία as a 'symbolic word-picture' (p. 210); Schnackenburg describes it as a 'cryptic discourse' (p. 283). Brown, whilst stating that there is no great difference between the two, also maintains that 'there may be more emphasis on the enigmatic in παροιμία' (1966, Vol. I, p. 385). The challenge to the reader of 10.1–21 is therefore to penetrate the hidden dimensions of the discourse.

(3) There is an overall setting implied in the narrative world of shepherds and sheep introduced in 10.1. All the action implied in this discourse takes place in and around an αὐλή (translated 'sheepfold' in most versions). Αὐλή denotes two possible scenarios: a sheepfold erected at pasture time out in the open and outside a village, or a yard pertaining to and adjoining a house (Schnackenburg, 1969, p. 279). The sheep are enclosed within this fold during the night, protected from wolves, robbers and other predators by a gatekeeper and by the shepherd. In the dark hours of the early morning, the shepherd goes in and out of the fold to lead his flock to pasture. The setting within the narrative world of John 10 is therefore as follows:

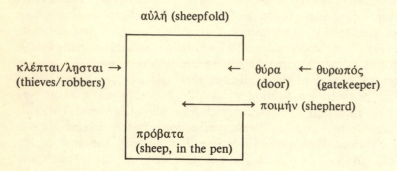

(4) The pastoral picture as a whole is constructed upon a number of significant character contrasts. These narrative oppositions are best expressed using Greimas's model for the study of all narrative performances, though I acknowledge the limitations of this model, as well as the fact that John 10.1–21 does not constitute a single narrative with a discernible plot:

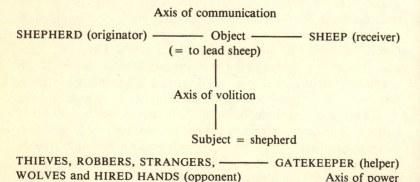

The top horizontal axis is what Greimas calls the 'axis of communication', which in this case is constituted by the shepherd (the originator) calling his sheep out of the fold to pasture. The middle vertical axis is the axis of volition, and the quest implied in this instance is the shepherd's (subject) desire to lead his sheep safely to and from their pen (object). The bottom line is the axis of power, and the struggle which the shepherd experiences in the attainment of his goal is caused by marauding thieves, robbers and wolves, and by incompetent hired hands and strangers (opponents). He is, however, assisted by the θυρωρός or gatekeeper (helper), who ensures that no one enters the fold by the gate except the shepherd.

What, then, has this rather terse set of images got to do with the narrative of Jesus' arrest and Peter's denials in John 18.1–27? If we take the narrative of Jesus' arrest first (scene one, 18.1–11), we can see that there are a number of narrative echo effects deriving from John 10 in these verses. First of all, the narrative settings are similar, with the action of 18.1–11 occurring in and around a walled enclosure during the hours of darkness. Secondly, Judas' approach to the garden enclosure mimics the approach of the κλεπτής in John 10, a connection which seems to be borne out by the description of Judas as κλεπτής in 12.6. Thirdly, Jesus' protective stance towards the disciples (he stands outside the walled garden whilst they huddle inside) imitates the protective conduct of the shepherd throughout John 10, as is indicated by the reference to 10.27ff. in 18.9. Fourthly, John 10 itself anticipates this first step towards the passion, with its recurrent stress on the shepherd laying down his life for the sheep. Thus, in diagrammatic form, the connections between John 10 and 18.1–11 look like this:

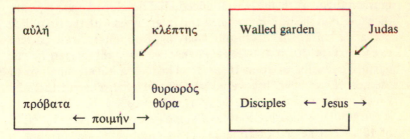

The connections between scene three (John 18.15–27) and the pastoral discourse in John 10 are more allusive than the above, and they centre on three details: (a) the courtyard of the high priest's house, which is described in John 18.15 with the same word which is used for the sheepfold in John 10.1, αὐλή; (b) the θυρωρός at the entrance of Annas' courtyard, which recalls the θυρωρός at the entrance of the sheepfold in 10.3 (which may explain why John 10 has this otherwise unnecessary detail); (c) the anonymous disciple goes in and out of the αὐλή in 18.15–16, just as the shepherd in 10.2–3 goes in and then out of the fold. The implication of these narrative echo effects is that the anonymous disciple functions as the shepherd of the symbolic word-picture in 10.1–5, whilst Peter functions as the hired hand who flees in the hour of danger (though Peter's flight is a metaphorical flight from confession, not a literal desertion). Peter is not yet a shepherd like his Master, willing to lay down his life for the sheep. That honour will be given to him later (John 21.15–19). Diagrammatically, these connections or narrative echo effects can be drawn up as follows:

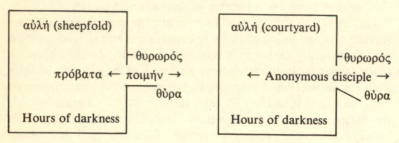

Conclusion

C. H. Dodd once wrote of John's story that 'the links which connect one episode with another are extremely subtle. It is rather like a musical fugue. A theme is announced, and developed up to a point; then a second theme is introduced and interwoven with the first, then perhaps a third, with fresh interweaving, until an intricate pattern is evolved' (1950, p.41). This is what we have discovered in our narrative reading of John 18.1–27. Through a holistic analysis of the gospel, we have discovered patterns of recurrence in 18.1–27 which derive from a much earlier part of the gospel, John 10. John 10 is certainly not the only source of some of the imagery and diction of 18.1–27 (the end of John 13 forms an obvious background to the theme of discipleship, betrayal and denial in John 18), but it is perhaps the most interesting quarry for an understanding of John 18.1–27 as narrative Christology. Looking at John 18.1–27 as *narrative* has led us to penetrate some of the rich poignancy of the

Jesus-as-shepherd image, and some of the severe irony of the Peter-as-hireling image – qualities which are overlooked in methods exclusively concerned with diachronic matters. Narrative criticism encourages the reader to provide those missing links which bring schemata together into an intelligible whole.

The trial of the king. John 18.28–19.16a

Narrative summary

Act two of the Johannine passion narrative comprises the story of Jesus' trial before Pilate. After the third denial of Peter, Jesus is led from Caiaphas' house to the palace of the Roman governor. Because the Jews want to eat the passover, they remain outside Pilate's residence. This forces Pilate into a situation where he has to come outside to the Jews if he wishes to question them, and to go inside to Jesus if he wishes to question him. Pilate begins his hearing by trying to ascertain the charges brought against Jesus. The Jews will not specify a charge, nor will they back down. So Pilate has to ask Jesus whether he is the King of the Jews. Jesus replies that he is a king, but not the sort of king either Pilate or the Jews have understood. Pilate, frustrated, goes back to the Jews and asks whether they want Jesus released. The Jews cry for Barabbas instead. Pilate then has Jesus flogged. His soldiers humiliate Jesus. Pilate brings Jesus out to the Jews again, but the chief priests and officials demand crucifixion. Pilate again pleads Jesus' innocence. The Jews, however, claim that Jesus has called himself God as well as king, thereby setting himself up against Caesar. The Jews eventually get their way with the statement, 'We have no King but Caesar.'

Narrative structure

R. H. Strachan was one of the first scholars to recognize the architectural subtlety of the narrative structure in this section. He pointed out that 'the trial is presented dramatically in a series of scenes, which are laid out alternately outside and inside the praetorium' (1941, p. 315). In scene one (18.28–32), Pilate meets the prisoner and his accusers outside the praetorium. In scene two (18.33–38a), Pilate conducts his first interview with Jesus inside the palace. He asks Jesus whether he is the King of the Jews. In scene three (18.38b–40), Pilate goes outside again to the Jews, who demand Barabbas instead

of Jesus. In scene four (19.1–3), Jesus is scourged and mocked inside
the palace. In scene five (19.4–7), Pilate takes the scourged Jesus
outside and exhibits him. In scene six (19.8–11), Pilate questions
Jesus inside the praetorium. In scene seven (19.12–16a), Pilate takes
Jesus outside to the Jews for the final confrontation. In other words,
Pilate goes 'back and forth from one to the other in seven carefully
balanced episodes' (Brown, 1966, Vol. II, p. 858). The first and the
seventh episode clearly correspond, since scene one presents the Jews
handing Jesus over to Pilate, whilst scene seven depicts Pilate handing
Jesus back over to the Jews. The purpose of this structure is twofold:
first, to give external expression to an inner struggle within Pilate's
soul, and secondly, to indicate the dubious nature of the trial through
the separation of accusers and defendant.

Characterization

Pilate

Pilate's characterization in John 18.28–19.16a is a masterful achievement and a superb example of how John the storyteller manages to
imply much with the greatest verbal economy. To begin with, Pilate
is a calm, political pragmatist. Without any hint of weakness he
enquires after the charge against Jesus (v. 29). Pilate's question here
is a legal and official formality. 'For him, Jesus is an ordinary man,
a case like many others' (Schnackenburg, 1982, p. 244). However,
the somewhat sarcastic response of the Jews ('If this fellow were
not a criminal ... we would certainly not have handed him over to
you', v. 30) upsets Pilate, so he responds rather gruffly that the Jews
ought to go and try Jesus themselves (v. 31a). This gesture now
succeeds in unsettling the Jews, who reveal the real reason why the
hearing has to be before Pilate: 'We are not permitted to put anyone
to death' (v. 31b). Aware that this request for the death penalty
implies a serious crime on Jesus' part, and presumably aware of the
rumours that Jesus has set himself up as a royal pretender, Pilate
decides to give up trying to discover the charge from the Jews and
ask Jesus himself. However, when Pilate asks Jesus whether he is a
king, he is confronted by the same apparently stubborn evasiveness
as he was with the Jews. Jesus does not answer his question. He throws
a question back, causing Pilate to lose his cool and cry angrily,
'Surely you don't think that I am a Jew?' (v. 35). As Strachan puts
it, 'his procuratorial dignity and impartiality are impugned' (1941,
p. 314).

Pilate's approach remains pragmatic and impartial, even though he has clearly been unsettled by the lack of response from both accusers and defendant. So he returns to the real issue in hand. 'What have you done?', he asks Jesus (v. 35), a question which promptly evokes a gnomic and somewhat esoteric non-sequitur on the subject of Jesus' other-worldly sovereignty: 'My kingdom does not belong to this world. If my kingdom belonged to this world, my subjects would be fighting to save me from being handed over to the Jews. But, as it is, my kingdom does not belong here' (v. 36). Pilate, latching on to the word king, then asks, 'So then, you are a king?', which again evokes a rather terse description of Jesus' royal purpose, which is to speak about the truth (v. 37). To which Pilate replies, 'Truth ... and what is that?' – not a cruel taunt, or philosophical playfulness, or even melancholic scepticism, but the frustrated exclamation of a man who has expended time and energy trying to get at the truth through a questioning of both accusers and defendants, but with absolutely no success. Truth for Pilate means 'the facts of the case'. Truth for Jesus connotes 'the eternal reality which is beyond and above the phenomena of the world' (Barrett, 1978, p. 448). Pilate and Jesus, in other words, are speaking at different levels. They are, to put it poignantly, at cross-purposes.

Pilate is now certain that the defendant is innocent and no real threat to the Roman state. Desperate to extricate himself from his unwelcome dilemma, he seizes on a passover amnesty in a moment of diplomatic inspiration and offers the Jews the opportunity to drop the charge and take Jesus back (vv. 38—40). However, a number of weaknesses in his approach betray the extent to which Pilate has been unsettled. First of all, by offering the Jews the opportunity to take Jesus under the amnesty, he in one breath declares Jesus innocent and yet proposes to treat him as guilty (Dods, 1903, p. 306). Secondly, if Pilate intends the passover amnesty to act as 'a bridge for the accusers so that they can withdraw from this farce without loss of face' (Schnackenburg, 1982, p. 252), he makes his task singularly difficult by referring to Jesus at this point as 'king of the Jews' (v. 39) – a title which he must have known would not endear him to the accusers. Inevitably, therefore, the Jews opt for Barabbas, and Pilate is consequently trapped into doing the very thing which he has taken the greatest trouble to avoid – punishing Jesus. Pilate is trapped by expediency into forsaking the very principles of justice which it is his duty to uphold.

Pilate's next move (19.1—5), in which he has Jesus flogged and in which he allows Jesus to be humiliated by his soldiers, is a further attempt to avert a judicial catastrophe. Bultmann sees the scourging and the mocking of Jesus as an attempt 'to make the person of Jesus appear to the Jews as ridiculous and harmless, so that they should drop their accusation' (1971, p. 658). That is why Pilate 'yields part of the way to the desire of the world' (1971, p. 658). 'Jesus arraigned and arrayed in this way is designed to awaken the pity of the Jews' (Haenchen, 1984, Vol. II, p. 180). However, Pilate's plan again misfires. Pilate's somewhat drastic attempt to evoke a spirit of pity in the Jews through such a cathartic spectacle is an indication of the extent to which he misjudges the perverse motivation of the accusing party. His 'Behold the man!' is intended to create sympathy out of pathos, but the gesture fails to take into account 'the common principle that when you have wrongfully injured a man you hate him all the more' (Dods, 1903, p. 307). Pilate's exhibition of this 'caricature of a king' (Bultmann, 1971, p. 658), far from diminishing the blood-lust of the Jews, actually seems to intensify it. The crowd, their vengeance unassuaged, cry in rabid unison, 'Crucify him! Crucify him!' (v. 6a). Pilate, no doubt deeply disturbed by the irrational violence of the clamour, tries to yield the initiative and responsibility back to the Jews. 'Take him yourselves and crucify him; I find no case against him' (v. 6b).

At this stage in the narrative, there is considerable dramatic tension. All along, the reader has suspected that the Jews are, in fact, playing a game with Pilate. Indeed, it is precisely this fact which has so unsettled him. The Jews have held back from making their most explicit and damning accusations. In 19.7, however, they begin the subtle process of suggesting hard, concrete charges to Pilate. They claim that Jesus has claimed to be God's Son. At this point, the narrator gives us an inside view of Pilate's psychology. He says, 'Pilate was more afraid than ever' (v. 8). Perhaps it was a fear arising from the threat to political stability and to his own safety which messianic pretenders habitually engendered. Or perhaps Bultmann is again correct in saying that the suggestion that Jesus might be some kind of *theios aner* means that, for Pilate, Jesus becomes a sinister figure (p. 658). All the way through the trial, Jesus' silence and bearing have made him an enigmatic figure surrounded by an aura of the uncanny. Now the idea of deity has been implanted in Pilate's mind by the subtle power of the accusers' suggestions. Pilate therefore timidly asks, 'Where do you come from?' (v. 9) — the key question about Jesus in the fourth gospel. Implicit in this is the more important question, 'Are you from heaven or from earth?' But Jesus, again, refuses to answer.

Pilate's fear now reduces him to a desperate remark about his authority to release or condemn Jesus (v. 10), a grandiose claim which hardly rings true when Pilate has already tried twice, unsuccessfully, to release Jesus (Marsh, 1968, p. 608). Jesus proceeds to point out the irony and indeed the implied blasphemy in Pilate's pompous and defensive remark by stating that Pilate's authority is given by God, and not something he wields of his own free will. As Lindars puts it, 'Pilate's unqualified claim to be above reason and justice, like an absolute monarch, makes him ascribe to himself almost the divine prerogative which is actually true of Jesus' (1972, p. 568). The effect which Jesus' analysis of Pilate's authority has is to reinforce the numinous fear which has already surfaced in him. So he tries to set Jesus free yet again (v. 12a). But the Jews point out that setting Jesus free would negate Pilate's status as friend of Caesar, since anyone who pretended to royal status automatically set himself up against the emperor (v. 12b). At this, 'fear of the world and fear of the mysterious come into conflict' (Bultmann, 1971, p. 663). In the end, Pilate's fear of being reported to the most suspicious of emperors engulfs even his anxiety before the numinous, and his resistance is broken. He appears to sit Jesus down on the judgement seat before the Jews and shouts, sarcastically, 'Look, here is your king!' (v. 14). Pilate's mockery goes unnoticed. The Jews respond with the words that constitute their trump card, 'We have no king other than the Emperor.' And the narrator laconically remarks that Pilate handed Jesus over to them to be crucified (v. 16a).

Pilate's characterization is a subtle and indeed a brilliant artistic achievement, which combines historical reminiscences with a sensitivity towards dramatic effect. For Culpepper, Pilate 'represents the futility of attempted compromise' (1983, p. 143). For Brown, 'Pilate's story ... illustrates how a person who refuses decisions is led to tragedy' (1966, Vol. II, p. 864). But Pilate is not ultimately a character whom the reader of this narrative is supposed to condemn. He may be an example of the impossibility of neutrality, but his dilemma is not so much of his own making as scholars have traditionally asserted. His indecisiveness may be a lamentable feature of his character, but that indecisiveness itself is directly caused by the fact that no one, at any point, answers the perfectly legitimate questions which he asks. Jasper has written that the characteristic of the Johannine trial narrative is its 'discontinuous dialogue' (1987, p. 45). As Jasper puts it, 'Pilate never gets a straight answer to his question', a fact which has a singularly dislocating effect since Jesus is consequently 'always slipping out of focus' (p. 46). Jesus' language seems to point to 'a realm which utterly transcends the assumptions underlying all such perfectly reasonable questions as those of Pilate' (p. 46). We should not, therefore, be too hard on Pilate. His rediscovery of composure, stature and dignity in 19.22 ('What I have written, I have written') reinforces the truth that the ones who handed Jesus over to Pilate were guilty of a greater evil (v. 11).

The Jews

The ones who handed Jesus over to Pilate were the Jews in 19.11, and it is to them that we now turn. Urban von Wahlde has shown that the Jews, when referred to in a hostile way in John, refer to 'a certain class (or classes) of persons within Palestinian society' characterized by a note of intense enmity towards Jesus (1982, p. 35). 'The Jews understood in this hostile sense do not refer to the Jewish nation as a whole, but to the Jewish authorities – as can be seen, for example, from the fact that in 11.45–52 the authorities are designated as Pharisees, whilst in 18.12–14, when the same passage is recalled, the same authorities are identified as 'the Jews'. Only 6.41,52 deviates from this norm, and these verses are rightly regarded as later, redactional additions. All other passages exemplify the uniquely Johannine reference to the authorities. As for the character of this collective, Culpepper has commented that the Jews are 'associated with all the negative categories and images in the gospel: the world, sin, the devil, darkness, blindness and death' (1983, p. 129). As Culpepper continues, 'through the Jews, John explores the heart and soul of unbelief' (p. 129). This is borne out in the second narrative unit of John's passion account.

The Jews in 18.28–19.16a are extremely cunning and perverse in the gradual way they persuade Pilate of the necessity of Jesus' execution. They begin by incriminating Jesus very generally as 'a criminal' (18.30). In 19.7 they progress to a charge that Jesus claimed that he was the Son of God. Finally, in 19.12ff., they accuse Jesus of being an enemy of Caesar. In this progression in their accusations, the Jews delay the most important charge (the one that will most persuade Pilate) until the end. The specific motivation for all this is to have Jesus crucified on a Roman cross, an incentive that will lead to a perverse neglect of Pilate's threefold protestation of Jesus' innocence. The utterly demonic nature of this rationale is suggested by the use of παραδίδωμι in 19.11, a verb normally reserved for Judas, who in John represents the incarnation of the cosmic forces of evil. As far as the Jews are concerned, the end thoroughly justifies the means, even if the means involve hypocrisy and apostasy on their part. That is why in 18.28, when they refuse to enter Pilate's house, they will show more concern for ritual purity than moral integrity. That is why they will falsely denounce Jesus as a political criminal in one breath and demand the release of a real political evil-doer, Barabbas, in the next (18.40). That is why they will misquote the passover Nismat in 19.15, changing the words 'We have no King but Thee' (Yahweh) to 'We have no King but Caesar!'

Jesus

Three important aspects of John's narrative Christology emerge in act two of the Johannine passion narrative. All three represent interpretative understandings of the character of Jesus. The three themes which emerge are: (i) Jesus as Judge, (ii) Jesus as King, (iii) Jesus as elusive God. The first theme in this section of the passion account is that of Jesus as the true Judge who is ironically under judgement. In some senses the whole of John could be described as an extended trial narrative, because there are very few moments when Jesus is not under judgement from the Jews, whilst at the same time being disclosed as the true Judge. This comes to a climactic ironical expression in 19.13 when the narrator leaves it highly ambiguous whether Pilate sits Jesus down on the judgement seat, or whether Pilate sits himself down (Brown, 1966, Vol. II, pp. 880–1). Although Pilate does not make Jesus a judge here, his mocking and acerbic gesture has a double meaning to it, revealing to the implied reader that Jesus really is the judge, which this prominence insinuates. During the trial proceedings before Pilate, furthermore, this seems to be suggested by the fact that it is very often Jesus who is interrogating Pilate, rather than vice versa. Jesus is ironically the judge who is judged.

The second theme of this section is the theme of Jesus as the true King – ironically, the very thing with which he is charged. This is given expression in a number of places, either explicitly or implicitly. In fact, just as act one (18.1–27) is in some senses a symbolic sequence depicting Jesus as the Good Shepherd, act two (18.28–19.16a) is a symbolic sequence depicting the proclamation and enthronement of a king (Appold, 1976, p. 131). If one were to ignore the tone of the narrative, one could read Pilate's question, 'do you want me to release the King of the Jews?' as the presentation of the king; the mocking of Jesus (in which a crown of thorns is placed on his head and a purple robe over his shoulders) as the investiture of the king; the continuous arraigning of Jesus with the words, 'Hail! King of the Jews!' as the reception of the king; the 'behold your king!' in 19.15 as the proclamation of the king; the crucifixion of Jesus with the royal *titulus* above his head as the enthronement of the king; and the burial in the garden amidst lavish gifts as the burial of the king. Kingship is the prominent theme in John 18–19. Jesus is called king eleven times in these chapters, and most of the references occur in this trial narrative – a narrative in which Jesus is quite explicit about the nature of his kingship and his kingdom. Thus, we should concur with Barrett's comment that 'John has with keen insight picked out the key of the passion narrative in the kingship of Jesus, and has made its meaning clearer, perhaps, than any other New Testament writer' (1978, p. 443).

Perhaps the most striking aspect of Jesus' characterization in act two is his elusiveness. We have already indicated that Jesus speaks elusively in so far as he uses discontinuous dialogue. A. D. Nuttall was the first to notice this aspect of Jesus' words in act two of the passion drama (1980). Nuttall rightly perceived that Jesus never answers questions directly. He tends to answer questions with questions ('Is that your own idea?', 18.34), or with mysterious statements that do not appear to be relevant ('My kingdom is not of this world', 18.36). Nuttall also points out that there are lacunae or logical gaps in what Jesus says. This systematic absence of logical fit in the dialogue seems to suggest that Jesus is employing a strategy of deliberate transcendence in his interrogation, with the result that Pilate emerges as someone thinking entirely on the wrong plane. This note of concealment in act two contrasts with the note of revelation in act one of the passion story. In act one, Jesus is the Revealer whose 'I ams' floor his opponents. Indeed, after all the evasions of Jesus in John one can understand why the arresting party fell over. It was as much the shock of finally catching up with Jesus as the expected reaction to a theophany. Elsewhere in act one Jesus stresses how public and open he has been (18.20). In act two, however, Jesus the Revealer becomes Jesus the Concealer. The elusive Word of God becomes elusive in his words.

Conclusion

The artistic achievement of the evangelist's narrative of the trial of Jesus before Pilate is evident in the structure and characterization in 18.29–19.16a. As we have already seen, the evangelist brilliantly creates two stages, one outside the praetorium and one inside, and presents Pilate toing and froing between the two. The momentum and pace of the plot is increased as the encounters between Pilate and the Jews, and between Pilate and Jesus, become progressively more confrontational. The artistry of act two consists of the way in which the evangelist suggests truths, particularly about Pilate, through artful reticence. John's picture of Pilate is indeed laconic, but much is suggested about his state of mind through his verbal gestures, a restraint not found in the replete descriptions of modern fiction. Everywhere, John suggests much in few words.

As a final example of this, we may notice the brevity of the sentence at the end of chapter 18: 'Now Barabbas was a bandit.' There have been previous examples of John's use of punchy, dramatic and terse sentences in the gospel. 'Jesus wept' (11.35) and 'It was night' (13.30) are two good instances of this narrative style. In all these cases, John evokes a wealth of meanings with the greatest economy. In the sentence, 'Barabbas was a bandit', there is first of all the irony of Barabbas' name in a gospel where Jesus' Sonship is stressed: Bar Abbas, son of abba (father). Secondly, John uses the word ληστής to describe Barabbas. This evokes the image of the sheepfold in John 10 again, where it is the robbers and the bandits (ληστής) who seek to destroy the sheep. Since Judas is clearly an embodiment of the robber figure, Barabbas must be an embodiment of the bandit figure. The artistry of John's storytelling is revealed particularly in the way in which he creates multi-story meanings through the fewest possible words.

The slaughter of the lamb. John 19.16b–42

Narrative summary

Having handed Jesus over, Pilate's soldiers escort Jesus, who carries his own cross, to the place of execution. He is crucified between two others. Pilate places a titulus above Jesus' cross which reads, 'Jesus of Nazareth, King of the Jews'. The Jews object, but Pilate remains undeterred. Meanwhile, the executing party divide Jesus' clothes amongst themselves. Jesus utters his last words to his mother and to the BD. After this, Jesus bows his head and dies. A while later the soldiers return to finish the victims off, but they find Jesus already dead. All the same, one of the soldiers pierces Jesus' side with a lance, bringing a sudden flow of blood and water. Later, two men collect Jesus' body, embalm it and bury it in a new tomb nearby. All this occurs on the Jewish day of Preparation, when the sacrificial lambs were being prepared for slaughter in the temple.

Narrative structure, plot and theme

Act three of John's passion account contains seven items of tradition: (i) vv. 16b–18 set the scene of the crucifixion; (ii) vv. 19–22 present the titulus and the reaction of the Jews; (iii) vv. 23–4 portray the division of Jesus' clothes by the four soldiers in the executing party; (iv) vv. 25–7 describe Jesus' provision for his mother and the BD; (v) vv. 28–30 concentrate on Jesus' last moments, his thirst and the handing over of his spirit; (vi) vv. 31–7 focus on the flow of blood and water from Jesus' side; (vii) vv. 38–42 depict Jesus' burial. The act as a whole falls into four parts with a dramatic contrast in each:

1. The crucifixion and the titulus, vv. 17–22
2. The four enemies and the four friends, vv. 23–7
3. The two words, 'I thirst' and 'it is finished', vv. 28–30
4. The hostile and the friendly petitions, vv. 31–42

Further evidence of structural activity can be seen in the fact that the setting of the last scene of the passion account in a garden (19.38–42) mirrors the setting of the first scene of the passion account (18.1ff.), creating a neat inclusio within the chapters as a whole. The last word of the passion narrative is Jesus, just as Jesus, if one takes out the redactional 'having said these things' in 18.1, would have been the first word. There is also the suggestion of an inclusio within this narrative section itself, since there is a deputation to Pilate very near its beginning (the chief priest's complaint in v. 21), and a deputation to Pilate very near its conclusion (Joseph of Arimathea's request for Jesus' body in v. 38).

What this structure presents us with is a narrative catena of seven logically sequential episodes arranged in four main sections, each with a contrast. The topography depicted within these seven episodes is confined to the area of execution until the burial scene in verse 41. The story time of 19.16b–42 is indicated in verse 31, where we learn that the execution took place on the Friday of passover week, with the passover sabbath near at hand. The actual hours of Friday which 19.16b—42 covers are discernible from the previous narrative section. In 18.28, we learn that Jesus was taken to Pilate's house very early in the morning. The early hour referred to would be between 3.0 a.m. and 6.0 a.m., though probably nearer 6.00 a.m., since the narrator reports a cock crowing at 18.27. In 19.14, we learn that Pilate's final capitulation to the Jews' demands for Jesus' execution occurred at 'almost noon of the day before the Passover', again underlining the fact that the execution of Jesus took place on the day of Preparation, the 'ereb pesah. Noon here means midday, since the fourth evangelist was almost certainly reckoning hours from daylight rather than from midnight. Thus, the story-time depicted in 19.16b and 19.42 is a period of approximately six hours (from about midday to just before nightfall). The story-time of the passion account as a whole should be seen as a twenty-four-hour period, beginning on Thursday evening and ending early on Friday evening. This period coincided with the vigil of the Sabbath from 6.00 p.m. Thursday until 6.00 p.m. Friday (Brown, 1966, Vol. II, p. 933).

The theological significance of John's chronology here is not easy to assess. It has often been pointed out that the evangelist's dating of the crucifixion means that Jesus is crucified at the same time as the paschal lambs are being slaughtered in the temple precincts by the Jewish priests (between noon and nightfall, when the lambs would have to be ready for the passover meals on that Friday evening). Since the hours of Jesus' execution extend from approximately midday to about 6.0 p.m. on this same day, we can see some poignancy in this coincidence of occurrences. Jesus has been referred to as 'the lamb of God' in 1.29. There are also a number of possible paschal nuances in the language used to describe Jesus' crucifixion — for example, the hyssop stalk which the soldiers use to offer vinegar to Jesus (which mimics the use of the hyssop to sprinkle blood from the paschal lambs), and the fact that Jesus' legs were not broken (which is redolent of Exodus 12.46). In the light of these details, I suggest that narrative chronology is here inseparable from narrative Christology, that the importance of John's story time derives from the fact that Jesus is implicitly depicted as the true paschal lamb. The idea of the death of Christ as a paschal sacrifice is therefore one theme in this final act of John's passion narrative (Howard, 1967, p. 337).

Along with this idea of Jesus as the true paschal lamb, the fourth evangelist has selected, combined and expressed his passion material in order to bring together the Christological theme introduced in John 18.1—27, and the Christological theme introduced in John 18.28—19.16a. In act one of John's passion account, the regulative idea is that of Jesus as the Good Shepherd who voluntarily lays down his life. As Reginald Fuller has put it, 'the keynote of John's presentation of the passion is struck in 10.17—18, "I have power to lay it (my life) down, and I have power to take it again." Jesus initiates the passion and calls the shots' (1986, p.57). In John 18.1—27, the voluntariness of the shepherd's act of self-giving is time and again stressed by Jesus' control over events. Jesus is depicted as the one who has the power and the initiative to master his predicament, but instead chooses to allow himself to become the passive victim of the world's perverse animosity. In act three of the passion account (19.16bff), this is again emphasized in three details. First, Jesus carries his own cross to Golgotha, whilst Simon of Cyrene helps him in the Synoptic versions. This physical feat reveals 'the all-sufficiency of Jesus' (Barrett, 1978, p.456) and the fact that he is 'sole master of his destiny' (Brown, 1966, Vol. II, p.917). Secondly, in verses 25—9, Jesus is portrayed as one who has the power and control to complete the task he has been given, even whilst on the verge of death. Thirdly, in verse 30, he is seen to bow his head at the moment of his death. Even here, he is again the subject of an active verb, implying that he 'deliberately chose the moment of his death by bowing his head, thus restricting his breathing, and causing life to become extinct' (Marsh, 1968, p.618).

The pastoral theme of act one of John's passion account is therefore brought to fruition in act three. But it is also true that the royal theme of act two (18.28—19.16a) is fulfilled here. In act two, the principal, regulative Christological theme is the notion of Jesus-as-king — ironically the very thing which the Jews use as the basis for his execution. As Brown writes, 'Jesus is crowned and hailed as King during his trial, and enthroned and publicly proclaimed as King on the cross' (1966, Vol. II, p.960). In John 19.16b—42, this royal Christology is dramatically fulfilled in three significant details. First, in v.18, the evangelist insists that Jesus is crucified in the centre, between two other victims, thereby signifying that he has a place of royal honour. As Schnackenburg puts it, 'even in the midst of the macabre scenery he is King' (1982, p.270). Secondly, Pilate's superscription, 'Jesus of Nazareth, the King of the Jews' (v.19), written in Hebrew, Latin and Greek, is seen by the evangelist as an ironic witness to Jesus' universal Kingship. The charge becomes 'a world-wide proclamation of enthronement' (Brown, 1966, Vol. II, p. 919). Thirdly, at the end of this third section (vv. 38–42), Nicodemus brings a royal gift of an immense quantity of myrrh and aloes in order to embalm Jesus' body. This lavish quantity of myrrh and aloes (about 75 lb in weight) signifies that 'in the evangelist's eyes, this is a regal burial, the burial of "the King of the Jews" ' (Strachan, 1941, p. 323). Thus, the two themes of Jesus-as-shepherd and Jesus-as-king are continued and fulfilled by six significant narrative details (three in both cases) in the emplotment of John 19.16b–42.

Symbolism

Commentators on the Johannine passion account have rarely been restrained in their symbolic readings of narrative details, and nowhere is this truer than in the context of John 19.16b–42. Four details have encouraged a particularly vast and sometimes eccentric interpretative literature: the seamless robe in 19.23b, the role of Jesus' mother in 19.26, the stalk of hyssop in 19.29, and the effusion of blood and water in 19.34. Of these, the most important is the incident in 19.34, as can be seen from the disproportionate amount of narrative its description, attestation and interpretation requires (19.31–7, the longest section in act three). At the historical level, what we have here is a reminiscence of an incident in which a soldier probed Jesus' body in order to make sure that he was dead, especially since death appears to have been unusually premature. This puncturing of Jesus' body brings forth not only a stream of blood but also a quantity of water – the water possibly being a residue of haemorrhagic fluid from the pleural cavity released during the scourging (Brown, 1966, Vol. II, p. 947). As so often in John's gospel, a detail in the life (or in this case the death) of Jesus becomes patient of a deeper, symbolic resonance. This brings us to the question of the symbolic meaning which the evangelist attaches to it. The insistent tone of 19.35, the eye-witness attestation and verification of the incident, makes it clear that the evangelist and his community regarded the matter as an awesome occurrence, perhaps even miraculous. But what symbolism did they see in the effusion, and can we penetrate that level of meaning?

   A first possibility is that 19.34 provides us with a further piece of paschal symbolism. There may be some paschal significance in the apparently casual adverb 'immediately' in 19.34. Since 'one of the strict requirements of Jewish sacrificial law was that the blood of the victim should not be congealed but should flow forth at the moment of death so that it could be sprinkled' (Brown, 1966, Vol. II, p. 951), it is possible to understand the immediate effusion of blood as yet another indication that Christ is the true paschal lamb here. A second possibility, advanced by Augustine, is that the blood and the water are symbols of the two Sacraments, Eucharist and Baptism, and that the incident symbolizes the birth of the church. Just as Eve was created out of Adam's side, so here the church, the New Eve, is created from the side of Christ, the New Adam (Brown, 1966, Vol. II, p. 949). A third possibility is that the effusion, along with the handing over of the spirit, was intended to point to the real humanity of Jesus. I John 5.7 reads: 'There are three witnesses, the Spirit, the water and the blood, and all three give the same testimony', i.e. that Jesus really was a human being. The spirit quitted Jesus at death (19.30). This meant that only the emission of blood and water would prove Jesus Christ's true humanness, that he really was the Word become flesh. The wonder of the incident derived from its concrete rebuttal of a proto-gnostic conception belief that the human body of Jesus was a phantom.

All three of these possibilities are plausible. However, each one requires ideas which are properly speaking extrinsic to the gospel for their justification. As so often in John's story, the symbolic explanations of concrete narrative details are usually provided within the gospel itself, so that the real question at issue is this: what significance does the evangelist give to blood and water elsewhere? The blood of Jesus in 6.53 is quite clearly a life-giving property. Jesus says, 'if you do not eat the flesh of the Son of Man and drink his blood, you have no life in you'. Very significantly, water is given the same life-giving property in connection with Jesus' body at 7.38–9. Jesus here quotes a Scripture which may refer to himself and to his death: 'As the Scripture says, "From him shall flow rivers of living water" ' The wonder of the incident in 19.34 therefore consists of the paradoxical association of life-giving properties with a dead man's body. Origen expressed the beauty of this paradox as follows: 'even in death, Jesus manifested signs of life in the water and the blood, and was, so to speak, a new dead man' (Hoskyns, 1940, p. 636). Barrett writes: 'it is highly probable that in the effusion of blood and water from the pierced side of Christ John saw a symbol of the fact that from the Crucified there proceed those living streams by which men are quickened and the Church lives' (1978, p. 463). Thus, even though an allusion to the Sacraments is by no means impossible, the primary significance of this incident is that 'no sooner is Jesus' sacrifice complete than the flow of life for the world begins' (Lindars, 1972, p. 586).

Minor characters

There are a number of minor characters in act three of John's passion story, the most important of whom are Joseph of Arimathea and Nicodemus. Nicodemus has appeared before as the secret enquirer in 3.1f. and as the opponent of the unlawful persecution of Jesus in 7.50—2, and he now appears in 19.38—42 as the disciple who venerates the dead Jesus as King. Joseph of Arimathea, on the other hand, has not appeared before. He is, however, well known in the earliest church as a rich man (Matthew 27.57) and as an opponent of the decision to crucify Jesus (Luke 23.51). Both men are paradigmatic of the aristocratic crypto-believer. Both are aristocratic first of all; Joseph provides a new tomb and Nicodemus a royal quantity of burial spices. Both are crypto-believers, secondly; the action here takes place in the evening after dark and it is said of Joseph that he was a secret disciple because he feared the Jews (19.38). Nothing in this short passage indicates that John's tone is hostile towards these minor characters. Indeed, there is something idyllic in this quiet garden scene. Is it possible that John the storyteller knew of the Lucan and Matthean nativity traditions and has, in this distinctive account of the burial, consciously set up ironic resonances with the birth stories of Jesus? Both John's burial scene and the Matthean/Lucan combined birth story have a pastoral setting, prominent men approaching Jesus, and spices (myrrh in both). If John intended such echoes, then he would be very subtly suggesting that the death of Jesus, far from being the end, was in fact the beginning, the birth, of something altogether new. This would tie in with the symbolic meaning of the effusion of blood and water above.

Conclusion

The artistry of John's storytelling is plainly visible in this narrative construction of Jesus' death and burial, and especially in his pervasive and highly sophisticated use of irony. I have not devoted a separate section to irony for two reasons: first because it is a device which is so fully integrated into the narrative superstructure that I have found myself examining it in the context of characterization, structure, emplotment, time, themes, and so on; secondly, because any comments on Johannine irony would, in any case, be little more than footnotes to the excellent literary studies done by Wead (1970), Culpepper (1983), O'Day (1986) and – particularly – Paul Duke (1985). However, in John 19.16b–42, irony plays a vital part in the shaping of the reader's response to the crucial subject of the death of Jesus, so some passing remarks must be made.

Irony itself is an oppositional structure which thrives on two orders of meaning contrasting with one another. For a word, a phrase or a sentence to be ironic, it must be possible to imagine someone or some group interpreting something superficially and missing completely the deeper dimension of truth. Defined this way, we can see that irony permeates the narrative world which the evangelist portrays in 19.16bff. For example, when the soldiers crucify Jesus in the middle of two other victims, they are unaware that they are testifying to Jesus' sovereignty. When Pilate puts the royal titulus above Jesus' cross, he is unaware that he is testifying to Jesus' universal Kingship. When the soldiers agree not to tear Jesus' garments, they are unaware that their restraint is a fulfilment of prophecy, and so on. At every opportunity, the narrator subtly insinuates the reader into the superior position of understanding meanings which are missed by characters within the narrative world itself. The narrator's post-resurrectional view-point leads the reader into understanding where his characters suffer from misunderstanding. As such, he nudges and guides the reader into a faithful and responsible interpretation of Jesus as the Christ, the Son of God – the very task he sets himself in 20.31. All the narrative strategies we have examined in this chapter – including irony – are subservient to the evangelist's Christology. Every narrative technique is employed with the rhetorical purpose of persuasion in mind. Truly, John 18–19 deserves the title 'narrative Christology'. Truly, John 18–19 is an excellent example of the artistry of John's storytelling.

6

A GENRE CRITICISM OF JOHN 18–19

The genre of the passion story

In chapter 5 I set about the task of examining the formal qualities of the story in John 18–19. The task we have before us now is to summarize the essential story of John's passion narrative and then to assess their family resemblances, story-types or *mythoi*. The main thrust of chapter 2 was that the structuralist understanding of narrative introduced by Vladimir Propp can be helpful in the establishing of gospel genres. Propp worked on over 100 Russian folk-tales, broke them down into invariable plot functions, and then produced a taxonomy of essential characters and functions within the genre. In gospel studies I showed how Nickelsburg uses a similar approach on the Marcan passion narrative. He too starts with the Marcan text, breaks it down into its essential plot functions, then relates the basic framework of Mark 15–16 with stories of persecution and vindication in Jewish literature which have the same basic story-pattern. All this implies the existence of deep plot-structures which transcend their actualizations in stories. One main thrust of structuralist narratology is that there is a distinction between narrative as a specific historical performance and narrative as an achronic system. With this in mind it is helpful to see John 18–19 as a particular manifestation in space and time of a supra-historical structure of possibilities. Just as a written sentence is an individual utterance (performance) which must obey the rules of a grammatical structure which is complete at any given time (competence), so John 18–19 is an individual performance which obeys the grammatical rules for narratives of a certain genre. The question is: which system of rules is John 18–19 obeying?

What we are after in this chapter is what Northrop Frye calls the archetype behind John 18–19. Northrop Frye's understanding of literature derives from the study of heroic stories by scholars like Joseph Campbell. Campbell's book, *The Hero with a Thousand Faces*, had argued that the stories of heroes tell the same single story, only with different characters and names. The stories are, as Propp would say in the context of Russian folk-tales, the re-enactments of a common pattern, a pattern in this case in which 'the hero sets out from his homeland on a quest, endures a perilous journey in which he encounters forces of evil that momentarily defeat him, eventually emerges triumphant and returns home to become king and marry the princess' (Ryken, 1979, p. 79). There is a sense in which the story of Jesus fits into this pattern. He too is the hero who leaves the homeland of heaven, sets out on the ultimate quest of saving mankind, endures a perilous journey through first-century Palestine with much supernatural and human opposition, is momentarily and apparently defeated in the crucifixion, but rises triumphant from death to return home as the highly exalted King and as the Groom of the church, the Bride of Christ. This, in a sense, is the story of stories. However, there is a major difference too. The main difference is that, in the story of Jesus, we are dealing with history, not with myth, with fact and not with fiction. Frye's understanding of what he calls the monomyth, the single story of literature, can be applied to the gospels if this difference is remembered. Frye's system of archetypal stories is important to NT genre criticism because each of the gospels is a manifestation or performance of a story-pattern which transcends it and which is visible in other narrative literature.

Frye would picture the one story or monomyth of literature in roughly the following way:

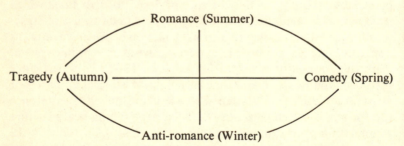

Ryken summarizes this as follows:

> Romance (which Northrop Frye calls 'the story of summer') pictures idealized human experience and is a wish-fulfilment dream of complete happiness. Its opposite, anti-romance ('the story of winter'), portrays unideal experience and is an anxiety dream of total bondage and frustration. Tragedy ('the story of fall/autumn') narrates a fall downward from

bliss to catastrophe, and comedy ('the story of spring')
narrates a rise from bondage to happiness and freedom.
These are the four kinds of story or poem material, and
together they make up the composite story of literature.

(p. 79)

Furthermore, each of these basic story-types has its own archetypes.
Frye defines an archetype as 'a symbol, usually an image, which
recurs often enough in literature to be recognizable as an element of
one's literary experience as a whole' (1971, p. 365). The identification
of the genre of John 18–19 depends therefore on our ability to
identify the basic image of Jesus, the hero of the story, and on our
subsequent ability to see which of the four basic story-patterns this
image belongs to: romance, anti-romance, tragedy or comedy. At this
point we therefore need to summarize the basic plot of John's story.

If we recall Greimas's model of narrative in chapter 2, we can see
that a basic narrative plot consists of three axes, an axis of communication, an axis of volition and an axis of power. These three
axes can be summed up in the words commission (the giving of the
task), quest (the undertaking of a task) and conflict (the opposition
to a task). The commission is given by a sender to a receiver. The
quest is undertaken by the receiver, who acts as a subject in search
of an object. The conflict derives from the opposition of opponents.
However, its fulfilment is greatly assisted by helpers. In diagram
form, Greimas's model of the basic shape of narratives looks like
this:

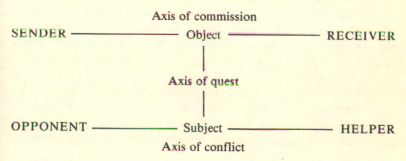

The essential ingredients of John's plot are as follows: first of all,
there is a commission. God the Father gives Jesus the task of bringing
eternal life into the world. The great commission text in John's story
is John 3.16: 'God so loved the world that he gave his one and only
Son, that whoever believes in him shall not perish but have eternal

life'. In the story, God the Father is the Sender, as can be seen by Jesus' constant references to him as 'him who sent me' (6.38, 7.16, 12.44, etc.) and to 'the Father who sent me' (5.37, 6.44, 8.16, etc.). Indeed, this use of the verb send makes God the archetypal narrative Sender and Jesus the archetypal Receiver.

The quest in the story is Jesus' desire to fulfil the Father's commission. He is the Subject whose Object is to bring men life. 'I have come that they may have life, and have it to the full', he says (John 10.10). Jesus' quest is to give the life of the age to come in the here and now. John 19.30, 'it is finished', signals the completion of this work which the Father has given.

However, in the undertaking of this task, opponents seek to destroy Jesus. This is the axis of conflict. The opponents of Jesus in John's story are 'the Jews' and Pharisees (understood as the hostile authorities, 5.18, 7.1, 10.31, 11.49—53, etc.), Judas (12.4—6, 13.27—30, 17.12, 18.1—11), the devil (12.31, 13.27, 16.11), the powers of darkness (1.5) and of this world (16.33), and finally the Roman state (18.3, 12, 28; 19.1—3, 19.23). In this conflict, Jesus is not exactly spoiled for helpers. Though the Father never leaves Jesus, and though the Spirit baptizes him, Jesus properly speaking stands alone in John's story, the solitary and heroic Stranger from heaven pitted against the world with all its hubris or dark rebellion against God.

This is the fundamental story of Jesus with which the reader is presented in the gospel. It can be summarized thus: Jesus' origins are with the Father in heaven before the world was made. Jesus was with God at the beginning, and everything was made through Jesus' creative agency. At a given moment in time, Jesus comes into the world he has made and assumes our humanity. The Word of God becomes flesh. However, though the world belongs to Jesus, when he comes into the world, even those who should have been expecting him fail to recognize him. He should have been welcomed as God and as King, but is rejected, and walks on earth as the Stranger from heaven. For the rest of the gospel, Jesus attracts to himself a group of disciples who recognize him as God, both women and men, but he is also hounded and persecuted by the Jewish leaders who, for the most part, do not accept his divinity in spite of the miracles he performs. There is an increase in the conflict between Jesus and these Jews, especially when Jesus travels to the city of Jerusalem for the third and final time. In the final week of his life, even though Jesus is welcomed as king when he enters Jerusalem, he is tried, mocked and tortured. He is led out of the city like a scapegoat, and at Golgotha, the place of the skull, he is hauled up on a wooden cross and crucified. The charge above his head reads, 'King of the Jews'. He dies with a universal witness to his royalty and in a manner befitting a great king. However, this is not the end of the story. Early on the first day of the next week, some women followers find that the tomb where Jesus was buried is now empty. The King has risen from the dead. He appears to his disciples on a number of occasions, the last of which is beside the Sea of Tiberias. It is here that Jesus gives his final instructions to his disciples. At this point the story ends.

Obviously the key moment in this story is the death of Jesus. The portrait of his death throughout John's story and particularly in chapters 18 and 19 can be summed up as follows: first of all, the death of Jesus is the killing of a king. Jesus' Kingship is, as we have seen in chapter 5, a strong theme in the passion narrative. Indeed, the titulus 'King of the Jews' is said to have been in three major languages of the civilized world.

Secondly, Jesus' death is the death of an innocent man. One of the poignant aspects of John 18–19 is Pilate's unease at the apparently irrational blood-lust of the Jews. This is borne out by his threefold protestation of Jesus' innocence (18.38, 19.4 and 19.6).

Thirdly, Jesus' death is, paradoxically, the death of a deity. Jesus stresses his unity with God the Father in John 10.30 (a unity of being, not just of doing) just as the narrator does at the beginning of the prologue. His crucifixion is therefore an act of deicide.

Fourthly, Jesus' death is depicted as the moment of departure to another world. John's story of the passion presents Jesus' death as the moment of return to the glory of the Father (13.1). That this return is a glorious phenomenon is suggested by the recurrent use of the verbs to lift up and to glorify in connection with Jesus' death. The verb lift up contains the double meaning of exaltation as well as crucifixion, and the verb glorify means 'to bring to a position of honour and clothe with splendour' (Lindars, 1977, p. 19). This means that the death of Jesus is more of a *triumphal exit* than a kathartic degradation.

What are the generic influences upon the fourth evangelist's formation of his passion narrative? Put another way, what is the story-paradigm which most influenced the evangelist's shaping of his historical tradition of the passion? Alan Culpepper has argued that this story approximates most closely to the *mythos* of romance. Quoting Frye, he says that typically the romance presents a successful quest with three main stages: 'the preliminary minor adventures; the crucial struggle, usually some kind of battle in which either the hero or his foe, or both, must die; and the exaltation of the hero' (1983, p. 83). However, this seems to me to be quite the wrong story-pattern. There is a sense of dreamy wistfulness in romances like *The Faerie Queene* which we certainly do not sense in John's gospel. Jesus' conflicts with the Jews are nothing like the knight's adventures with dragons and other fictive creatures. They are concrete, flesh-and-blood encounters with real, societal evils. Culpepper himself admits that 'the fit is certainly not perfect' (p. 84). Culpepper, I believe, has simply made the wrong classification.

A number of scholars throughout this century have suggested that John's story most closely corresponds to tragedy, not romance. In 1925 Strachan wrote that 'the ominous note of tragedy is struck in the Prologue (1.1–18) itself, "He came unto his own, and his own received him not" ' (p. 16). In 1923, F. R. Hitchcock argued that John is 'a tragedy, real, intense, progressive' (p. 317). In 1930, Clayton Bowen wrote that the gospel is not really narrative at all, but a form of drama close to Greek tragedy (p. 293). In 1937, F. Pfister discovered some interesting parallels between the pseudo-Senecan tragedy *Hercules Oetaeus* and the fourth gospel. As recently as 1983 W. R. Domeris proposed that the evangelist 'fashioned his Gospel after the model of the Greek dramas and particularly the Tragedies' (pp. 29–30).

Northrop Frye himself would say that the gospel story corresponds more closely to his *mythos* of autumn (tragedy) than to romance, though there are elements of both comedy and romance in the story of Jesus. In his *Anatomy of Criticism* he writes:

> tragic stories, when they apply to divine beings, may be called Dionysiac. These are stories of dying gods, like Hercules with his poisoned shirt and his pyre, Orpheus torn to pieces by the Bacchantes, Balder murdered by the treachery of Loki, Christ dying on the cross and marking with the words, 'Why hast thou forsaken me?' a sense of his exclusion, as a divine Being, from the society of the Trinity.   (p. 36)

Indeed, throughout *Anatomy*, Frye alludes to the passion as tragic. For example, he writes about the typical tragic hero as follows:

> The tragic hero is typically on top of the wheel of fortune, halfway between human society on the ground and the something greater in the sky. Prometheus, Adam and Christ hang

between heaven and earth, between a world of paradisial
freedom and a world of bondage. Tragic heroes are so much
the highest points in their human landscape that they seem
the inevitable conductors of the power about them, great
trees more likely to be struck by lightning than a clump of
grass. Conductors may of course be instruments as well as
victims of the divine lightning.   (p. 207)

Another example of this description of the gospel story as tragedy
is on p. 211, where Frye asks: 'is an innocent sufferer in tragedy (i.e.
poetically innocent), Iphigenia, Cordelia, Socrates in Plato's
Apology, Christ in the Passion, not a tragic figure?' Frye seems
to be suggesting throughout these sections that there is something
Dionysiac about the story of Jesus. Both Dionysus and Jesus were
sons of divine and human parents. Both came into the world but
were not recognized. Both sought to alleviate suffering. Both were
killed (the sparagmos) and both ascended into heaven. The story of
Jesus, one might say, evokes the very roots of tragedy. It is tragic
myth become fact.

What, then, is 'the central story, the essential myth or fable, that
underlies those great actions that most fully exemplify the tragic genre'
(Scott, 1966, p. 122)? Definitions of tragedy are numerous. Aristotle
regarded tragedy as a story of the change of a hero's fortunes from
happiness to misery. Diomedes regarded it as a narrative of the
fortunes of semi-divine characters in adversity. Isidore of Seville saw
tragic stories as sad stories of commonwealths and kings. Chaucer
thought of tragedy as a story of someone 'in greet prosperitee' who
falls 'out of heigh degree/ Into miserie', and Shakespeare as 'sad
stories of the death of kings' (Leech, 1969, pp. 1—2). One thing is
certain: tragedy is not simply 'anything that is bad or unfortunate,
however deeply it may tear at our hearts' (the celebrated 'toothache'
view of tragedy) (Humphreys, 1985, p. xiii). Tragedy begins with
the myth of the dying god. Out of these Dionysiac roots, the myths
and rituals of the killing of the god-king turn into a drama with a
recognizable story-pattern. Richard Holloway describes this pattern
as follows: over the course of the whole story, a protagonist is
taken from being 'the cynosure of society to being estranged from
it' (1961, p. 135). This same protagonist undergoes a process of
increasing alienation, 'to a point at which what happens to him
suggests the expulsion of a scape-goat, or the sacrifice of a victim,
or both' (p. 135).

It seems, then, that even though there is an element of variation in the cause of a tragic protagonist's suffering, there is an essential invariability in the general pattern of each tragic story. Kenneth Burke has described the central moments in the dialectic of tragedy as 'poiema, pathema, and mathema' (the act, the sufferance or state, the thing learned). As Burke puts it, 'we can discern something of the "tragic" grammar behind the Greek proverb's way of saying "one learns by experience"; "ta pathemata mathemata", the suffered is the learned' (1952, p. 39). In tragedy, an act engenders opposition ('brings to the fore whatever factors resist or modify the act'), which an agent then suffers 'and as he learns to take the oppositional motives into account, widening his terminology accordingly, he has arrived at a higher degree of understanding' (pp. 39–40). Fergusson's categories are perhaps clearer than Burke's. He reduces tragic action into the following motifs: purpose (for example, Oedipus' desire to find Laius' killer), passion (the suffering that results from Oedipus' purpose) and perception (the new understanding of the mystery of the human situation which emerges from Oedipus' experiences) (1949, p. 18). The paradigmatic tragic story is thus one which manifests an inexorable movement from a specific purpose to an extreme experience of suffering to a new perception, either by the protagonist, or by his social group, or by the reader/spectator.

The picture of the archetypal tragedy which develops out of these summaries is one of a protagonist (originally a king and/or a god) who undergoes an extreme transition from prominence to disaster (the *peripeteia*) through some *hamartia* or *agnoia* (failure of recognition). This leads to a situation of intense suffering (the *pathos*), and results in the expulsion or death of the protagonist, either preceded by or followed by a recognition (anagnorisis), by the hero, his familial group, or the reader. The invariable functions of the paradigmatic tragic story therefore seem to be the following: (1) (a) the introduction of a protagonist of exceptional standing, sometimes a king, sometimes a semi-divine being (Hercules), sometimes even a god (Prometheus); (b) the introduction of a purpose; (2) (a) a *peripeteia*, or a change in fortune, in which the protagonist comes into dissonant collision with the family, society or cosmos which had seemed initially neutral or even cooperative; (b) a passion, that is, a catastrophe resulting from some *hamartia/agnoia* (this *pathos* is usually characterized by an estrangement, humiliation and murder on the part of the protagonist's family, society or gods): (3) a perception, a new understanding of the moral order, of humanity or of society resulting from the extremity of the protagonist's sufferings. These aspects (purpose/passion/perception) constitute 'the conceptual system underlying the creation and appreciation of individual, existing tragedies' (Berke, 1982, p. 1). In a sense, such an abstraction is inevitably an over-simplification. However, it will serve for the time being as an outline of the achronic system of which each tragic story, including John's story, is a performance.

The passion as tragic story

Before we turn to look at John 18–19 in relation to the *mythos* of tragedy, it is important that we take time to justify looking at the gospels as tragedy. Surely, some would say, the gospels are much nearer to comedy, because they end with resurrection, not with death? This is one of the common misconceptions that have traditionally hindered an appreciation of the tragic vision behind John's story of Jesus. This first misconception really centres on the view that Christianity is fundamentally incompatible with tragedy because the former embraces the ultimate hope of a happy ending (a characteristic of comedy). I. A. Richards once proposed that 'tragedy is only possible to a mind which is for the moment agnostic or Manichean' because 'the least touch of any theology which has a compensating Heaven to offer the tragic hero is fatal' (Leech, 1969, p. 8). On the surface of it, this argument is appealing. However, it is much too simplistic to claim that a system of belief which regards suffering as redemptive or as a prelude to glory precludes a kathartic spectacle of human misery. The not yet character of the Kingdom of God is characterized by an eschatological tension in which extreme Christian suffering is very much a reality (witness Paul's catalogue of hardships in II Corinthians 11). Furthermore, a tragedy can still be a tragedy and end on a note of hope and even with the notion of apotheosis and ascension. *Oedipus at Colonus*, for example, ends on a highly positive, redemptive note (as does *Philoctetes, Alcestis*, etc.). In fact, tragedy actually requires an element of redemption so that a new knowledge of the human condition can be acquired.

A second misconception that has hindered a tragic reading of John and specifically of the Johannine passion narrative is expressed as follows: 'tragedy is a Graeco-Roman phenomenon, how then can it be a characteristic of the Hebrew Bible and of a Jewish Gospel like John?' One answer is that John's gospel is not a pure Jewish work exempt from Greek literary characteristics. It is eminently possible to over-emphasize the Jewishness of John and to overlook the fact that the same gospel employs Greek techniques to treat themes of primarily Jewish concern. For example, 'the ironic techniques of the Fourth Gospel are far more akin to the techniques of Greek drama' (Duke, 1985, p. 140).

Another answer is to say that tragic stories are not the exclusive property of Greek culture: they are much more widespread than Greece and Rome. For example, a number of scholars have seen a close correspondence between the tragic vision and certain aspects of the Hebrew tradition in the Old Testament, most recently in the case of I Samuel 9−31 (Gunn, 1980; Humphreys, 1978). The story of Saul has been read by at least one scholar as a terrifying transition from fame and royal prosperity to a desperate tragic isolation, and Saul's suicide as a tragic attempt to wrench meaning from his destiny (comparable to the self-blinding of Oedipus).

A third misconception that has hindered an interpretation of John's passion as tragic is the view that tragedy is only to be found in the medium of drama. If this were true, it would prevent us from reading John 18−19 as tragedy, since the literary form of the passion account is self-evidently narrative, not drama. Clayton Bowen, thinking on the one hand that tragedy is exclusive to drama, and on the other that John's gospel is a tragedy, argued that 'in no sense is the Fourth Gospel in form a narrative at all', but rather a sequence of 'dramatic scenes' (1930, p. 293). However, Scholes and Kellog have shown that a narrative is identifiable by virtue of 'the presence of a story and a story-teller', whilst a drama is 'a story without a story-teller; in it characters act out directly what Aristotle called an "imitation" of such action as we find in life' (1966, p. 5). Since John's gospel quite clearly has a storyteller, Bowen cannot argue that it is drama. In truth, there was never any need for him to do this. Tragedy is not confined to drama but is a kind of story which is found in many different works, from the plays of Aeschylus to the novels of Malcolm Lowry. As Humphreys puts it, 'the tragic vision can inform to a greater or lesser degree a wide range of literary genres' (1985, p. 2), including Hebrew narrative and NT gospels.

The grounds for denying that a Christian narrative like John 18−19 could be tragic are refutable. Indeed, it is likely that John knew Mark's story of Jesus (probably in an oral form), which has often been described as tragedy (Bilezikian, 1975). Furthermore, I am not the first Johannine specialist to employ a broadly structuralist approach to prove that John's story has tragic dimensions.

Hitchcock's 'Is the Fourth Gospel a Drama?' (1923) was a ground-breaking study in this regard. His argument is that the fourth evangelist closely follows the canons of Aristotle – canons which I would want to say provide us with a proto-structuralist grammar of rules for tragic story. Like a tragedy, John's gospel has a complete and unified plot with a beginning, a middle and an end. The beginning is the ideal beginning of the Word (John 1.1). The middle or complication (*desis*) is the raising of Lazarus and the reaction it evokes. The end or denouement (*lusis*) is the resurrection, and the pronouncement of Thomas. Like a Greek tragedy, John has five divisions with prologue and epilogue: act one is 1.19–2.12; act two is 2.13–6.71; act three is 7.1–11.57; act four is 12.1–19.42; and act five is 20.1–31. The *lusis* is begun in 18.1 with the arrest of Jesus. The attempted *anagnorisis* or discovery of Jesus occurs more than once; it is begun by the soldiers (18.4), continued by Pilate (18.28ff.) and achieved by Thomas (20.28). The *peripeteia* occurs throughout these scenes, but particularly when the Jews reject Jesus in favour of Barabbas. The *pathos* is obviously the crucifixion in 19.16ff., and the final *anagnorisis* is Thomas's climactic confession in 20.28. As Hitchcock concludes, 'every occurrence contributes to the advance of the drama; at every step the tragedy grows to climax' (p. 317).

Another important piece of evidence in defence of the argument proposed in this chapter is what I call the history of Dionysiac interpretations of passages in John's gospel. As early as the second century we see Origen in *Contra Celsum* drawing attention to the parallels between the arrest of Jesus in John 18 and Euripides' story of Dionysus in the *Bacchae* (Hengel, 1989, p. 191, n. 86). Celsus quotes the *Bacchae* when he complains that Jesus, when he is bound and arrested, fails to act like a real god in disguise. If Jesus really was a concealed deity, then, like Dionysus, he would have burst his bonds and scattered his enemies. As Celsus asks: 'Why, if not before, does he not at any rate now show forth something divine, and deliver himself from this shame, and take his revenge on those who insult him and his Father?' Celsus also complains that Annas and Pilate are allowed to get away with their unlawful interrogations of Jesus. Unlike the *Bacchae*, where Pentheus is most severely punished for the same presumption, the interrogators are allowed to get away with their trials. Thus Celsus complains, 'the one who condemned Jesus does not even suffer any such fate as that of Pentheus by going mad or being torn into pieces'. There is therefore an ancient precedent for examining the Dionysiac poetics of John's story. This has continued to this very day. Rudolf Bultmann draws attention to the same texts as Celsus in his commentary on John 18—19 (1971, p. 639, n. 7). Fortna's interpretation of the wine miracle in John 2 is also based on a long-standing observation of Dionysiac parallels. He writes: 'we have here in the source a legendary account, possibly imitating the deed of a god (the Dionysus tradition of water-changed-into-wine), that displays his astonishing power and status. Just like Dionysus, Jesus shows who he is, what he can accomplish, and in that way reveals a kind of divinity' (1989, p. 52; Broer, 1983, pp. 103—23).

Whether or not we agree with Fortna's description of the wine miracle as legendary (it is, after all, possible that the miracle is historical and that the storyteller has given it a Dionysiac resonance), it is significant that Dionysiac echoes have been noticed throughout centuries of fourth-gospel research. The identification of these parallels underlines the legitimacy of mapping John's gospel against our paradigm of tragic story, which itself has its roots in Dionysiac mythology. However, further evidence is needed for regarding John as tragic performance. This evidence can be found in the parallels between John's gospel and the *Bacchae*. What we therefore need to do now is to look at the Euripidean revision of the Dionysiac myth in more detail in order to trace the possible influence of Dionysiac poetics on John's storytelling.

The story of the *Bacchae* proceeds as follows: at the beginning of the play, the god Dionysus enters and speaks the prologue. He describes himself, in the first line, as 'the son of Zeus' (the father of the gods) and he explains his presence thus: 'I have come back to Thebes, the land where I was born ... And here I stand, a god incognito, disguised as man' (lines 2—6). We learn from this prologue that Dionysus is divine because his father is the father of the gods, but we also learn that his mother was human (Semele), and that her tomb is outside the royal palace of Thebes. Dionysus has come to the city because Semele's sisters, who are still alive, are slandering her and suggesting that Dionysus is not divine, is not the son of Zeus. Only Semele's father, Cadmus, has protected Dionysus' name by honouring Semele's tomb. Dionysus therefore returns to his home city, strikes Semele's sisters into a wild frenzy, and begins the task of revealing himself to mortal eyes as the god Semele bore to Zeus.

The principal antagonist of Dionysus is introduced at the end of the prologue. He is Pentheus, the new King of Thebes, and the grandson of Cadmus. Dionysus claims that this unbelieving Pentheus 'revolts against divinity' (line 45, the sin of hubris) because he neglects the true worship of Dionysus. When this same Pentheus enters the scene it is to criticize the 'obscene disorder' (line 232) which Dionysiac worship is producing, and to slander Dionysus as a 'charlatan magician' (line 234). Seeing Cadmus and the blind Teiresias in their Dionysiac costumes, he mocks them too. Teiresias rebukes Pentheus with a warning. Dionysus, the son of Semele, is the supreme blessing of mankind because he is the inventor of the wine that bears away the suffering of mankind (lines 278ff.). He is the provider of the true 'medicine for misery' (line 283). The worship of Dionysus is therefore to be encouraged, because it is through Dionysus' intercession before Zeus that his followers 'may win the favour of heaven' (line 285). Teiresias warns Pentheus not to mock Dionysus, not to 'flout the will of heaven' (line 325), by suggesting that Dionysus is not a son of Zeus. Cadmus urges Pentheus to agree. If Dionysus is not divine, then 'the fiction is a noble one' because it confers honour on Cadmus' and Pentheus' family. Pentheus, however, does not hear the warning, not even the warning of a terrible revenge by Dionysus, such as Actaeon received because of his blasphemy against Artemis. Pentheus dismisses the two old men, charging them not to contaminate him with their madness (line 344).

Pentheus, furious at the gullibility of his grandfather and of the blind prophet, commands his attendants to arrest the effeminate stranger (the disguised Dionysus) who has duped the old men. Dionysus voluntarily accepts arrest and is brought before Pentheus. There follows an acerbic and stichomythic exchange which results in Pentheus incarcerating Dionysus in a dark prison inside his palace. However, Pentheus has underestimated his adversary, and his palace is soon in ruins, destroyed by a great earthquake out of which Dionysus walks unscathed. At this point a messenger enters and describes the orgy of indulgence and frenetic activity which Pentheus' mother (Agave) and her sisters are enjoying outside the city on the hills. Pentheus, eager to put a stop to such embarrassing frenzies, decides to take an army and rout the women. Dionysus persuades him, however, that it would be more interesting to go there in disguise and observe the full splendour of a Bacchic party. In order to be even more inconspicuous, Dionysus persuades Pentheus to wear women's clothes, and off he goes to the hills. When there, Dionysus tells him that he would have a better view up in a tree. Pentheus agrees, is hoisted up into a fir tree, seen by the women, and torn to pieces. His mother, Agave, takes his head back to Thebes, thinking that it was a lion which she and her women butchered. Before long, the women awake from their madness and Agave sees the full extent of their 'awful murder' (line 1245). Dionysus metes out severe penalties on them all, and his powerful divinity is re-established.

Looking more closely at Euripides' revision of the Dionysiac myth, we can see how it fits into our deep structure of tragic story introduced at the end of the last section. Indeed, the *Bacchae* is an interesting manifestation of the paradigm of tragic story. It is a story which focusses on the murder of a king, and which conforms to the paradigmatic sequence of purpose/passion/perception. It begins with the introduction of a divine protagonist, Dionysus, and with the overt statement of a purpose: namely, Dionysus' task of making certain members of the Theban royal family recognize his divinity. It proceeds to the introduction of the antagonist, the unbelieving Pentheus, who establishes a purpose directly in opposition to Dionysus': that is, to disprove Dionysus' divinity (even though they are members of the same family) and to quash the Bacchic uprising in his land. Pentheus' purpose is a direct cause of his *hamartia* or *agnoia* — his inability to acknowledge Dionysus as the son of Zeus and to recognize the effeminate stranger in his city as Dionysus. 'You do not know what you do', says Dionysus (line 506), in language which reminds us of the later Lucan passion account. The *peripeteia* which inevitably follows this error occurs when Pentheus makes his stand against Dionysus by attempting to imprison him. From that moment on, Pentheus is estranged from his family, his society and his cosmos. His passion ensues, and takes the form of a humiliation (being mocked in women's clothes), a journey from his city to the 'accursed hill' (line 1386), an elevation in a high tree, and a terrifying *sparagmos* (separation and scattering of his limbs) — the *pathos*. The perception occurs at the conclusion of the play, when Pentheus' head is recognized by his mother, and when Dionysus' divinity is finally re-established.

From this summary we can detect some broad similarities with the story of Jesus in John's gospel. The following is a list of very general parallels:

1. The prologue of both stories concentrates upon the same theme: a divine being goes to his home but is rejected by members of his family — in Jesus' case, his earthly and his spiritual family (1.11 and 7.5).
2. In both stories, the protagonist is an unrecognized deity, a stranger from heaven, who faces intense hostility and unbelief from the ruling party of the city.

3. In both stories, the goal of the deity is basically philanthropic, for it is Dionysus' desire to share the wine that alleviates man's sufferings, whilst it is Jesus' desire that man should drink of his life-giving blood (John 2, where the wine has been seen as a Dionysiac symbol, and John 6, where the blood of Jesus arguably points to the wine of the Eucharist).

4. In both stories, the tragic *hamartia* consists of the antagonist's failure to recognize one who is really a member of the same family. In the *Bacchae*, Pentheus' grandfather Cadmus is the father of Semele, making Pentheus and Dionysus, in some sense or other, brothers. In John, both the Jews (the antagonist) and Jesus (the protagonist) share the same Father in heaven (making them in a spiritual sense brothers), though the protagonist's filial relationship is unique and fulfilled, whilst that of the Jews is shared and unfulfilled.

5. In both stories, the *pathos* consists of the victim being dressed up in humiliating garb (John 19.2—3), led out of the city to an accursed hill (19.17), hoisted up on to a 'tree' (19.18) and then killed.

6. In both stories, women fulfil the role of true worshippers of the visiting deity.

7. In both stories, the *theomachus*, the enemies of the deity, attempt to stone the god.

8. In both stories, the deity is ambiguous and elusive, often speaking and acting in such a way as to escape definition and capture.

9. In both stories, the place of the city is important as a symbol of institutionalized religion and the loss of the immediacy of belief.

10. In both stories, the divine stranger has thaumaturgic powers.

11. In both stories, the tragic action is not centred upon one person. The *Bacchae* is not called *Dionysus*, nor is it called *Pentheus*, even though both titles would have been possible given the prominence of these protagonists. In John's story too, the tragic action centres not only on Jesus but also on the Jews and on Pilate.

It is not possible here to explore each of these parallels in detail in order to highlight both the differences and the similarities between John's story of Jesus and Euripides' story of Dionysus. However, a brief examination of the prologue to the *Bacchae* reveals some interesting parallels with John's gospel. Here is a very brief excerpt:

I am Dionysus, the son of Zeus,
come back to Thebes, this land where I was born.

And here I stand, a god incognito,
disguised as man, beside the stream of Dirce
and the waters of Ismenus.

Like it or not, this city must learn its lesson:

Cadmus the king has abdicated,
leaving his throne and power to his grandson Pentheus;
who now revolts against divinity, in me;
thrusts me from his offerings; forgets my name
in his prayers. Therefore I shall prove to him
and every man in Thebes that I am god indeed.

(lines 1–2, 4–6, 39, 43–8)

The differences are, first of all, glaringly evident. Dionysus' prologue presupposes a pagan pantheon of deities, whilst the Johannine prologue portrays two divine persons, the Word and God. The former depicts a deity of aggression and hedonism, whilst the latter depicts a divine figure who is full of grace and truth. The former is spoken by the god in the first person, whilst the latter is spoken by the narrator about the deity, and so on. However, there are also similarities. Both texts are poetic prologues. Both centre upon a divine being who has assumed mortal flesh (in the *Bacchae*, Dionysus introduces himself as 'the son of Zeus' and speaks of exchanging his divine form for a mortal one; in John, the storyteller boldly announces in line 14, 'the Word became flesh and dwelt among us'). In both prologues, the idea of revelation is important (in the *Bacchae*, Dionysus speaks of how he is 'to be a manifest god to men'; in John, we hear of the Light coming into the world). In both prologues, the idea of *anagnorisis*, or of recognition, is deemed crucial to the plot (Dionysus is appalled at Pentheus, the new King of Thebes, who refuses to recognize him as a deity, refuses to worship him, and 'nowhere addresses me in his prayers'; in John 1.10–11, John openly states that the world did not recognize Jesus and that his own people did not receive him). In both prologues, one man is singled out for praise on account of his public recognition of the deity. King Cadmus, Pentheus' grandfather, is commended by Dionysus. John the Baptist is introduced as witness to the Light in John 1.6. These literary parallels are very general ones, but it is perhaps possible to see why the note of tragedy is struck in the words, 'He came to that which was his own, but his own did not receive him.'

It is important to recognize at this point that I am not arguing that John necessarily knew the *Bacchae* by heart and that he consciously set up a number of literary echoes with the prologue of that play, or indeed the rest of the play. What I am arguing is that John unconsciously chose the *mythos* of tragedy when he set about rewriting his tradition about Jesus and that general echoes with Euripides' story of Dionysus are therefore, in a sense, inevitable. Hayden White has shown in his *Metahistory* that every historical reconstruction is fictive in form (not in content). In the writing of history, the historian – like the storyteller in literature – must choose from the four different modes of emplotment: romance, tragedy, comedy, satire (anti-romance). As White puts it, 'a given historian is forced to emplot the whole set of stories making up his narrative in one comprehensive or *archetypal story* form' (1973, p. 8). Indeed, 'every history, even the most "synchronic" or "structural" of them, will be emplotted in some way' (p. 8). Thus, Francis Cornford argued that when Thucydides came to write his history of the Peloponnesian war, he structured it on the model of Aristotelian tragedy. The work started out as a textbook in strategy and politics but ended up with the shape of tragedy, a shape inwrought into the very structure of the author's mind. As Cornford put it, 'Even his vigilant precaution allowed a certain traditional mode of thought, characteristic of the Athenian mind, to shape the mass of facts which was to have been shapeless, so that the work of science became a work of art' (p. viii). The reason why John's gospel therefore appears to us as tragedy is that John the storyteller, like Thucydides, lived in a culture in which the tragic form was deeply embedded. When John narrated his tradition, something inevitably tragic emerged in his story of the killing of the king.

It is for this reason that it is possible to map John's story of the death of Jesus against our kernel plot sentence of tragic story (purpose, passion, perception). In John's gospel, the protagonist, Jesus, is introduced in the prologue as the creative Word of God who comes to his own people as a human being but is not recognized as the Father's only Son. The purpose of his coming is to give those who receive him and believe in him the right to become the children of God. However, this purpose is threatened because a highly persistent antagonist raises itself up against him, namely, the Jewish leaders in Jerusalem. Their *hamartia* consists of the fact that they seem resolutely blind to the truth that Jesus is God's Son. Their hubris consists of the fact that they are stubbornly rebellious in the face of divinity. As the *theomachus* of the fourth gospel, they are the embodiment of tragedy's most perverse emotions. Not only do they suffer from lack of recognition and pride, but they also suffer from *agnoia*: they are ignorant throughout the story of the identity of the Son who points them to their Father. Indeed, the very suggestion that Jesus is God's only Son makes the same Jewish authorities bent on killing Jesus from very early on in the story (5.18). The *peripeteia* inevitably comes after the raising of Lazarus in John 11. Jesus' popularity, which in 6.15 had almost led to him being crowned king by the people, ironically disappears after the Jewish council decides to have Jesus killed on the very same charge of kingship. He is arrested, humiliated and executed on the instigation of the Jews. Perception is denied to Pilate and the Jews and placed instead on the lips of Thomas in 20.28, who exclaims 'My Lord and my God!'

In this light we can see how John's story resonates with the essential *mythos* of tragedy. John's story is a tragic performance. The evidence I have produced in this section to support this proposal is made up of the following:

1. There are similarities between John's story of Jesus and the deep story-structure of tragedy.
2. A number of Johannine scholars have drawn attention to the similarities between John's gospel and Greek tragedy during the course of this century.
3. There have been a number of very influential secular literary critics and theorists who have regarded the gospel story of Jesus as the archetypal tragic story.
4. John's story of Jesus is closer to Mark than to the other gospels, and Mark has often been described as a tragedy (unlike Matthew and Luke, which have been likened to other genres).
5. John's story of Jesus has been subjected to a number of Dionysiac interpretations, especially with regard to John 2.1—11 and John 18.12—27. I have shown that the resonances with the story of Dionysus are set up right at the beginning of John, in the prologue.
6. There are some interesting parallels between John's gospel and Euripides' story of Dionysus.

In the final section of this chapter we turn to some interesting parallels between John 18—19 and the *Bacchae*.

John 18–19 and the myth of Dionysus

We now turn to the text of John 18–19 and the *Bacchae*. There are essentially three interesting points of comparison, one from each act of John's dramatic passion narrative. In act one of John 18–19, I shall be looking at the parallels and differences between the arrest and binding of Jesus in John 18.12–27, and the arrest and binding of Dionysus in *Bacchae* 616–36. In act two of John 18–19, I shall be examining points of contact between the interrogation of Jesus by Pilate in John 18.28–19.16a, and the interrogation of Dionysus by King Pentheus in *Bacchae* 462–80. Finally, in act three, I shall be looking at the similarities and contrasts between the crucifixion of Jesus in John 19.16b–42 and the *pathos* of Pentheus in *Bacchae* 1084–1136. It is important to repeat at this stage that I have nowhere put forward the argument for a direct literary dependence of John on Euripides. That, in fact, would be the simplest but the least likely solution. What I have proposed throughout this section is that there was something intrinsically tragic in what John knew of the story of Jesus. John, more than any other New Testament storyteller (with the possible exception of Mark), has cleverly evoked the tragic nuances inherent within Jesus' life-story. Hence, there are inevitably parallels with tragic stories from the world of Graeco-Roman drama. The same deep structure that generated tragic stories in ancient Athens – the purpose, passion, perception paradigm centring on the killing of a king and derived from the myth of Dionysus – has greatly influenced John's retelling of Jesus history. To use Northrop Frye's and Hayden White's terminology, John has narrated his history using the *mythos* of autumn (tragedy).

In act one of John 18–19, it is the arrest and binding of Jesus which most closely resembles an episode in Euripides' story of Dionysus – a parallel to which Bultmann draws our attention in a footnote in his commentary (p. 520). In John 18.12–27, the evangelist is at pains to stress Jesus' willing passivity: the fact that, after being in sovereign control of events throughout the story, Jesus now allows himself to be taken captive. In verse 12 the narrator informs us that 'the detachment of soldiers with its commander and the Jewish officials arrested Jesus. They bound him and brought him first to Annas.' It is important at this point to notice that only John, of all the evangelists, mentions that Jesus was bound. After a brief description of Peter's entrance into Annas' palace, the interrogation of Jesus is described in verses 19–24. Annas, the high priest, questions Jesus about his disciples and his teaching. Jesus stresses that he has spoken openly to the world; that he has not been given secret, politically subversive talks to a select group of bandits. He qualifies this by adding that he always taught in synagogues or at the temple, and never in secret. Jesus then suggests that his inter-rogators question his disciples and others who have heard his teaching. At this point, one of the officials nearby strikes Jesus. Jesus' response is to defend himself verbally. He says, 'if I said something wrong, then testify as to what is wrong. But if I spoke the truth, why did you strike me?' The trial seems at this point to end in stalemate, and the narrator informs us that 'Annas sent him, *still bound*, to Caiaphas the high priest.' Again, John's second reference to Jesus being bound (δεδεμένον, 18.24) is unique to the fourth gospel. It stresses the voluntary passivity of a most powerful divinity.

Now compare John 18.12—27 with *Bacchae* 616—36, where Dionysus is also arrested, bound, and taken inside a palace at night-time. Dionysus is speaking to the chorus, which has just enquired how Dionysus came to be free from Pentheus' imprisonment. Dionysus replies:

> DIONYSUS:
> There I made a mockery of him. He thought he was
>   binding me;
> But he neither held nor touched me, save in his deluded
>   mind.
> Near the mangers where he meant to tie me up, he found
>   a bull;
> And he tied his rope round the bull's knees and hooves,
>   panting with rage,
> Dripping sweat, biting his lips; while I sat quietly by and
>   watched.
> It was then that Dionysus shook the building, made the
>   flame
> On his mother's tomb flare up. When Pentheus saw this,
>   he supposed
> The whole place was burning. He rushed this way, that
>   way, calling out
> To the servants to bring water; every slave about the
>   place
> Was engaged upon this futile task. He left it presently,
> Thinking I had escaped; snatched up his murderous
>   sword, darted indoors.

Thereupon Dionysus — as it seemed to me; I merely
  guess —
Made a phantom hover in the courtyard. Pentheus flew
  at it,
Stabbing at the empty sunlight, thinking he was killing
  me.
Yet a further humiliation Bacchus next contrived for him:
He destroyed the stable buildings. Pentheus sees my
  prison now
Lying there, a heap of rubble; and the picture grieves his
  heart.
Now he's dazed and helpless with exhaustion. He has
  dropped his sword.
He, a man, dared to take arms against a god.

In other words, Dionysus explains that his binding was an illusion.
Pentheus thought he was binding Dionysus, but in reality he tied up
a bull nearby. Through his supernatural powers, Dionysus broke free
from captivity, destroying Pentheus' palace and sending Pentheus
mad in the process.

In John 18.12–27 and this part of the *Bacchae*, the initial circumstances are similar. Both stories focus upon a divinity whose power
is unquestioned by the reader, but who is not recognized by the
ruling powers of the city which owes him honour. Both divine men
are bound by ruling figures (Pentheus and Annas), and both are led
into the palace of these men to be imprisoned. However, it is just
at this point of *peripeteia* that the two stories go in entirely different
directions. First of all, in the *Bacchae*, we are not allowed to entertain the notion that Dionysus is in any danger for one moment.
Dionysus reveals that he was never really tied up in the first place:
'There I made a mockery of him. He thought he was binding me; /
But he neither held nor touched me, save in his deluded mind.' In
John 18.12ff., on the other hand, Jesus' arrest, binding and abuse
are no illusion (the blow which he receives from the official is real
enough). Secondly, in the *Bacchae* we are not allowed to entertain
the notion that Dionysus will remain passive in the face of imprisonment. Dionysus reaps the nemesis of divine revenge upon Pentheus
and his palace for the terrible hubris described in 635: 'He, a man,
dared to take arms against a god.' In John 18.12ff., on the other
hand, there is no such action taken by Jesus, even though we know
from his power over the arresting party in 18.6 (perhaps the Johannine
equivalent of Dionysus' thaumaturgic power over his captors) that

Jesus is more than able to break free from human hands if necessary. In other words, at the moment when Jesus' predicament seems most Dionysian, his behaviour becomes truly anti-Dionysian. John says, in a very significant aside, that Jesus is *still bound* at the end of this interrogation. As Celsus noticed, there is no powerful escape. The Dionysiac paradigm is seemingly subverted.

There are, then, both similarities and differences between the two stories of Jesus and Dionysus in act one of John 18–19. The same is true in act two (John 18.28–19.16a), where the interrogation of Jesus by Pilate has some points of resemblance with the interrogation of Dionysus in *Bacchae* 462–80. In John's gospel, Jesus is taken before Pilate. Pilate interrogates Jesus, but Jesus, who has proved to be elusive throughout, becomes even more evasive by answering questions with questions or with statements of a transcendence which Pilate is incapable of penetrating. The ironic double entendre in John 19.13 (where it is left ambiguous as to who is sitting on the judgement seat) reveals that it is really Pilate on trial, not Jesus. In a similar scene in the *Bacchae*, we see the same dynamic at work:

> Ah, well; first tell me who you are. What is your
>   birth?
>
> DIONYSUS:
>   Your question's easily answered, it is no secret.
>   Perhaps you have heard of Tmolus, a mountain decked
>   with flowers.
>
> PENTHEUS: A range that curves round Sardis? Yes, I
>   know of it.
>
> DIONYSUS: That is my home. I am a Lydian by birth.
>
> PENTHEUS: How comes it that you bring these rituals to
>   Helas?
>
> DIONYSUS: Dionysus, son of Zeus, himself instructed me.
>
> PENTHEUS: Is there a Lydian Zeus, then, who begets new
>   gods?
>
> DIONYSUS: I speak of Zeus who wedded Semele here in
>   Thebes.
>
> PENTHEUS: Did he possess you in a dream, or visibly?
>
> DIONYSUS: Yes, face to face; he gave these mysteries to
>   me.
>
> PENTHEUS: These mysteries you speak of: what form do
>   they take?
>
> DIONYSUS: To the uninitiated that must not be told.

PENTHEUS: And those who worship – what advantage do they gain?

DIONYSUS: It is not for you to learn; yet it is worth knowing.

PENTHEUS: You bait your answer well, to arouse my eagerness.

DIONYSUS: His rituals abhor a man of impious life.

PENTHEUS: You say you saw him face to face: what was he like?

DIONYSUS: Such as he chose to be. I had no say in that.

PENTHEUS: Still you side-track my question with an empty phrase.

DIONYSUS: Just so. A prudent speech sleeps in a foolish ear.

There are some revealing similarities and differences between the two interrogation scenes. In both, the one on trial is an un-acknowledged deity. In John, Jesus is unacknowledged as the Son of God by the Jews (Pilate's fear in 19.8 seems to suggest some latent sense of Jesus' divinity in him). In the *Bacchae*, it is Pentheus who fails to acknowledge Dionysus as a god. Secondly, in both cases, the interrogator is a ruling figure in the city where the deity should be worshipped. The respective cities are Jerusalem and Thebes. The respective interrogators are Pilate and Pentheus – men with very different motives behind their actions. Thirdly, in both cases the one on trial is really the judge. In John, this is brought out in the ambiguity in 19.13 and in the Jesus-as-Judge theme throughout the gospel. In the *Bacchae* it is brought out clearly in the gnomic statement which Dionysus makes, 'A prudent speech sleeps in a foolish ear.' This functions as more than just a proverb: it is a judgement upon Pentheus. Fourthly, in both interrogation scenes the deity proves extremely elusive, so that the interrogator finds him hard to understand. In the *Bacchae*, this is achieved structurally through stichomythic dialogue. In John it is achieved through the two-stage setting. In both scenes, the deity uses language evasively:

PENTHEUS: And those who worship – what advantage do they gain?

DIONYSUS: It is not for you to learn; yet it is worth knowing.

PENTHEUS: You bait your answer well, to arouse my eagerness.

There are other parallels, such as the question of the deities' origins (John 19.9/*Bacchae* 461–3), but we need now to draw attention to one very significant difference between the two interrogations. At the beginning of chapter 19, the evangelist presents us with a vivid, shocking and dramatic spectacle: the mockery of Jesus. Indeed, of all the scenes in the gospels, this one comes closest to achieving that quality of katharsis which Aristotle identified. The evangelist writes as follows:

> Then Pilate took Jesus and had him scourged. And the soldiers wove a crown out of thorns and fixed it on Jesus' head, and they threw around him a cloak of royal purple. Time and again they came up to him, saying, 'All hail, "King of the Jews"!' And they would slap him in the face.

In the *Bacchae*, we have a similar humiliation scene, involving Pentheus being dressed up as a woman just before his appalling death:

> PENTHEUS: What kind of dress did you say you would put on me?
> DIONYSUS: First I'll adorn your head with locks of flowing hair.
> PENTHEUS: And after that? What style of costume shall I have?
> DIONYSUS: A full-length robe; and on your head shall be a snood.
> PENTHEUS: Besides these, is there anything else you'll put on me?
> DIONYSUS: A dappled fawnskin round you, a thyrsus in your hand.

There are some similarities between the two scenes, but it is more important that we recognize this supreme difference, that, whilst in the *Bacchae* the humiliation is experienced by Pentheus, in John the humiliation is experienced by Jesus, the unrecognized divinity. It is precisely at this point that John subverts the conventions of the tragic *mythos*. As Euripides' play clearly shows, the unrecognized god, at the moment of greatest conflict with the city's authorities, rises up to bring nemesis upon them. In John's story, Jesus allows himself to suffer the punishment which, in literary and in moral terms, the reader regards as belonging to the Jews. Little wonder, then, that Celsus found the passion narrative in John such an offence.

Finally, the similarities and differences between act three of the Johannine passion narrative and the *Bacchae* further reveal how John subverts the tragic *mythos*. In both cases, the story ends with the killing of a king. In the case of the *Bacchae*, the scene is described graphically by the second messenger. Here is the centre-piece of his report:

> And then I saw that foreigner do an amazing thing.
> He took hold of a pine-tree's soaring, topmost branch,
> And dragged it down, down, down to the ark earth.
>   It was bent
> In a circle as a bow is bent, as a wheel's curve,
> Drawn with a compass, bends the rim to its own shape;
> The foreigner took that mountain-pine in his two hands
> And bent it down – a thing no mortal man could do.
> Then seating Pentheus on a high branch, he began
> To let the tree spring upright, slipping it through his hands
> Steadily, taking care he should not be flung off.
> The pine-trunk, straightened, soared into the soaring sky,
> Bearing my master seated astride, so that he was
> More visible to the Maenads than they were to him.
> He was just coming into view on his high perch,
> When out of the sky a voice – Dionysus, I suppose;
> That foreigner was nowhere to be seen – pealed forth:
> 'Women, here is the man who made a mock of you,
> And me, and of my holy rites. Now punish him.'
> And in the very moment the voice spoke, a flash
> Of dreadful fire stretched between earth and the high heaven.
>   The air fell still. The wooded glade held every leaf
> Still. You could hear no cry of any beast. The women,
> Not having caught distinctly what the voice uttered,
> Stood up and gazed around. Then came a second word
> Of command. As soon as Cadmus' daughters recognized
> The clear bidding of Bacchus, with the speed of doves
> They darted forward, and all the Bacchae after them.
> Through the torrent-filled valley, over the rocks, possessed
> By the very breath of Bacchus they went leaping on.
> Then, when they saw my master crouched high in the pine,
> At first they climbed the cliff which towered opposite,
> And violently flung at him pieces of rocks, or boughs
> Of pine-trees which they hurled as javelins; and some

Aimed with the thyrsus; through the high air all around
Their wretched target missiles flew. Yet every aim
Fell short, the tree's height baffled all their eagerness;
While Pentheus, helpless in this pitiful trap, sat there.
Then, with a force like lightning, they tore down branches
Of oak, and with these tried to prise up the tree's roots.
When all their struggles met with no success, Agauë
Cried out, 'Come, Maenads, stand in a circle round the tree
And take hold of it. We must catch this climbing beast,
Or he'll disclose the secret dances of Dionysus.'
They came; a thousand hands gripped on the pine and tore it
Out of the ground. Then from his high perch plunging, crashing
To the earth Pentheus fell, with one incessant scream
As he understood what end was near.
                                          His mother first
As priestess, led the rite of death, and fell upon him.
He tore the headband from his hair, that his wretched mother
Might recognize him and not kill him. 'Mother,' he cried,
Touching her cheek, 'It is I, your own son Pentheus, whom
You bore to Echion. Mother, have mercy; I have sinned,
But I am still your own son. Do not take my life!'
    Agauë was foaming at the mouth; her rolling eyes
Were wild; she was not in her right mind, but possessed
By Bacchus, and she paid no heed to him. She grasped
His right arm between wrist and elbow, set her foot
Against his ribs, and tore his arm off by the shoulder.
It was no strength of hers that did it, but the god
Filled her, and made it easy. On the other side
Ino was at him, tearing at his flesh; and now
Autonoë joined them, and the whole maniacal horde.
A single and continuous yell arose – Pentheus
Shrieking as long as life was left in him, the women
Howling in triumph. One of them carried off an arm,
Another a foot, the boot still laced on it. The ribs
Were stripped, clawed clean; and women's hands, thick red
    with blood,
Were tossing, catching, like a plaything, Pentheus' flesh.

There are some broad similarities between this scene and the
pathos in John's story. In both, a king is led out of the city. In both,

a king is led out to a hill/mountain (Golgotha in John's gospel and the mountain in the *Bacchae*). In both stories, a king is lifted up. In both stories, women play an important role at the site of the *pathos*. However, the differences are just as striking as the similarities. In John's gospel, the sufferings of Jesus are not presented in an extreme and horrifying way. Indeed, as many scholars have pointed out, the suffering of Jesus seems to be understated. In the *Bacchae* the description of Pentheus' death is drawn out and extreme where John's is laconic and restrained. Furthermore, whilst the women in John 19.25f. are merely witnesses of Jesus' death, in the *Bacchae* the women are the instruments of death. Even worse still is the fact that Pentheus' mother actually dismembers her son, whilst Jesus' mother merely functions as a by-stander, Compare Pentheus', 'Mother, it is I, your own son Pentheus' with Jesus', 'Look, your mother!' What this reveals is the striking fact that, even though John's story is a manifestation of tragedy, it is also the subversion of it. This is why John is happy to play down the suffering of Jesus and to resist opportunities for tragedy in the penitence of Peter and the catastrophic end of Judas. John has cleverly seen that Jesus suffers the nemesis he ought to have reaped on others, and that this single fact alone, in spite of all the tragic nuances in Jesus' passion, signals the death of tragedy.

7

A SOCIOLOGICAL READING OF JOHN 18–19

Ecclesial imagery in the Johannine passion account

Having exposed the Johannine passion account to practical and genre criticism (the two aspects of the synchronic approach to NT narratives), we now come to the first diachronic approach to John's story. When we approach a text such as John 18–19, narrative criticism is concerned not only with literary qualities and deep generic structures, but also with the function of John's narrative Christology in its original, proposed social milieu. I recognize that the task of identifying the social function of narrative has sometimes been a rather arbitrary and subjective exercise. One of the problems with Johannine redaction criticism is that it tends to allegorize details of the gospel into incidents from the community's reconstructed history. In chapter 3, I indicated the circularity of this thinking, and the disrespect for Jesus-history which such approaches entail. Instead of treating John's story as an allegory of community history, I suggested a more cautious method in which rigorous literary analysis and sociological explanation work together in harmony. For example, instead of regarding John 9 as an allegory of an incident in the life of John's community (in which a Christian minister runs foul of the Jamnia edict by healing a Jew and leading him to Christ), I would want to begin with a close analysis of the language in the narrative and then infer its plausible sociological function in the Johannine *Sitz im Leben*. Following the method suggested by Kenneth Burke, I am therefore interested in socially significant language in John 18–19. As is so often the case in John's storytelling, this may lead us into other parts of the fourth gospel where similar images are employed.

Only one scholar has recently examined John 18–19 with regard to its social function. Rensberger's 'The Trial of Jesus and the Politics of John' (in Rensberger, 1989) is a ground-breaking study because it attempts to reveal how political pressures at the time of John's community have influenced the telling of John's story. Rensberger summarizes his argument as follows: 'My contention will be that

John's handling of the story must be studied in relation to the concrete political climate of the late first century in order to appreciate his true intentions' (p. 90). Rensberger regards the role of the Romans in John 18–19 as crucial. In John 18.1–27, John emphasizes that the Romans were officially involved in the arrest of Jesus (18.3,12). This, along with the fact that there is no Jewish trial, means that John 'rests the *formal* responsibility for the humiliation and condemnation of Jesus squarely on the Roman prefect Pilate' (p. 91). 'There is no exculpation of the Romans at the expense of the Jews' (p. 91). In John 18.28–19.16, Rensberger argues that Pilate is a cold, calculating and hostile figure, not the sympathetic judge which so many commentators have defended. There is anti-Roman feeling coming through here, especially in Jesus' comment that Pilate would have no authority had it not been given from above. As Rensberger states, 'There is here a clear refusal to acknowledge the authority of Rome, as a power limited to this world, over those who by believing in Jesus have become children of God and so gained the ascendancy over this world' (p. 98). Throughout John 18–19, Rensberger looks at the treatment of political subjects in the light of the political situation of Jews and Christians in the late first century. He argues that the first-century reader had to decide between Jesus' and Caesar's authority, and between Jesus' and Barabbas' freedom.

Rensberger's political reading of John's passion narrative leads him to infer the overall *Sitz im Leben* and purpose of the gospel. He states: 'The Fourth Gospel confronts the issue of Israel's freedom in the late first century Roman Empire with an alternative to both zealotry and collaboration, by calling for adherence to the king who is not of this world, whose servants do not fight but remain in the world, bearing witness to the truth before the rulers of both synagogue and Empire' (p. 100). John 18–19 is a vital key to this interpretation because 'the political nature of the charges against Jesus is given far more emphasis in the Fourth Gospel than elsewhere in the New Testament' (p. 87). However, whilst Rensberger's political approach to John 18–19 has much to commend it, I shall be employing a different method as I seek to provide a sociological reading of John's passion story. Rensberger's method seeks to map John's political issues in the story world against issues in the real world of the late first century. This is an important insight, although it does depend upon a literary evaluation of Pilate's characterization which is questionable. For my part, I am more interested in looking at the imagery of John 18–19, isolating those images which are social in character, and then inferring their sociological function for John's readers. The difference between our two approaches is as follows: the redaction and political criticism of Martyn and Rensberger regards the behaviour of Jesus as an allegory of actual or idealized community history. The situation of Jesus is the situation of the Christian at the hands of anti-Christian Jews and/or Romans in the late first century. In my approach, I am more interested in the way the language in John 18–19 operates as an index of the community's value-system.

The first step in any sociological study of narrative must be to identify parts of John 18–19 where John the storyteller uses language to reflect, establish or correct social values. In John 18.1–27, the language of the sheepfold, which I highlighted in chapter 5, seems to me to be socially insignificant. This ecclesial image is evoked twice in 18.1–27. First of all, in 18.1–11 Jesus is implicitly and symbolically depicted as the shepherd, his followers as the sheep, the walled garden as the sheepfold, and Judas as the thief. Jesus standing at the entrance of the garden to defend his followers against the Jews and the Romans is a picture which speaks of a community closing ranks against the attack of outsiders; it speaks of a community in crisis. Secondly, in 18.15f., the conduct of the BD reveals the qualities of the shepherd whilst Peter's reveals the qualities of the hireling. The BD passes freely in and out of the door of the high priest's courtyard because he is recognized by the door-keeper. Again the sheepfold (αὐλή) functions as a symbol of a closed community. This time the emphasis falls upon the BD, founder of the community, who shows that he is a reliable and courageous pastor – like the Good Shepherd himself. In 18.1–27, therefore, the author is using imagery which is socially significant. The fold-image speaks of a social group which feels threatened from the outside by the political forces of both Judaism and the Roman Empire – forces intent on doing harm. It speaks of a group of disciples who have become defensive to official religion and to the state, and who even have a sectarian attitude towards the apostolic church (symbolized by Peter). In other words, the fold-image is used to express and reinforce the community's identity under pressure.

The sheepfold imagery in act one of John's passion story therefore has an important sociological function. Perhaps the most overt social imagery in John 18–19 as a whole, however, is the language of family relationships, especially in act three (John 19.16–42). In Kenneth Burke's programme, one of the most obvious and forceful images for social cohesion is the image of family and kinship ('familistic images', as Burke calls them). In John 18–19, the evangelist betrays something of an interest in familial relationships at a number of points. First of all, in 18.13, the narrator explains that Annas was the father-in-law of Caiaphas. This is no fiction on John's part; it is well attested in Josephus' *Ant.* XVIII.26–35. Secondly, in 18.15, the narrator explains that the anonymous disciple was 'well-known' to the high priest. Whilst γνωστός does not imply a blood-relationship, it certainly indicates a close intimacy, as Barrett has demonstrated from other uses of the same word in the LXX (1978, pp. 525–6). Thirdly, in 18.26, the narrator tells us that the high priest's slave who interrogates Peter was 'a relative of the man whose ear Peter had cut off' – a detail which the Synoptic gospels omit. Finally, in 19.25–7, we see a number of by-standers by the cross, mostly women. The narrator explains the relationships between these witnesses of Jesus' death: 'his mother, and his mother's sister, Mary the wife of Clopas, and Mary Magdalene'. Added to these women is the disciple whom Jesus loved, and it is upon him and Jesus' mother that the subsequent action focusses. Jesus, as his final task here on earth, turns to his mother and says of the BD, 'Woman, here is your son!' Then he turns to the BD and says, 'Look, your mother!' In giving these two people to one another, Jesus begins a new family at the moment of his death.

The familistic images provided by the narrator in 18.13,15 and 26 do not strike any of the commentators as particularly significant, and indeed the narrative would not suffer a great deal from their omission. However, most of the commentators are agreed upon the centrality of the familistic picture in John 19.25–7, since the BD is seen by many as the founding figure of the Johannine community. Most of the commentaries and a number of articles agree that this narrative pericope has a place of key importance within the passion narrative and indeed the gospel as a whole. Raymond Brown brings this point forcibly home when he analyses the structure of act three (John 19.16–42). He sees this part of the passion story as composed of seven episodes in a chiastic arrangement (1966, Vol. II, pp. 910–11). The fourth scene, the scene at the foot of the cross involving the BD, is the centre-piece of this structure. However, the task of assessing the precise narrative and sociological significance of 19.25f. is more complex than it might appear at first sight. This text is only a very small passage, yet there has, over the centuries, been much written on John 19.25–7, especially by Roman Catholic scholars interested in the role of Jesus' mother (Langkammer, 1968).

However, it is not John's intention to encourage wild symbolic interpretations of the mother of Jesus here. The meaning of the pericope
is clear: 'Jesus savours the proximity of those close to him' and
crowns his life by creating new relationships (Haenchen, 1984, Vol. II,
p. 193). The story, which dwells on Jesus' filial devotion and the
future of his followers, 'suggests a new beginning at the moment
when all is over' (Lindars, 1972, p. 573). Here Jesus fulfils 'the last
office of filial piety' (Westcott, 1892, p. 276; Lindars, 1972, p. 580)
by creating a new family.

This narrative of the final instructions of Jesus to those standing
by creates the 'effect of a testamentary disposition' (Schnackenburg,
1982, p. 278) in which Jesus, after leaving his meagre garments to
the soldiers in fulfilment of Scripture, provides for his mother and
his dearest friend in the last clause of his spoken will. Put this way,
we can see that 19.25ff. does contain one of Burke's familistic images,
for 'at the time of the Lord's death a new family is brought into
being' (Hoskyns, 1940, p. 631). 'Together, mother and son, they
form the nucleus of the new family of faith. The other disciples are
"brothers" and members of his family; all believers are the children
of God' (Culpepper, 1983, p. 122). It is important to realize that,
with the creation of this new family, a new status and a new role are
assigned to the BD. The new task given to the BD has been defined
by commentators in different ways. Many scholars describe it in terms
of succession (Grassi, 1986, p. 73). Since 'the mother of Jesus and
the beloved disciple are to stand in the relation of mother and son',
'the beloved disciple moves into the place of Jesus himself' (Barrett,
1978, p. 459). Thus Maynard writes that 'the Beloved Disciple is the
earthly successor to Jesus' (1984, p. 539), as does Grassi, who argues
that the pericope is designed to authenticate John's teaching by
suggesting a line of succession from Jesus to the BD (1986, pp. 72—3).
Other scholars, such as Dauer and Barrett, prefer the concept of
adoption, claiming that 'Woman, here is your son!' and 'Look, your
mother!' are adoption formulae actually used in the ancient world.
They argue that Jesus, at the hour of his death, is depicted as employing an adoption formula in his creation of a new spiritual family
(Dauer, 1967, pp. 222—39; Barrett, 1978, p. 458).

Both ideas, that of succession and that of adoption, are present
in 19.25—7. Let us look at these two interpretations in more detail,
first the adoption motif. Is Jesus citing an existing, known adoption
formula in the words 'here is your son!'? The answer is probably
no. None of the suggested parallels is exactly the same. In the Jewish

literature, Psalm 2.7 is often referred to, as is the LXX of Tobit 7.12 (at the engagement of the young Tobit to Sarah: 'From now on you are her brother, behold she is your sister!'), but neither of these is really close – nor are the extra-biblical parallels which have been suggested (Schnackenburg, 1982, p. 278). The evangelist wants us to understand Jesus' behaviour as a metaphor for spiritual adoption rather than as a literal adoption process. What, then, of the concept of succession in this passage? In 19.25f., it is clear that the BD becomes Jesus' earthly successor as well as his adoptive brother. This idea is introduced in 13.23f., where the BD is seen lying on 'the bosom of Jesus', a phrase which recalls the comment in 1.18 about Jesus being 'in the bosom of the Father'. As commentators have pointed out, the implication is that the BD shares the same kind of relationship with Jesus as Jesus enjoys with the Father; that is, a distinctive and highly intimate relationship. Furthermore, there is an interesting parallel between John 13.23f. and Jubilees 22.6f. According to Jubilees 22.6, when Abraham gave Jacob his final blessing and last will, both Abraham and Jacob 'lay down together on one bed, and Jacob slept on the bosom of Abraham, his father's father'. Brownlee has argued from this that lying on the testator's bosom was an ancient ceremony of adoption (Robinson, 1985, p. 98). If that is true, then we can see why nuances of 'adoption' and 'succession' surround some of the BD passages in John's story.

The picture of 19.25–7 is one in which Jesus creates a new family of faith by adopting the BD as his true successor on earth. This pericope, so easily overlooked in a hasty reading of John's passion narrative, turns out to be more than just a casual incident in Jesus' last moments. As Lindars rightly says, 'a great depth of meaning is indicated by means of a very few words, composed with the utmost restraint' (1972, p. 579). A number of factors reveal the centrality of 19.25–7: first of all, as I have argued already, act three of the passion narrative is made up of seven scenes, with the present pericope forming the centre-piece of that structure. Secondly, the μὲν ... δέ clause in verse 24 draws attention to 19.25f. because it sets up a contrast between the four soldiers in vv. 23–4 and the four women in v. 25. As Lightfoot puts it, these women represent 'the believing counterpart of the four unbelieving soldiers' (1956, p. 316) ('the faithful counterpart of the four unbelieving soldiers', Hoskyns (1940, p. 631)). Thirdly, the narrator's comment, directly after this adoption, about Jesus knowing that his work was now finished (19.28) suggests that 'Jesus' words to his mother and to the disciple which are a single whole, have something to do with the completion of his work' (Schnackenburg, 1982, p. 278). More than that, the μετὰ τοῦτο in 19.28 indicates that the adoption of the BD into his mother's family really constitutes the climactic work in his ministry. John 19.25–7 is therefore a crucial narrative episode in the Johannine passion account. It is a fulfilment in action of the truth enunciated by the narrator in 13.1: 'Jesus was aware that the hour had come for him to pass from this world to the Father. Having loved his own who were in this world, he now showed his love for them to the very end.'

Source and redaction in John 19.25–7

Source

From our narrative criticism of John 19.25–7 so far it is evident that the issues of source and redaction are important for our understanding of the social function of this pericope. I shall leave the question of sociology until the next section, since it merits a detailed discussion on its own. However, in the present section, we want to address ourselves to two questions: first, what historical source and tradition lie behind John 19.25–7? Secondly, what is the function of John 19.25–7 in the Johannine redaction? The first of these two questions (whether John 19.25f. actually happened) will lead us to ask further questions — such as who the BD was, whether this incident can be harmonized with the Synoptic passion stories, and whether the Roman executing party would have allowed friends and family so close to the cross in the first place. The second issue, the function of John 19.25–7 in the Johannine redaction, will involve a literary analysis of the network of familistic images of which it forms both part and conclusion. It is my belief that the evangelist is here depending upon reliable eye-witness testimony, and that his redactional purpose is to depict the BD's family as the true family of faith, over and against the earthly family of Jesus, and the Jewish family deriving from father Abraham (Israel). The sociological significance of such an image for John's community will be the topic of the next section.

The historicity of 19.25–7 depends partly on an understanding of the true identity of the BD, and his part in the composition of this story. All the evidence of the gospel itself suggests that the BD was an historical, Judaean disciple, not one of the Galilean Twelve. In this respect it is interesting to see how some Johannine scholars have rejected the traditional interpretation of the BD as John bar Zebedee in favour of the Judaean disciple hypothesis (Brown, 1979, p.33). In more recent writings they have been following Oscar Culmann's lead. In his *Johannine Circle* (1976), Culmann contended that Irenaeus' argument about the authorship of the fourth gospel could no longer be reconciled with the general evidence of the gospel itself (p. 75). He therefore turned from the evidence external to the fourth gospel to evidence internal to it. He began by stating that 'we must first of all rid ourselves of the expectation that the disciple must be sought among the Twelve' (p.75). Indeed, Culmann argues that the Twelve do not play any essential role anywhere in John's story. He then goes on to portray the BD as follows:

> As he only appears in scenes which take place in Judaea, at the beginning and the end of the gospel, we must assume that he comes from this region and that Jesus met him in Judaea. He is a former disciple of John the Baptist. He began to follow Jesus in Judaea when Jesus himself was in close proximity to the Baptist. He shared the life of his master during Jesus' last stay in Jerusalem. He was known to the High priest ... The fact that the final redactor published or completed his work and made a declaration about it in the first person plural ('we know') seems to indicate that the disciple collected a whole group of followers about himself.
>
> (p. 78).

According to Culmann, the internal evidence of the gospel indicates that the BD was a Judaean disciple whose name has not been recorded but who was sufficiently important to attract a Johannine circle around him. As I have argued in chapter 4, Lazarus fits this description perfectly.

If one attempts to read the fourth gospel as a narrative in its own right, forgetting for a moment second-century apologies for the identity of the BD, then Lazarus has to be the BD. Even the casual reader cannot help but notice that the BD makes his appearance in chapter 13, at the beginning of the book of Christ's passion (though it is arguable that he makes his first appearance at 1.35 as one of the two unnamed disciples, especially since the same phrase appears again at 21.2). In 13.23 we saw for the first time a disciple 'whom Jesus loved' leaning on Jesus' breast at the last supper. In 18.15 he is introduced again at the gate to Annas' courtyard as 'another disciple'. In 19.26 he is seen at the foot of the cross and called 'the disciple ... whom Jesus loved'. In 20.2, in the run to the empty tomb with Peter,

he is described as 'the other disciple wh...
is 'the other disciple'. In 20.4, he is a g...
disciple'. In 21.2, he is one of the 'other...
Tiberias. In 21.7 he is described as 'the...
loved'. In 21.20 he is again 'the discipl...
one character in John's story who is esp...
of Jesus is Lazarus, who features prom...
immediately before the appearance of t...
described to Jesus as 'the one whom you...
lines this love-relationship in the appare...
11.5 that Jesus loved Martha and her si...
more, when Jesus returns to Lazarus' hor...
dead, he weeps. The reaction of the Jew...
bereavement yet again confirms Jesus'...
They remark, ἴδε πῶς ἐφίλει αὐτόν — '...
him'.

My proposal is that John the story telle...
of the BD, a Judaean disciple called La...
about Jesus (possibly even a written...
fashioned into a gospel, and it was his pro...
standing which united a distinctive grou...
7.3 of the existence of a group of disc...
during the time of Jesus' ministry, and v...
of the Twelve highlighted by Mark (and...
and Luke). Jesus' brothers say to him, 'I...
so that your disciples too may get a look...
forming.' Since most of the Twelve we...
presume that this group of Judaean foll...
munity. That Lazarus figured in this grou...
likely if we recall that the BD may well...
followers of John the Baptist who tran...
Jesus in 1.37 (the narrator makes a poin...
was operating in Bethany when this hap...
to be the Bethany of 11.1, Lazarus' ho...
there was in Judaea a group of disciples,...
in which Lazarus was a key figure. This gr...
and basis of what present-day scholars hi...
nine community'. Its own centre at Bet...
house, may explain the focus on Jerusal...
story. Its leader's personal experience o...
indicate why the fourth gospel became...

in favour of the Judaean disciple hypothesis (Brown, 1979, p. 33). In more recent writings they have been following Oscar Culmann's lead. In his *Johannine Circle* (1976), Culmann contended that Irenaeus' argument about the authorship of the fourth gospel could no longer be reconciled with the general evidence of the gospel itself (p. 75). He therefore turned from the evidence external to the fourth gospel to evidence internal to it. He began by stating that 'we must first of all rid ourselves of the expectation that the disciple must be sought among the Twelve' (p. 75). Indeed, Culmann argues that the Twelve do not play any essential role anywhere in John's story. He then goes on to portray the BD as follows:

> As he only appears in scenes which take place in Judaea, at the beginning and the end of the gospel, we must assume that he comes from this region and that Jesus met him in Judaea. He is a former disciple of John the Baptist. He began to follow Jesus in Judaea when Jesus himself was in close proximity to the Baptist. He shared the life of his master during Jesus' last stay in Jerusalem. He was known to the High priest ... The fact that the final redactor published or completed his work and made a declaration about it in the first person plural ('we know') seems to indicate that the disciple collected a whole group of followers about himself.
>
> (p. 78).

According to Culmann, the internal evidence of the gospel indicates that the BD was a Judaean disciple whose name has not been recorded but who was sufficiently important to attract a Johannine circle around him. As I have argued in chapter 4, Lazarus fits this description perfectly.

If one attempts to read the fourth gospel as a narrative in its own right, forgetting for a moment second-century apologies for the identity of the BD, then Lazarus has to be the BD. Even the casual reader cannot help but notice that the BD makes his appearance in chapter 13, at the beginning of the book of Christ's passion (though it is arguable that he makes his first appearance at 1.35 as one of the two unnamed disciples, especially since the same phrase appears again at 21.2). In 13.23 we saw for the first time a disciple 'whom Jesus loved' leaning on Jesus' breast at the last supper. In 18.15 he is introduced again at the gate to Annas' courtyard as 'another disciple'. In 19.26 he is seen at the foot of the cross and called 'the disciple ... whom Jesus loved'. In 20.2, in the run to the empty tomb with Peter, he is described as 'the other disciple whom Jesus loved'. In 20.3 he is 'the other disciple'. In 20.4, he is again described as 'the other disciple'. In 21.2, he is one of the 'other two disciples' beside Lake Tiberias. In 21.7 he is described as 'the very disciple whom Jesus loved'. In 21.20 he is again 'the disciple whom Jesus loved'. The one character in John's story who is especially honoured as *beloved* of Jesus is Lazarus, who features prominently in the two chapters immediately before the appearance of the BD. In 11.3, Lazarus is described to Jesus as 'the one whom you love'. The narrator under-lines this love-relationship in the apparently redundant statement in 11.5 that Jesus loved Martha and her sister and Lazarus. Further-more, when Jesus returns to Lazarus' home to find Lazarus four days dead, he weeps. The reaction of the Jews to this demonstration of bereavement yet again confirms Jesus' special love for Lazarus. They remark, ἴδε πῶς ἐφίλει αὐτόν – 'behold, how much he loved him'.

My proposal is that John the storyteller drew on the reminiscences of the BD, a Judaean disciple called Lazarus. It was his testimony about Jesus (possibly even a written, early gospel) which John fashioned into a gospel, and it was his profound Christological under-standing which united a distinctive group of disciples. We learn in 7.3 of the existence of a group of disciples who lived in Judaea during the time of Jesus' ministry, and who were evidently not part of the Twelve highlighted by Mark (and subsequently by Matthew and Luke). Jesus' brothers say to him, 'Leave here and go to Judaea so that your disciples too may get a look at the works you are per-forming.' Since most of the Twelve were Galileans, we can only presume that this group of Judaean followers was a separate com-munity. That Lazarus figured in this group from its inception is quite likely if we recall that the BD may well have been one of the two followers of John the Baptist who transferred their allegiances to Jesus in 1.37 (the narrator makes a point of saying that the Baptist was operating in Bethany when this happened (1.28), which I take to be the Bethany of 11.1, Lazarus' home (Parker, 1955)). Thus, there was in Judaea a group of disciples, separate from the Twelve, in which Lazarus was a key figure. This group was to form the nucleus and basis of what present-day scholarship has christened 'the Johan-nine community'. Its own centre at Bethany, possibly in Lazarus' house, may explain the focus on Jerusalem and Bethany in John's story. Its leader's personal experience of new life after death may indicate why the fourth gospel became the gospel of eternal life.

Indeed, since the testimony of Lazarus is so crucial to John's story, there is a sense in which the latter could be called *The Gospel According to Lazarus.*

To return then, to the adoption scenario in John 19.25−7, it is my argument that Jesus gave his mother to Lazarus, the one he loved, who in turn took her to Bethany (the place where Mary and the disciples say farewell to Jesus in Luke 24.50f.). We can suppose that Lazarus testified to this fact many times in the presence of the story-teller who wrote the gospel. In the light of this judgement, I cannot agree with those commentators who dismiss the adoption scenario in 19.26−7 as historically implausible. C.K. Barrett's commentary on John 19.25−7 is fairly typical in this respect. He dismisses the natural explanation of 19.25f. (i.e. that it is a 'simple historical reminiscence due to the beloved disciple himself') on the grounds that 'the presence near the cross of friends of Jesus is improbable' (p.458). Barrett opts instead for the view that the evangelist was here following 'bad tradition' (p.455). In other words, convinced that there seems to be no great theological symbolism in the incident, and assured that such an event is at the same time historically im-probable, Barrett claims that the evangelist must have incorporated a suggestive item of tradition which was really invented rather than historical. However, there are very real problems with an argument like this. Barrett himself displays an apparent inconsistency when, after claiming that it is improbable that Jesus' family and friends would have been at the cross, he says, 'it is not inconceivable that Jesus, as the head of the family ... should have made provision for the care of his mother' (p.459). Now, either it is improbable that such an event occurred, or not; it cannot be both! Furthermore, if the adoption scenario really was a piece of fiction, then for what ecclesiological purpose and in what context was it created? Barrett remains silent on this issue.

Stauffer's estimation of the historicity of John 19.25f. provides a fair though somewhat general counter-argument to Barrett's scep-ticism. Speaking of the words from the cross in all four gospels, she asks, 'Are all these words historical?' (1960, p.111). In defence of their historical probability, she cites scholars whose research has revealed that 'at the place of execution crucified persons are often surrounded by relations, friends and enemies, and in the long and painful hours until their death have often said some word or other' (pp.111−12). The argument that the soldiers would not have allowed anyone near Jesus' cross is therefore mistaken. As a result, Stauffer regards it as by no means impossible that Jesus spoke the words which traditional accounts of the crucifixion preserved, including Jesus' words in 19.25f. Stauffer thus reconstructs the historical incident in 19.25f. as follows:

> Mary's presence at Golgotha is an act of confession. She confesses that she belongs to the community of the accursed one. That means cutting herself off from James and his brothers who still hold aloof from Jesus. In the Palestine of antiquity that means for a woman complete lack of a home and of protection — at the very moment when, having already lost her husband, she is also losing her son, the son with whom she has especially close ties. Jesus knows this. A crucified man has the right to make testamentary dispositions, even from the cross. Jesus now makes use of this right and with the official formula of the old Jewish family law he places his mother under the protection of the apostle John.   (p. 113)

Though I disagree with Stauffer's identification of the BD, her argument supports my view that John the storyteller has drawn on 'good tradition' in his restrained description of the creation of a new family of faith at the foot of the cross. However, the matter is not so easily resolved as this, since it is often objected that the Synoptic accounts of the crucifixion depict the women standing far off, with no sign of any male disciples anywhere near the cross. Thus Haenchen remarks that the scene in 19.25—7 'is not only unknown to the synoptics, it is even impossible as they represent matters. They report only that women watch how Jesus was crucified from afar' (1984, pp. 197—8). This is, however, a simplification of the Synoptic pictures. Mark mentions that the women were standing at a distance from Jesus, but only after his death (15.40). This would not rule out the possibility of an incident such as the one depicted in John 19.25—7, since it occurs before Jesus' death. As Brown has said, 'one can harmonise by claiming that during the crucifixion the women had stood close to the cross (John), but as death approached they were forced to move away' (1966, Vol. II, p. 904). Furthermore, the Synoptic pictures of the death of Jesus do not rule out the presence of the BD, since they are most concerned about the presence or absence of the Galilean Twelve (of whom Lazarus was not, of course, a member). The presence of male disciples at the crucifixion should not be dismissed, especially since Luke indicates that there were men who knew Jesus nearby (γνωστοί is masculine in Luke 23.49).

Redaction

Bultmann's claim that this scene is the evangelist's own composition
because 'in the face of the Synoptic tradition' it 'can make no claim
to historicity' (1971, p. 673) is suspect. In his narrative reconstruction
of tradition in 19.25–7, John the storyteller drew upon an oral or
a written source which derived from Lazarus' eye-witness testimony
and which was either omitted by the Synoptic evangelists or unknown
to them. What, then, was the evangelist's aim in incorporating this
incident in such a central way into act three of his passion account?
The sure way of answering this question is by finding other familistic
images in John's story which resonate with 19.25–7 and then establishing the network of meanings which such images suggest. The first
of such images occurs in 1.11, where the narrator tells us that Jesus-
the-Word came to his own home (τὰ ἴδια), but his own people (οἱ
ἴδιοι) did not receive or accept him (παρέλαβον). Verbal parallels
with 19.25f. immediately suggest themselves, for in 19.27 the narrator
reveals that the BD received or accepted Mary (ἔλαβεν) and took
her to his own home/people (τὰ ἴδια). The main point of 1.11, however, is that Jesus is said to be rejected by the spiritual family of the
Jews, his own people, in his own homeland. That the Jews in John's
story understand themselves as a kind of racial family is seen in the
familistic language of chapter 8, where they claim to be the seed of
Abraham and the children of Abraham, and where they claim that
Abraham is their father.

The picture evoked in chapters 1–12 is therefore one in which
Jesus comes to his own racial family (the Jews) but is subjected to
increasing hostility and rejection by them. However, the parenthesis
in 7.5 indicates that Jesus was not only rejected by this vast racial
family of Judaism but also by his particular, localized family. As the
narrator puts it, 'not even his brothers believed in him'. Thus Jesus
is rejected by both a spiritual family (Israel) and by his own natural
family in Nazareth. It is this fact which contributes so much towards
the sense of tragedy in John's story (tragedy often focusses on extreme
familial conflict). Jesus becomes not only a Stranger from heaven but
a Stranger on earth, isolated from all natural and earthly familial
relationship by his insistence on his own unique familial relationship
with God the Father (10.30). However, to all those who believe in
him and who face a similar isolation from their racial and natural
families (such as the man born blind in John 9), Jesus promises a
new family and a new home. As the narrator puts it in the prologue,

'all those who did accept him he empowered to become God's children. That is, those who believe in his name – those who were begotten, not by blood, nor by carnal desire, nor by man's desire, but by God' (1.12f.). Jesus offers a new family and a new 'home' (14.1) to those who are willing to accept him. It is because of this that Jesus can promise to his disciples in 14.18 that he will not leave them ὀρφανούς. Jesus will adopt the BD at the cross, and will not leave them vulnerable and homeless.

Jesus' coming leads to the breakdown of the family of Judaism, to a disruption of families and homelessness for his disciples, but also to the construction of a new family of faith defined by belief in Jesus. The destruction of the family of Judaism is depicted in 8.35 as homelessness for the Jews. In a very terse parable, Jesus warns the Jews that 'While no slave has a permanent place in the family, the son has a place there forever.' The slave in this context is an individual symbol representing a collective entity – the Jews. The son is obviously Jesus. The family, by implication, is the body of people who constitute the true children of God. Jesus' brief parable is therefore a warning to the Jews that they are on the point of losing their spiritual home and family centred upon God the Father. That right will now be given to the disciples. To them, Jesus promises a new family which will understand itself as the true brothers of Jesus and the true children of God. This new family is born out of the suffering of the cross, as yet another distinctive Johannine familistic image indicates. In 16.21 Jesus says, 'When a woman is in labour, she is sad that her hour has come. But once the baby is born, her joy makes her forget the suffering, because a child has been born into the world!' In this extraordinary parable Jesus suggests that the crucifixion will mark the birth of the true community of God; the child in the parable represents the new family which emerges from Jesus' quasi-maternal sacrifice.

The verbal parallels between 16.21 and 19.25f. (the use of the words woman and hour) indicate that the cross is supremely the place where God's old family is deconstructed and his new family is born. The cross is the place of adoption, as we have already seen. It is the fulfilment in narrative of the promise made in discourse (14.18): 'I will not leave you as orphans.' The dramatic and indeed tragic character of John's passion narrative is seen in the apostasy of the Jews in 19.15, for here they at last relinquish any right to be the children of God by claiming Caesar instead of Yahweh as king. But in this tragic rejection of their true king, the Jews unwittingly make the way clear for a new family, a true Israel, to replace the old unbelieving Israel led by the chief priests and rulers. It is at this point, in 19.25–7, that the new family of faith emerges. At the cross, Jesus establishes new relationships and a new community. By adopting the BD as his successor, Jesus establishes Mary and Lazarus as the human foci of the new spiritual family that can claim God as Father. Here earthly, natural ties are replaced by new familial relationships and a new home is created at Bethany, the οἰκία τοῦ πατρός.

The social function of John 19.25–7

A number of recent studies have sought to demonstrate, both from an exegetical and a sociological basis, the disruption of families and the consequent loss of home which discipleship caused. Martin Hengel's *Charismatic Leader and his Followers* (1981) showed just how drastic following Jesus could be for the first disciples. As he put it, 'decision for Jesus did not bring peace but disruption ... to families' in a way that conflicted dramatically with Jewish law, piety and custom (p. 13). Hengel argued that no adequate parallel to the special features of being a disciple of Jesus exists in any of the known, relevant sources. Instead, he proposed that Max Weber's sociological description of the charismatic leader offers the most revealing insights into Jesus' character and demands. Weber had claimed that 'those who are the bearers of the charisma – the master and his disciples and followers – must, if they are to do justice to their mission, stand outside the ties of this world, outside the everyday vocations and also outside the everyday family duties' (Hengel, 1981, p. 34). Hengel, in the light of this remark, attempted to rationalize the apparently severe Q saying, 'Let the dead bury their dead' (Matthew 8.21/Luke 9.59), by describing Jesus as an eschatological charismatic whose mission required a dramatic disruption of family and a loss of home. Indeed, Hengel maintains that Jesus demanded freedom from family ties.

Gerd Theissen's book *The First Followers of Jesus: A Sociological Analysis of Early Christianity* (1978) in many ways supplemented Hengel's 1968 book in that it sought to describe in greater detail the sociological implications of Jesus' life as a wandering charismatic. In Theissen's book, however, the focus is not so much on Jesus as the itinerant prophet but on those who sought to carry the Christian revelation from place to place. Theissen painted a picture of the earliest Christian church as a large number of communities which were visited by wandering charismatics, who in turn became those communities' spiritual authorities. He points out that Jesus did not primarily found local churches but rather called into being a movement of wandering prophets who lived a homeless, nomadic existence. From the Synoptics, it is clear to Theissen that their lives were characterized by homelessness, lack of family, loss of possessions and lack of protection. Howard Kee's *Community of the New Age*, published in the same year, went a stage further than this by showing that homelessness and loss of family were hallmarks of the communities as well as its charismatic leaders. Following Jesus, for both the Christian in the local community as well as the wandering charismatic, required 'a break with one group in which the individual finds his most important attachments and his true identity: the family' (p. 89). The need in the Christian communities was therefore for a 'new concept of the true family' (p. 89), and this — in Mark's gospel — was achieved in the picture of the church as an eschatological family (p. 109) (Mark 3.20f., 10.28f., etc.).

Perhaps the most detailed study of this phenomenon of homelessness in primitive Christianity is J. H. Elliott's sociological exegesis of I Peter, *A Home for the Homeless* (1981). Elliott draws attention to some of the distinctive language of I Peter which helps us to situate the letter. The present existence of Christians is described in 1.17 as παροικία or homelessness (p. 14). In the Graeco-Roman world, the πάροικος or *peregrinus* was a resident alien permanently without rights of citizenship because of status by birth. Placing the actual social setting of the letter in central and Northern Asia Minor, Elliott draws on other historical data concerning rural labouring classes to suggest that the language of homelessness is more actual than figurative in I Peter (p. 39). Homeless Christians founded sects, according to Elliott, whose group cohesion was strengthened by persecution (3.13—17, 4.12—19, 5.10). The purpose of I Peter was consequently to exhort the readers to remain resident aliens, not by offering some picture of a heavenly home, but by helping them to recognize the home which these Christians already possessed. The central ecclesiological image which the author used was therefore the image of the household, since it 'supplied powerful social, psychological and theological symbols' (pp. 222—3). The idea of the church as the household of God was imaginative because it enhanced social cohesion, appealed to the universal experience of family life, and evoked 'the common memory of and quest for home, companionship and a place of belonging' (p. 230).

These four writers — Hengel, Theissen, Kee and Elliott — have succeeded in delineating the effect on family and home which primitive Christianity caused. They portray Jesus as a homeless, charismatic nomad who was forced by the nature of his mission to relinquish his natural family ties. They depict the post-resurrection itinerant teachers as homeless prophets who cut themselves off from their families in obedience to (and imitation of) their Master. They describe the communities themselves as social groups in which conversion had resulted in the disruption of families and the loss of a sense of home. Above all, they show the writers of NT texts as sensitive and imaginative pastors who sought to reorientate their flocks to a sense of true belonging by using 'family' and 'home' as potent ecclesiological images. Thus, Mark orientates his readers to an awareness of their present existence as members of an eschatological family by reporting Jesus' statement that 'whoever does the will of God is my brother, and sister, and mother' (3.35), and his promise that 'there is no one who has left house or brothers or sisters or mother or father or children or lands, for my sake and for the gospel, who will not receive a hundredfold now in this time, houses and brothers and sisters and mothers and children and lands, with persecutions, and in the age to come eternal life' (10.29—30). In other words, the second evangelist compensates for his reader's alienation by offering them a powerful, familial legitimation of their present existence.

That these sociological studies of NT texts have a bearing on John 19.25—7 can be borne out by citing one of Barrett's remarks on the passage in his commentary. He writes at one point that the creation of a new family of faith in John 19.25—7 is an illustration of Christian unity, since 'the Christian receives in the present age houses and brothers and sisters and mothers and children and lands (Mark 10.30)' (p. 459). Barrett is not suggesting that John 19.25—7 is an allegorical illustration of the promise made by Jesus in Mark 10.30. Rather he is suggesting that the adoption scenario at the cross is an example of that redefinition of family and home which the earliest Christian disciples had to face. This redefinition is particularly evident in 19.25—7 because Jesus' brothers, whom one would have considered the logical and natural guardians of Mary, are noticeable for their absence. The BD is chosen in preference to the brothers of Jesus. Indeed, he takes their place because he truly believes in Jesus whilst they only misunderstand him (7.5). Thus, faith in Jesus is the criterion for adoption into Christ's family, not natural kinship. Spiritual relationships within the new family of faith take priority over natural ties. The church is a family of faith, not primarily of blood relationships.

So how would the first readers or hearers of John's passion narrative have responded to this powerful little narrative about the adoption of the BD? It is my contention that this narrative would have provided a forceful legitimation of the Johannine Christians' present existence and an effective consolation for the loss of family and home which they themselves had faced. There is evidence in the fourth gospel that belief in Jesus — if overtly confessed — resulted in alienation from the family of Judaism and indeed from one's own family. The statement of the narrator in John 9.22 demonstrates this truth translucently. In this context, the parents of the man born blind refused to cooperate with the synagogue authorities because they feared the Jews, because the Jews had already agreed that if any one should confess Jesus to be Christ, he was to be expelled from the synagogue. Why did the evangelist feel that it was necessary to include the parents at all? The answer is first of all because they were present in his historical source. This much is suggested by the word already in 9.22, which indicates a desire by the storyteller to remind the reader that discipleship was causing disruption of families and excommunication even during Jesus' ministry. Just as importantly, however, the evangelist includes the parents because the division between parents and children was a critical reality in the lives of those Christians for whom he was writing. Thus, the implied division of a family in John 9 would have been a focus of poignant identification for the gospel's first readers.

Just as the Johannine Christians would have identified with the disruption of a family in John 9, so they would have identified with the creation of a new family of faith in John 19.25—7, especially since the BD seems to have been the central and originating figure in their communal history. John 19.25—7 therefore functioned as a familistic image which enhanced the sense of religious belonging amongst Johannine Christians. Every religious community requires a group image if successful socialization is to be achieved (Carrier, 1965, p. 208). The degree of social affiliation depends on the reality and relevance of the group image within the consciousness of the collectivity concerned. As Carrier puts it, 'the image projected by a group plays a decisive role in strengthening the sense either of belonging or its rejection' (p. 210). Such group images are most frequently expressed in the form of a community narrative. As the Christian social ethicist Stanley Hauerwas puts it, 'the form and substance of a community is narrative-dependent and therefore what counts as "social ethics" is a correlative of the content of that narrative' (1981, p. 10). As he continues, 'a people are formed by a story which places their history in the texture of the world. Such stories make the world our home by providing us with the skills to negotiate the dangers in our environment in a manner appropriate to our nature' (p. 15). What I am suggesting in the context of John 19.25—7 is that this narrative creates a sense of 'home' amongst Johannine Christians by showing that their fraternity derives from an act of love by Jesus himself at the cross.

The psycho-social phenomenon of religious belonging is best achieved by the concentration upon and repetition of the images of family and home. This is particularly obvious in first-century Jewish communities, where religious affiliation was realized through the idea of a familial bond. As Bossmann has argued, in much of the Judaism of this period, family terms and family-based symbols of tradition and authority were used in order to stabilize Judaism during a period of dangerous social unpredictability. In other words, the Pharisees used the extended-family model because it was 'the safest and most effective context for the practice and transmission of Judaism' (Bossmann, 1987, p. 5). However, this characteristic of regarding the community as a family was not confined to first-century Judaism. As Anne Marie Ohler has shown, Jewish society from the earliest times composed family sagas designed to reinforce the sense of community identity, and these sagas were successfully passed on from generation to generation. Ohler gives some space to what she calls the 'family saga'. She shows how 'the narratives collected in Genesis 12—50 represent the beginnings of the people of Israel in the guise of a family history', and how, from then on, stories emphasizing the family history of the community were treasured and repeated (1985, p. 93). Such parallels in Jewish stories both prior to and contemporary with the fourth gospel suggest that 19.25—7 may well have acted as a kind of family history similar to those family sagas which the Jewish Johannine Christians treasured before their conversion — though (as I have demonstrated in the preceding section) John 19.25—7 is based on historical tradition. It is neither legend nor saga.

The adoption narrative in John 19.25—7 is therefore a good example of the way John's passion story functions at a sociological level. In a nutshell, this text functions as a legitimation of the present family life of Johannine Christians. When I call 19.25—7 a legitimating narrative, I mean that it objectifies the kind of knowledge necessary for explaining and justifying the present social order of Johannine Christianity. Peter Berger has shown that such legitimations are necessary in community life because 'not only children but adults as well "forget" the legitimating answers. They must ever again be "reminded". In other words, the legitimating formulas must be repeated' (Berger and Luckmann, 1984, p. 31). Berger goes on to add that *ritual* is the crucial instrument for 'reminding' society (p. 40). This is interesting in the case of John 19.25–7, because it has been argued that the passion narratives in all four gospels are precisely the kinds of story which would have been recited in the earliest Christian liturgies. Trocmé has stated that 'the Sitz im Leben of the original Passion narrative … was … the liturgical commemoration of Christ's death by Christians during the Jewish Passover celebration' (1983, p. 82). Whether or not we agree that the first passion story or stories were only recited at passover, the fact remains that the passion narratives in the gospels would have been used early on in liturgical settings. This liturgical function should caution us against neglecting the primary oral situation when assessing the artistry of John. It should also warn us that the purpose of John 18–19 was, in part, to remind Johannine Christians of legitimating answers, through the narrative form, and in a ritual context.

Summary

In this chapter I have tried to imagine some of the first reader responses to John 18–19. My aim has been to highlight the relationship between narrative and social identity in John's story, and the way in which John 19.25–7 is composed not only for its historical value but also for its community resonances. To Johannine Christians, no doubt facing the social and psychological bereavement of alienation from the family of Judaism as well as from their own natural families, such an adoption narrative would have provided consolation. No doubt it would also have reinforced the authority both of the BD and his testimonies. But its primary function is to recreate the sense of family and home in a people faced with the crisis of metaphorical and actual homelessness. Put another way, with the liturgical recitation of John 19.25–7, Johannine Christianity would have constantly experienced a sense of what Winquist calls 'homecoming'. In *The Act of Storytelling and the Self's Homecoming* (1978), Winquist argues that 'without a history or without a story there is very little that we can say about ourselves' (p. 2). As he continues, 'The story can be viewed as an integrating structure that organizes our feelings and forms a sense of continuous identity. To live without a story is to be disconnected from our past and our future' (p. 2). 'Only in the imaginative extension of story or myth can the unfinished self approximate a homecoming' (p. 9). It is in the light of these thoughts that I propose the following thesis: that the Johannine act of story-telling in John 19.25f. would have resulted in a sense of homecoming in the Johannine community. As I have argued throughout this book, the gospel's narrative form cannot therefore be separated from its social function.

8

A NARRATIVE-HISTORICAL APPROACH TO JOHN 18–19

Narrative and history

My aim in this chapter is to explore the journey from narrative history through narrative source to narrative gospel. As with the corresponding chapter in part I (chapter 4), my headings to each section reflect this tradition history. In this section I shall be looking at the issue of narrative and history in John 18–19, and in doing so I shall be asking the same two questions which I asked about John in general in chapter 4: (1) In what sense can we speak of history at the heart of John 18–19? (2) In what sense was this history already narrative in form? In the second section I will want to take the reader on the journey from history to source. Having argued in this first section that John is narrating valuable historical data in John 18–19, I shall show in the second section how this history was very early on redescribed in the form of a primitive passion narrative, the general character of which can be discerned by distinguishing between tradition and redaction. The reader will have already spotted that I detect two main narrative sources behind John's gospel: a catena of miracle stories from Galilee and, most significantly, a primitive gospel narrative based on the reminiscences of Lazarus, the disciple whom Jesus loved. The question left unanswered in my hypothetical reconstruction is this: where does the passion fit into this picture? In the third section of this chapter ('Narrative and gospel') I shall look at John's contribution. Having established that we have a reliable record of the passion which was early on collected into a narrative source, I shall show in the third section how John interpreted this narrative history and narrative source. Many of the subtleties analysed in chapters 5 to 7 above are his inspired contribution.

In what sense, then, can we speak of history within and behind John 18–19? At the outset I need to stress that I am making the assumption that the historical arguments for the facts of Jesus' arrest, trial and execution are known. The evidence comes from outside the NT canon (in Roman and Jewish historiography) as well as inside the NT. Indeed, it is with the passion of Jesus that the four gospels are most agreed. All four agree that Jesus was arrested, that Peter denied him, that Jesus was taken before Caiaphas, that he was then tried by Pilate, that he was handed over to be crucified, that he died between two others outside Jerusalem, and that he was buried in a tomb nearby. In very general terms, there is the kind of consensus between the four evangelists which leads us to regard their basic stories as fact rather than fiction. However, the reader of John 18–19 should not be deceived by these broad similarities into believing that there are no tensions between the four NT passion narratives. In reality, John 18–19 bristles with difficulties for the historical critic. In act one (18.1–27), we have the involvement of the Romans in the arrest of Jesus, the omission of any mention of Judas approaching Jesus to kiss him, the lack of any note of agony at Jesus' mention of the cup of suffering, the mention of Annas rather than Caiaphas as high priest, the interrogation before Annas, the lack of any formal Jewish trial, and so on. In act two (18.28–19, 16a), we have the following difficulties: whether or not the Jews could put someone to death, the source of the details of the private conversation between Jesus and Pilate, the place of Jesus' scourging, and the question of blasphemy. In act three (19, 16b–42), there are problems connected with Jesus carrying his own cross, the seamless robe, the friends near the cross, the hyssop branch, the time of Jesus' death and the effusion of blood and water.

In the following pages it is my aim briefly to show that some (not all) of the arguments against the historicity of John 18–19 are merely presumption, to use John Robinson's word (1985, p. 1). To do this I shall be using a charge and response approach in which the charges reflect the kinds of argument often levelled against John's historical value, and the responses my own attempt to vindicate some of John's story of the death of Jesus as a window on to facts.

1. Charge

In 18.3 John tells us that a detachment of soldiers came to arrest Jesus. The word used for 'detachment' is σπεῖρα, which means a cohort (about 600 Roman soldiers). There are two problems here. First of all, it is not likely that the Romans would have been involved in the arrest of Jesus. As Barrett says, 'The participation of Roman forces at this stage of the proceedings against Jesus seems improbable, since the first step was apparently for the Jews to frame a charge that might be brought before the Governor, and Roman soldiers would have taken Jesus at once to Pilate, not to the high priest' (1978, p. 518). Secondly, even if Roman soldiers had been involved in the arrest of Jesus, 600 men would have been an absurd number to send. A whole cohort sent to apprehend one Galilean preacher would not only have been a waste of manpower, it would also have left the Antonia fortress dangerously undermanned. The only solution is that John has fabricated the Roman involvement in the arrest because he wants the reader to see Jesus as sovereign over the world's power (Rome) and ecclesiastical power (the Jews) (Bultmann, 1971, p. 633). The involvement of the Romans is a purely symbolic one: the arrival of the Romans is a fulfilment of John 14.30: 'the ruler of this world is coming'.

1. Response

On the first issue, the involvement of the Romans in the arrest of Jesus, the following needs to be said in defence of the historical plausibility of this detail. First, John's tendency throughout the gospel and indeed in the passion account is to load the responsibility for the death of Jesus on to the Jews. In 19.11 Jesus openly states before Pilate that the one who handed him over was guilty of a greater sin. This is clearly a reference to Caiaphas as representative of the Jewish leaders who had decreed that Jesus must die. Since the participation of the Romans at the arrest of Jesus goes against this Johannine tendency to implicate the Jews, the detail concerning the detachment is likely to be historical. Secondly, it is likely that the Romans would have been involved in the arrest because the Jews would have persuaded them that Jesus was a danger to the peace at a volatile time. The Roman soldiers in this instance are therefore acting as the law-enforcement officers for the Jewish supreme court who in 11.50 decide that Jesus must die if the Jewish nation is to survive under Roman occupation. On the second issue, the quantity of soldiers, it has been pointed out that σπεῖρα is also used for 'maniple', which would be 200 men (Brown, 1966, Vol. II, p. 807). That would not be an implausible number of soldiers to use during the passover festival, with the threat of bandits like Barabbas on the mind of the Roman governor. The involvement of the Roman maniple is therefore a probable historical detail and not a purely symbolic feature.

2. Charge

In Mark 14.44 we read that Judas had arranged a signal with the arresting party: 'The one I kiss, is the man.' Judas goes at once to Jesus when they arrive at Gethsemane and kisses him, thereby identifying Jesus as the one to be led away captive. The same situation is depicted in Matthew 26.48 and Luke 22.47. In John 18.4, however, no such signal is given. Indeed, Jesus goes out to the arresting party and identifies himself as the one they want. The actions of Jesus in this episode clearly serve theological purposes. This is not an historical reminiscence.

2. Response

There is no doubt that this episode has been redescribed by the storyteller with narrative licence. A number of John's favourite narrative themes surface here: for example, the supernatural γνῶσις of Jesus ('knowing all that was going to happen'), the initiative of Jesus ('he went out'), the theme of seeking ('who is it you want?'). I have already shown in chapter 5 how the whole of act one has been artfully depicted so as to suggest resonances with the shepherd imagery of John 10. The behaviour of Judas in this passage corresponds to that of the κλεπτής. The behaviour of Jesus corresponds to that of the Good Shepherd. Clearly there is more interpretation than history in the movements of Judas and Jesus in 18.4.

3. Charge

The response of the arresting party in 18.6 is symbolic rather than historical. It is highly improbable that a maniple of 200 men and the temple guards would have drawn back and fallen to the ground when Jesus identified himself. This is 'the normal effect of a theophany' (Lindars, 1972, p. 541), and not an historically reliable detail.

3. Response

This detail is an obvious example of dramatic hyperbole rather than historical reportage. Though there may be some basis in historical fact (perhaps the soldiers really were floored by Jesus' confidence), the reaction of the soldiers here serves narrative purposes. The commentaries fail to point out the resonances with John 11.9–10 which must form part of the background for 18.6: 'Are there not twelve hours of daylight? A man who walks by day will not stumble, for he sees by this world's light. It is when he walks by night that he stumbles, for he has no light.' There are some interesting implications for John 18.6 in these words. They show that the arresting party are of the world and that they lack spiritual illumination, in spite of all the lanterns and torches which they bring (18.3), because they stumble at night. Furthermore, no one has pointed out that this incident is the climax to all the negative seeking which goes on in John's story. After countless instances in which the elusiveness of Jesus is emphasized, we now have a situation in which Jesus freely presents himself to those seeking him ('whom do you seek?', 18.4). The reaction of the arresting party is meant to signify their surprise at the ease of the divinity's capture. It is hardly an historical reminiscence.

4. Charge

There is a total omission of any agony scene in the garden in John 18. In the Synoptic gospels, Jesus agonizes over the cup of suffering from which he is about to drink (Mark 14.35–6, Matthew 26.39, Luke 22.42). In John, the cup is mentioned, but in a much more confident tone, Jesus, castigating Peter for his aggression says, 'Shall I not drink the cup the Father has given me?' Jesus' words in 18.11 reveal an awareness of the Gethsemane prayer, but depart from it in two respects: first, Jesus' words are a question, not a prayer; secondly, the cup represents the Father's appointed work for him ('the cup the Father has given me' is loaded with Johannine theology). This departure from the Synoptic Gethsemane tradition is a further argument against the historicity of John 18.

4. Response

Although John omits Gethsemane and the prayer of agony, there are in John 18 and elsewhere in the fourth gospel elements of this tradition. The vocabulary of 18.11 is close to that of the common tradition (see Mark 14.36, 'Abba, Father'/'cup'). Also, there are elements of the Synoptic agony scene in John 12.27–8, where Jesus' heart is troubled and where he ponders whether to pray, 'Father, save me from this hour'. John therefore knows of the agony scene, but chooses to emphasize Jesus' sovereignty in 18.11.

5. Charge

The trial before Annas is historically improbable in 18.12–23. Annas was not the high priest at the time, and in any case it would have been inappropriate for Jesus to have been examined by him on two grounds: first of all, nocturnal trials were against Jewish law; secondly, such an interrogation should have been undertaken by Caiaphas. The whole scene is therefore historically incredible.

5. Response

There has been much written in defence of the historicity of John's sequence of events (Strachan, 1941, pp. 307–8). There is nothing to suggest that 18.12–23 is not historical. We know from Josephus that Annas was an extremely influential high priest. His rule extended from AD 6 to AD 15, and he was succeeded not only by his son-in-law Caiaphas, but also by five sons (Josephus, *Ant.* XX.198). As Robinson concludes, 'there is little doubt that John is historically accurate in depicting Annas thus as very much a power behind the throne and one who still enjoyed the courtesy title of "high priest"' (1985, p. 246). Furthermore, the interrogation before Annas is not a formal trial (which the later Mishnah tractate, *Sanhedrin*, suggests would have been illegal), but an informal interrogation of Jesus before he is sent to Caiaphas for a trial in the very early hours of the morning (18.24, 18.28). Matthew and Mark are therefore wrong to describe what happened at night as a meeting of the Sanhedrin, since a properly constituted Council meeting could only have taken place in the morning. The scene involving Annas presents us with no difficulties if we see it as 'a police interrogation of a newly arrested criminal before any formal trial procedures are begun' (Brown, 1966, Vol. II, p. 834). The informal interrogation before Annas is based on good historical tradition which may well derive from the eye-witness accounts of the BD, who was well known to Annas.

6. Charge

The whole of act two (18.28–19, 16a) is based on interpretation rather than on fact. It is impossible to see how an eye-witness could have reported what primarily amounts to private conversations between Jesus and Pilate. In any case, some of the details in this trial narrative suggest that the incident is pure drama rather than historiography.

First of all, the Jews did have the right to execute people, in spite of what John has them claim in 18.31. Secondly, there is no evidence outside of John, Matthew and Mark for the passover amnesty cited in 18.39. Thirdly, John has the scourging and mockery of Jesus in the middle of his trial (19.1—3), and not as a prelude to his execution (Mark 15.16—20/Matthew 27.27—31). These factors tell against the historical value of act two.

6. Response

Even though it is hard to see how there could have been an eye-witness at the trial of Jesus before Pilate, there have been many scholars who have argued that we have good historical tradition in act two. Robinson has stated that, 'Far from being a distortion of the primitive record there is, I believe, nothing in the Johannine story that is palpably unhistorical and a great deal that makes the other accounts *when taken alongside it* intelligible' (1985, p. 275). Dodd argued that the trial narrative in John 'represents an independent strain of tradition, which must have been formed in a period much nearer the events than the period when the Fourth Gospel was written, and in some respects seems to be better informed than the tradition behind the Synoptics, whose confused account it clarifies' (1963, p. 120). In an important article on 'The Trial of Jesus in the Fourth Gospel' (1980), F. F. Bruce has put forward some of the reasons why scholars have defended the historical value of John's trial narrative. First of all, Bruce claims that the fourth gospel alone explains why the Sanhedrin referred Jesus to Pilate. According to John 18.31b, the Sanhedrin lacked the authority to carry out the death sentence. Bruce claims that this is very probably true. He cites Sherwin-White's comment that 'The capital power was the most jealously guarded of all the attributes of government, not even entrusted to the principal assistants of the governors' (p. 12). Bruce also cites a text in the Palestinian Talmud which proves the Sanhedrin's loss of capital jurisdiction: 'Forty years before the destruction of the temple the right to inflict the death penalty was taken away from Israel' (p. 12). Secondly, Bruce argues that the agreement between John and Mark on the matter of the passover amnesty supports the view that the release of Barabbas is historical. 'In our ignorance of the background to this custom, we can but note that its independent attestation in the Johannine alongside the Markan tradition strengthens the case for its historicity' (p. 15). Thirdly, the position of the scourging in John's story is not implausible. In Luke 23.22, Pilate proposes to chastise and then release Jesus on the grounds that he has done nothing wrong. In John 19.1, Pilate has Jesus scourged. 'This scourging (*mastigosis*) is not the *phragellosis* of Mark 15.15, which was a preliminary stage in the process of crucifixion, but a less severe beating, a punishment in itself, intended to teach the accused to be more prudent in future' (p. 15). These and other details lead Bruce to the following conclusion: 'John's framework for the Roman trial is judicially accurate, though he fills it in with theological as well as historical content (the theological interpreting the historical)' (p. 14).

7. Charge

In John 19.17, Jesus is depicted carrying his own cross, whilst in the Synoptic tradition Simon of Cyrene carries Jesus' cross. The independence of Jesus here is theologically motivated: it is meant to reinforce the impression of his sovereignty and control over events.

7. Response

There are two possible arguments in favour of the historicity of this detail. First of all, it has been argued (combining Luke and John's versions here) that Jesus carried the patibulum whilst Simon carried the back part of the cross (Brown, 1966, Vol. II, pp. 898–9). Secondly, it has been proposed that Jesus carried the patibulum for as long as he was able and that Simon took over the task when Jesus became exhausted. Of the two solutions, the second is more likely to be the truth. John has simply omitted mention of Simon for theological reasons.

8. Charge

In John 19.23–4, the soldiers share Jesus' clothes at the foot of the cross. They divide them into four shares but cast lots for the tunic (χιτών) or undergarment because it is woven without seam. The χιτών is clearly a symbolic detail. The background for the incident is Psalm 22.18, which is cited in 19.24: 'They divided my garments among them and cast lots for my clothing.' This is an example of Hebrew parallelism. To divide garments and cast lots for clothing are synonymous: they are one and the same act. What John has done is to take the second statement, 'they cast lots for my clothing', and make a separate, fictional incident out of it. Whilst it is likely that the quaternion of soldiers shared Jesus' clothes four ways, and that this was seen as a fulfilment of Psalm 22.18, the second incident, concerning the casting of lots for Jesus' χιτών, was invented on the basis of Psalm 22.18b. Therefore, the sharing of the clothes is an historical reminiscence, but the casting of lots for the χιτών is symbolic and based on Psalm 22.18b.

8. Response

Whilst the idea of the tunic is the centre of theological symbolism in this episode, there are good reasons for regarding it as an historical reminiscence, again deriving from the BD. If John was inventing the incident on the basis of Psalm 22.18, then why does he not use the same verbal expressions as in the psalm? He prefers the verb toss to the simpler expression, 'to roll dice'. Moreover, how could the words *labus* or *himatismos* in Psalm 22.18 have suggested χιτών? As Brown concludes: 'it seems more likely that the interpretation of the psalm is stretched to cover an incident that the evangelist found in his tradition rather than vice versa' (1966, Vol. II, p. 920).

There are other details in act three which we could also look at, such as the arguments that the friends and relatives of Jesus would not have been allowed near the cross (19.25–7), that the sponge with vinegar on it could not have been lifted up to Jesus on a hyssop branch (19.29), that the date of the crucifixion on the eve of the passover (19.14, 19.42) is incorrect, and that the effusion of blood and water in 19.34 is pure symbolism. I have already looked at one of these (19.25–7, in chapter 7). I shall be looking at others later. What I wish to stress here is that John 18–19 can justly be regarded as being a window on to facts even if there has been narrative and theological elaboration of history in these chapters. This judgement is supported by the fact that there is much in John 18–19 which fills in gaps in the Synoptic accounts of the passion. (1) For example, in 18.2 we learn exactly what it was that Judas knew about Jesus which proved so useful to the Jews: the secret meeting place of Jesus and his disciples. The Synoptics never make it clear what piece of information Judas had which could have been so valuable. (2) In 18.10, John provides us with the names of those involved in the incident at the arrest where a disciple cut off a guard's ear. John tells us that the two men were Peter and Malchus. (3) In 18.13f. John clears up the confusion in the Synoptics about the illegal, nocturnal trial before the Council by explaining that the trial at night was really an informal interrogation. (4) At 18.15, John explains how Peter managed to gain access to the environs of the nocturnal proceedings (i.e. through the BD), something left unstated in the Synoptic accounts. (5) In 18.26, John explains how Peter was recognized at his denials. The man who accuses him was a relative of the man whose ear Peter had cut off. (6) In 18.31, John again explains what the Synoptics leave unexplained, namely, why Jesus was brought before Pilate by the Jews. John tells us that the Sanhedrin did not have capital jurisdiction. These and other details fill in the lacunae left in the Synoptic passion narratives and strongly support the assertion that John 18–19 is history as well as interpretation.

But we are still left with the question about the narrative character of Jesus-history. Were Jesus' arrest, trial and execution already a story calling out to be narrated? In chapter 4 I argued that history does have a rudimentary story-like character; that it already possesses the order and direction of an emplotted narrative, but that the historian must seek to discover the followability inherent within past events if that story-like quality is to be revealed. At this point, it is helpful to pause and explore some analogies between John's use of his passion traditions and criminal detection. The analogy between historical enquiry and detection has been noticed before. Collingwood, in his seminal work on *The Idea of History* (1953), wrote: 'the hero of a detective novel is thinking exactly like an historian when, from indications of the most varied kinds, he constructs an imaginary picture of how a crime was committed, and by whom' (p. 243). Collingwood does not elaborate on the analogy, but it is important in this context to spell out the similarities. When a murder is committed, all that is immediately visible at the crime-scene is the murdered victim. There is no obvious story of how, why, when and by whom the murder was committed. However, the detective begins a period of intensive research in which the minutest clues are subjected to the intensest scrutiny, in order that the story of the murder can be recreated. The overall sequence of cause and effect is then imagined from the flimsiest of details: a fragment of curtain material, an inconsistency in hand-writing, and so on. In successful detection, someone is arrested whose response confirms the validity of the reconstruction, at least in its outline, and a trial can begin. If a jury is persuaded that the narrative reconstruction of the crime corresponds beyond reasonable doubt with the actual facts, then a sentence can be carried out and the murderer can be imprisoned.

The point Collingwood is making is this: there is a similarity between the way in which the detective reconstructs a followable and logical narrative out of clues, and the way in which an historian perceives and redescribes the narrativity intrinsic to past history. We can apply these insights now to John's gospel. The Roman Catholic priest and scholar Raymond Brown (arguably the finest living scholar of the fourth gospel) has already explored some of the implications of this analogy in the matter of John's authorship. He writes: 'It is notorious that many biblical scholars are also passionate readers of detective stories. These two interests come together in the quest to identify the author of the Fourth Gospel' (1966, Vol. I, p. lxxxvii). Brown does not, however, develop this thought. In the context of Jesus' passion, though, the analogy is very instructive. What John had before him when he came to compose his passion narrative was a number of details about the death of Jesus (in a sense the most obscene homicide that has ever been committed). These may already have been part of a passion story in the BD's ur-gospel. They function for him as concrete clues. John's keen eye for such details is self-evident: the scene of the arrest as an orchard or walled garden; the lanterns, torches and weapons of the arresting party; the names of those involved in the scuffle in 18.10 (also the mention of Peter's dagger, and of the fact that it was Malchus' right earlobe which Peter severed); the relationship between Annas and Caiaphas; the charcoal fire in Annas' courtyard; the time of day when Pilate spoke with Jesus (18.28); the charge that Jesus was a criminal (18.30); the time of Pilate's decision to hand Jesus over to be crucified (19.14) – all these and other details speak of a storyteller who has a truly perceptive view of details surrounding the murder of his protagonist.

What John does with these clues is to create a followable story of the passion from clues in his tradition. That this corresponds to a teleology within the history of Jesus' passion itself is, I believe, supported by the arguments of this book. John's story has an internal logic and coherence to it when read in its own right, and this logic and coherence are intrinsic to the events themselves, not imposed ab extra. It has much to commend it as historiography when read in the light of the Synoptic passion narratives because it fills in the lacunae between cause and effect in many places in the Marcan, Matthean and Lucan accounts. What John the storyteller has created in John 18—19 is a model of actuality. It is not an exact documentary reconstruction or a photographic copy. It is a bold and perceptive attempt to evoke the meaning inherent within the historical events of the passion *as he knew them*. The narrative-historical critic plays a significant part in all this because he functions as a juror, assessing the evidence available, and then passing a verdict on the accuracy and reliability of the storyteller's model. For some jurors, particularly Frank Kermode (1979, pp. 101ff.), but also non-narrative specialists such as Bultmann, the verdict passed on the text is one of guilty. If the charge levelled against John is one of falsifying history, then Kermode and Bultmann would support that plea. But for others the matter is much more complex. Whilst there is agreement that John has handled his tradition creatively and at times inspirationally, there is also a body of scholars who would say with me that John's story-plot evokes something intrinsic to the historical death-plot. In the final analysis, the fourth gospel will continue to provoke much discussion about its historical tradition, but the narrative-historical critic who sees it as valuable in terms of its historical reference has a good case to make.

Narrative and source

In chapter 4 I proposed that the fourth gospel is a complex and creative adaptation of sources: a Bethany tradition deriving from Lazarus, a signs source, a Samaritan mission source, sayings collections and a selection of controversy episodes handed down in the form of dramatic dialogues. It is my belief that the passion and resurrection narratives of John 18–20 have their origins in the Bethany tradition of Lazarus, the BD. In support of this, it is important to note that Lazarus appears shortly before the Book of the Passion begins, and that he appears again as the BD in chapter 13, at the last supper. Lazarus does not figure again in chapters 14–17 (nor would we expect him to, since these chapters are, for the most part, dramatic monologues of Jesus). But he does appear as *another disciple/the disciple whom Jesus loved* at key, strategic moments during the passion narrative. In chapter 18 it is said that the BD was well known to Annas, and that it was consequently he who guided Peter into the courtyard of the high priest's palace. The informal interrogation of Jesus by Annas, as well as the denials of Peter by the charcoal fire outside, must therefore be regarded as based on the eye-witness reporting of the BD. In chapter 19, the BD is near the cross with Mary and three other women. The incidents connected with the crucifixion, indeed everything from 19.16 to 19.37, should be regarded as based on the eye-witness reporting of the BD. This is confirmed by the forceful testimony of the community in 19.35 that the effusion of blood and water from Jesus' dead body is true because the BD has testified to it. The tradition within the majority of acts one and three should therefore be seen as deriving from the BD. If the BD was well known to Annas, then it is not impossible that he came to know of the Roman trial too.

My proposal is that the passion source used by John was a narrative of the arrest, trial and death of Jesus deriving from the reminiscences of the BD. Two presuppositions are, however, implied in this value judgement. First of all, I am implying that John's passion source came from a Judaean disciple known as the BD and that it was therefore not based on the written Synoptic passion narratives. Peter Borgen, after a minute, scientific analysis of the comparative texts, concludes:

> John is based essentially on an independent tradition. Some synoptic pericopes or parts of pericopes have been assimilated in this Johannine tradition. Within these pericopes, or parts of pericopes, various elements from the several synoptic accounts have been fused together. When John appears dependent upon the Syn. only in certain pericopes, it is probable that oral tradition has brought to John this material already fused. This explains the relative freedom with which John has reproduced the synoptic material.
>
> (1959, p. 259)

This means that Ivor Buse (1957) is wrong to see John 18—19 as dependent upon pre-Synoptic or Synoptic narratives. Buse argued that there are parallels between the Johannine passion narrative and one of the two sources which Vincent Taylor saw behind the Marcan passion narrative. These two sources Taylor called A (a basic narrative) and B (Petrine and mainly Semitic material with which A was expanded). Buse draws attention to similarities between John 18—19 and the pre-Marcan B source. He argues for close parallels in the assault on the high priest's servant, Peter's denial, the trial before Pilate, the Barabbas story, the handing over of Jesus to be crucified, and the mocking. In reality, however, these similarities are insignificant and debatable. Buse's argument that John is dependent upon a pre-Marcan passion source is not convincing.

My first presupposition is that John's passion story is based on a source which existed independently from the pre-Synoptic passion traditions but which has some parallels with them. This can be seen if we take the Johannine story of the crucifixion and compare it with the parallel Synoptic accounts. Looking at John 19.16b–30, we find the following details in the following order: (a) Jesus is crucified (19.17); (b) between two criminals (19.18); (c) the royal titulus is fastened above his head (19.19–20); (d) the Jews object to the titulus (19.21–2); (e) Jesus' garments are divided (19.23–4); (f) Jesus adopts the BD into his family (19.25–7); (g) Jesus utters his last words and expires (19.28–30).

Of these, the Marcan passion narrative only has (a), (b), (c) and (e), but it has them in a different order: (a), (e), (c), (b). Matthew has the same. Luke has (a), (b), (c) and (e) but in the order (a), (b), (e), (c). The Synoptics, in other words, do not narrate the objection of the Jews to the titulus (d), the adoption of the BD (f), or the last words as found in John's story (g). John's account, similarly, lacks many of the details found in the Synoptics. The following details in Mark are absent in John: Simon of Cyrene, the refusal of the drugged wine, the abuse from by-standers, the darkness over the land, the cry of dereliction, the rending of the temple curtain, the centurion's confession. Some details in Matthew are also absent in John: all of Mark's details, plus the soldiers keeping watch (27.36) and the earthquake (27.51ff.). Luke has details which John lacks: Simon of Cyrene, the drugged wine, the abuse from by-standers, the darkness over the land, the rending of the temple curtain, the centurion's confession, plus the lamenting daughters of Jerusalem, Jesus' prayer of forgiveness, the scornful and the penitent thief, the prayer of commendation and the repentant crowd.

Five important conclusions can be drawn from these findings: (1) Matthew and Luke have both used Mark's passion narrative as the major source for their own passion narratives, but they have also added details from their own special sources, M and L, respectively. (2) John has not followed Mark, Matthew or Luke, but has some points of contact with them in items (a), (b), (c) and (e). (3) John's source represents a tradition independent of the traditions behind the Synoptic passion narratives (this would have to be the case because John would certainly have included the darkness over the land and the rending of the temple curtain had he known these items of tradition; both would have suited his theological purposes admirably). (4) John used a passion source which had its roots in the eye-witness accounts of the BD, and this is his only source. He does not copy and elaborate the written Synoptic passion accounts. (5) The reason why there are some similarities between John's story of the passion and the stories told by Mark, Matthew and Luke is that John's source may have had some contact with the pre-Synoptic oral passion traditions at a very early stage.

My first presupposition is therefore that John's passion source derived from a tradition independent of the written Synoptic passion narratives: the eye-witness tradition of the BD. My second is that this tradition was very early on formed into a connected narrative. In *From Tradition to Gospel* (1934), Dibelius argued that 'we must presuppose the early existence of a Passion narrative complete in itself, since preaching, whether for the purpose of mission or of worship, required some such text' (p. 23). 'The Passion story is the only piece of Gospel tradition which in early times gave events in their larger connection' (p. 179). In relation to John 18–19, I propose that the storyteller drew upon a source which was a continuous narrative right from the beginning. John's passion did not derive from different fragments from all sorts of different sources, as Maurice Goguel argued in *Les Sources du récit Johannique de la Passion* (1910). Dodd rightly points out that 'The attempt to explain the Passion Narrative as an aggregation of originally independent units is fundamentally misguided.' As he continued, 'each incident is intelligible only in its place within the continuous sequence, depending on what has gone before and preparing for what comes after' (1963, p. 21). The source at John's disposal was already a narrative with a beginning, a middle and an end. My two presuppositions, in summary, are as follows: that John draws on his own distinctive source to redescribe the story of Jesus' death (a source deriving from Lazarus, the BD), and that it was a continuous narrative from the beginning.

However, this leaves us with a vital question: What did this narrative source look like? The two most recent attempts to reconstruct 'PQ' or the narrative passion source behind John 18–19 have been made by Urban von Wahlde and Robert Fortna, whose work we looked at in chapter 4. The chart below compares their respective passion sources:

Robert Fortna's SG		*Urban von Wahlde's SG*	
The arrest	18.1–3,4c–5,10–12	The arrest	18.1–3, 7–8, 10–11
Interrogations	18.13,24,15,16a,19,20,21a, 22,16b,17,18,25b–27	Interrogations	18.19–24
Trial by Pilate	18.28a,29,33,37b,38c,39–40, 19.6ac,13,14a,1–3,16a	Trial by Pilate	18.28–9,33–5
		Scourging	18.39–19.6a
		Judgement	19.13–14a,15b–16
Crucifixion and burial	19.16b–18,19b,20c,23–4, 25a,28–30,25b,31–4,36–8, 40b,41–2	Crucifixion	19.17–25a
		Burial	19.39–42

Fortna reconstructs his narrative passion source by peeling away everything that he regards as the theological contribution of the evangelist. His version of PQ (which is more thorough than von Wahlde's) therefore reads as follows:

18 [1]Jesus went out with his disciples across the Wadi Kidron, where there was a garden. [2]Now Judas his betrayer also knew the place, since Jesus often gathered there with his disciples. [3]Therefore Judas brought a troop of soldiers, and guards from the chief priests, and came there with lanterns and torches and weapons. [4c]So Jesus said to them, 'Who is it that you want?' [5]They said, 'Jesus the Nazarene.' He said to them, 'I'm he.' [10]So Simon Peter, since he had a sword, drew it and struck the slave of the high priest and cut off his right ear. And the slave's name was Malchus. [11]So Jesus said to Peter, 'Put back your sword; shall I not drink the cup the Father has given me?' [12]So the soldiers and their captain and the guards seized Jesus and bound him. [*The disciples flee.*]

18 [13]And they led him first to Annas, for he was the father-in-law of Caiaphas, who was high priest that year. [[[24]So Annas sent him bound to Caiaphas.]] [15]Now Simon Peter and another disciple followed Jesus. That disciple was known to the high priest, and he went into the courtyard of the high priest along with Jesus, [16a]but Peter stood outside at the door. [19]The high priest (asked Jesus about his teaching. [20]Jesus answered him, 'I have taught in the Temple where all are gathered; [21a]why do you ask me?') [The high priest said to him, 'If you are the Christ, tell us', and he said, 'If I told you, you would not believe.' ... And Jesus said, 'Do you say, "You are blaspheming" because I said that I am the Son of God?'] [22]When he had said this one of the guards standing there struck Jesus a blow and said, 'Is that how you answer the high priest?'

[[[16b]So the other disciple, the one known to the high priest, went out and spoke to the doorkeeper and brought Peter in. [17]And the maid who was doorkeeper said to Peter, 'Are you one of this man's disciples too?' He said, 'No, I'm not.' [18]Now the slaves and guards had made a fire, since it was cold, and were standing and warming themselves. And Peter also stood with them and warmed himself.]] [25b]So they said to him, 'Are you also one of his disciples?' He denied it and said, 'No, I'm not.' [26]One of the high priest's slaves, a relative of the one whose ear Peter had cut off, said, 'Didn't I see you in the garden with him?' [27]Again Peter denied it. And immediately the cock crowed.

18   [28a]So they led Jesus from the house of Caiaphas into the Pretorium; it was early morning. [29]Pilate said, 'What charge do you bring against this man?' [The Jewish leaders answered, 'He has made himself out to be king.'] [33]So Pilate called Jesus and said to him, 'Are you the king of the Jews?' [[37b]Jesus answered, 'You say I am a king.' *Perhaps a second question, to which Jesus remains silent.*] [38c]He said to them, 'I find no crime in him, [39]but it is your custom that at Passover I release one man to you. Do you want me to release "the king of the Jews" for you then?' [40]They shouted back, 'Not this man but Barabbas!' Now Barabbas was an [insurrectionist]. [*Pilate asks what he should do then with Jesus.*] 19 [6ac]The chief priests and the guards cried out, 'Crucify him! crucify him!' Pilate said to them, 'I find no crime in him.' [*They call again for Jesus to be crucified.*] [13]So Pilate took Jesus out and sat down in the judgment seat in the place known as the Stone Pavement, or in 'Hebrew' Gabbatha. [14a]It was Friday, about twelve noon. [[[1]Then Pilate took Jesus and had him whipped. [2]And the soldiers wove a crown of thorns and put it on his head and put a purple cloak on him, [3]and they came up to him and said, 'Hail! the king of the Jews!' and they hit him.]] [16a]So [Pilate] then turned him over to them to be crucified.

19   [16b]So they took Jesus [17](and carrying the cross himself he went out) to what was known as the Place of the Skull, which is called Golgotha in 'Hebrew,' [18]where they crucified him, and two others with him, one on either side. [19b]And there was written, JESUS OF NAZARETH, KING OF THE JEWS. [20c]And it was written in 'Hebrew,' Latin, and Greek.

[23]When the soldiers had crucified Jesus they took his outer garments and divided them in four parts, one to each soldier, also his tunic. But the tunic was seamless, woven from top to bottom; [24]so they said to each other, 'Let's not tear it but

instead toss to see whose it will be' — that the scripture might be fulfilled which says, 'They divided my garments among them, and for my clothing they cast lots.' [25a]So that is what the soldiers did. [28]After this, that the scripture might be fulfilled, Jesus said, 'I thirst.' [29]There was a bowl of vinegar there, so they filled a sponge with the vinegar and putting it on a stick they held it to his mouth. [30]And when he had received the vinegar Jesus said ... And bowing his head he breathed his last.

[[[25b]Now standing by Jesus' cross were his mother's sister, Mary wife of Clopas, and Mary Magdalene.]] [31]Since it was Friday, lest the bodies remain on the cross on the Sabbath, they asked Pilate that their legs be broken and that they be taken away. [32]So the soldiers came and broke the legs of the first and then of the other who had been crucified with him. [33]But when they came to Jesus and saw that he was already dead, they did not break his legs, [34]but one of the soldiers stabbed his side with a spear and at once there came out blood and water. [36]For these things took place so that the scripture might be fulfilled, 'His bone shall not be broken', [37]and again another scripture says, 'They shall look on the one they have pierced.'

[38]After this Joseph of Arimathea, a disciple of Jesus, asked Pilate that he might take Jesus' body down, and Pilate consented. So [they] came and took down his body, [40b]and they bound it in burying cloths with (the) spices, [[[39d]about seventy-five pounds.]] [41]Now in the place where he had been crucified there was a garden, and in the garden a new tomb in which no one had yet been buried. [42]So since it was Friday and because the tomb was nearby they buried Jesus there.

The narrative elements which are regarded as the work of the evangelist (and therefore absent in the source) are as follows:

1. Connecting or linking phrases, such as 'When he had said these things' in 18.1.
2. Anachronisms, such as the reference to the Pharisees in 18.3, which refers to the evangelist's situation.
3. References to Jesus' supernatural knowledge (18.4, 19.28).
4. The initiative of Jesus in 18.4.

5. The use of the divine name in 18.5ff.
6. The flooring of Jesus' opponents in 18.6.
7. The Good Shepherd echoes in 18.8—9.
8. Parentheses, such as 'Judas the traitor was standing there' in 18.5.
9. References to the disciples (18.1, 18.19), who stand for the Christian community.
10. Redundancies, such as the phrase 'where all the Jews met together' in 18.20.
11. Forensic language centring on the idea of 'witness' (18.23).
12. References to the eve of the passover (18.28, 19.14, 19.31, 19.42).
13. References to Pilate going in and out of his palace (18.29ff.).
14. Much of the conversation between Pilate and the Jews (including 19.20—1) and between Pilate and Jesus.
15. The adoption of the BD in 19.25—7.
16. The BD's testimony in 19.35.
17. The reference to Joseph of Arimathea's secrecy and fear of the Jews (19.38).
18. Allusions to Nicodemus (19.39).

Furthermore, Fortna (I think wrongly) regards the sequence of events in the passion source as different from what we find in John 18—19. The two main examples of this are in his reconstruction of 18.12ff. (he has 18.24 straight after 18.13) and the trial (he has the scourging of Jesus — 19.1—3 — after 19.14).

There is little doubt in my mind that Fortna's reconstruction of the narrative source behind John 18—19 is plausible, however hypothetical we may feel it is. The connecting or linking phrases, as well as the parentheses, are evidently the work of the evangelist, who is trying to bring greater clarity and coherence to the final narrative. The passages where the evangelist's prominent themes are evident are also unlikely to have been in the source: the sovereignty, initiative and supernatural power of Jesus in 18.4ff., the shepherdly conduct of Jesus in 18.8ff., the language of discipleship in 18.1/19 and in 19.38, the language connected with witness and testimony in 18.23 and 19.35, the synchronization of the passion with the slaughter of the passover lambs, the references to Jesus' other-worldly Kingship and to truth in 18.36—8 — all these passages are likely to be the work of the evangelist, who has already shown in the rest of the gospel a marked interest in these themes. The dramatic structure of the trial narrative, with the insecure toing and froing of Pilate, is also very likely the authorial contribution of John the storyteller. The only items which Fortna omits from the source and which I would include there centre on the BD and on Nicodemus. Since the BD is the eye-witness responsible for PQ in my compositional hypothesis, I would want to include the adoption scenario (19.25–7) in the passion source. The storyteller's support for the BD in 19.35 may well be a later addition, so that passage need not necessarily be included in PQ. As far as Nicodemus is concerned, I see no reason for excluding him from PQ at all. Like Nathaniel and Lazarus, Nicodemus is one of those characters who are peculiar to the distinctive Johannine tradition. He is not a fictional creation of the evangelist's.

There are also several items in Fortna's PQ which I would suggest are the work of the evangelist. First, the use of the verb ζητεῖν (to seek) in 18.4, 'Whom are you seeking?', is the work of the evangelist. As I showed in chapter 4, John has made a distinctive contribution to the Jesus tradition by employing a hide-and-seek theme throughout his gospel. The use of ζητεῖν in 18.4 is part of this pattern and is the work of the evangelist. Secondly, the references to various characters 'standing' in John 18 are the work of the evangelist. Judas, in verse 5, is said to be *standing* with the arresting party. Peter in verse 18 is said to be *standing* with the servants and officials by the fire in Annas' courtyard. Fortna regards 18.5 as the work of the evangelist, but not 18.18. In fact, both are the work of the storyteller. Both details are homiletical devices; both reveal where and with whom Judas and Peter are standing spiritually; they stand with the servants of the world. Thirdly, the reference to the Sanhedrin's lack of capital juris-diction in 18.31b must have been in the source. As I have shown, it is historically correct and explains why the Jews referred the matter to Pilate. The same goes, fourthly, for the *amicus Caesaris* charge in 19.12, which is also historical and which explains why Pilate readily yields to the Jews. Apart from these minor disagreements, I would propose that Fortna's thorough source analysis has uncovered as much of the BD's passion story as we are likely to find. Fortna's analysis reveals that John the storyteller had access to a continuous historical narrative which he has carefully and artfully redescribed. In the next section we shall look at one of the ways in which the storyteller develops his narrative source.

Excursus: The special affinities between John and Luke

It has been proposed by a number of scholars this century that John knew a version of Luke's story of Jesus, and that this knowledge is particularly obvious in the case of the Johannine passion narrative. J. Schniewind published his classic work on *Die Parallelperikopen bei Lukas und Johannes* in 1914. Here he contended that John's story is similar to Luke's at the following points:

1.	John 1.19f., 26, 28; 3.22–4.3	Luke 3.3–20
2.	John 21.1–19	Luke 5.1–11
3.	John 4.46–54	Luke 7.1–10
4.	John 12.3–8	Luke 7.36–50
5.	John 12.12–19	Luke 19.28–40
6.	John 13.36–8	Luke 22.31–4
7.	John 18.1–11	Luke 22.39, 47–53
8.	John 18.12–27 (10.24; 3.12; 8.45)	Luke 22.54–71
9.	John 18.28–19.16	Luke 23.1–25
10.	John 19.16–42	Luke 23.26–56
11.	John 20	Luke 24

What is immediately obvious from this list of parallels is the fact that Schniewind spots a number of similarities between John 18–19 and the Lucan passion narrative. H. Klein has recently devoted a whole study to these parallels in his 'Die lukanisch-johanneische Passionstradition' (1976). More recently still, R. Maddox has high-lighted similarities between John 18–19 and Luke's passion narrative in his *Purpose of Luke–Acts* (1982):

1. John 18.2//Luke 22.39: Jesus and his disciples are said to frequent the Mount of Olives (this thought absent in Mark and Matthew).
2. John 18.8ff.//Luke 22.49ff.: the disciples try to prevent the arrest of Jesus (absent in Mark and Matthew).
3. John 18.10//Luke 22.50: only John and Luke mention that it was the right ear of the High Priest's slave that was severed.
4. John 18.13–24//Luke 3.2; Acts 4.6: Annas as High Priest. Both John and Luke hesitate about the position of Caiaphas. In Mark the High Priest is never named. In Matthew it is Caiaphas.
5. John 19.12–15//Luke 23.2: the charge of sedition brought against Jesus by the Jewish authorities. In Mark and Matthew the charge is kingship.

6.   John 18.38, 19.4, 6//Luke 23.4, 14, 22: Pilate declares Jesus innocent three times. In Mark and Matthew he does so only once.
7.   John 18.33–8, 19.9//Luke 23.6–12: only in John and Luke does Pilate show any interest in where Jesus has come from.
8.   John 19.1–12//Luke 23.16: the scourging in the middle of the trial as opposed to Mark and Matthew, who depict it as a preliminary to execution.
9.   In neither Luke nor John is there a cry of dereliction from the cross (cf., however, Mark 15.34//Matthew 27.46).

In spite of these apparently impressive similarities, it is important to emphasize that none of the above scholars (Schniewind, Klein and Maddox) has argued for John's literary dependence upon a written version of Luke. Schniewind concluded his research with the view that the affinities between John and Luke are best explained by oral tradition. Both evangelists, he proposed, were drawing on a common oral tradition. Klein and Maddox take a similar line. We can conclude with the judgement that John's oral passion tradition was similar to Luke's. The current consensus does not encourage us to argue for John's dependence on a written version of Luke's passion narrative (though see J. Bailey's *The Traditions Common to the Gospels of Luke and John* (1963)). To take just one example, if John was dependent upon Luke, then why does he use different vocabulary in pericopes where there is parallel tradition? For instance, both Luke and John point out that it was the right ear of the servant which Peter cut off. However, Luke's word for ear is οὖς, whilst John uses the diminutive, ὠτάριον. Differences such as these reinforce Gardner-Smith's argument (1938) for John's dependence on an oral tradition which has similarities with that behind and within the Synoptic gospels.

Narrative and gospel

From what we have seen so far in this chapter it is clear that a narrative-historical approach to John 18–19 is important if we are to appreciate the storyteller's artistry. In the first section I argued that John 18–19 is based on valuable historical tradition and that the actual events of Jesus' arrest, passion, death and burial were not a random, meaningless sequence of episodes but were already in a sense narrative in form. They had a coherence and a logic that one associates with stories. In the first section, therefore, I proposed that we see Jesus-history, at least in relation to the passion, as narrative history: as intrinsically story-shaped. In the second section I looked at the passion source behind John 18—19, using Fortna's generally helpful and perceptive source reconstruction. There I made the point that it is not only passion history that is story-shaped; the passion source is also narrative or story-shaped. The passion source is a narrative redescription of narrative history. In this final section, I wish to underline a point which by now will be evident: that John the storyteller is not content merely to reduplicate PQ in an unchanged way; he redescribes it in order to evoke meanings which he believes are inherent within the past but which have been revealed to him by the Paraclete (14.26). Thus, for example, he takes Jesus' 'I am' in 18.5 — which is no doubt in his source merely as a statement of identification — and he interprets it as a revelation of the divine name. In John's highly creative imagination, a statement of human identification becomes redolent of divine disclosure. We see this happening everywhere in John 18—19: Jesus' protective attitude towards his disciples in the source behind John 18 stimulates him into recreating the scene as an enacted parable of Jesus as Shepherd. PQ for John is the springboard for charismatic history.

My point is this: John's narrative source of the passion was a very rudimentary narrative. As Dibelius said of the earliest passion story, it 'was neither stirring nor heroic. It contained no word speaking of the human greatness of Jesus in suffering, none intended to appeal to the human feelings of the reader' (p. 185). Thus, John does not incorporate PQ's narrative interpretation without comment or addition. He actively redescribes it by making explicit the rich Christological nuances within his source. I have discussed many items of John's inspired contribution in this book, but I have not made mention of one vital piece of evidence of his artistry as storyteller, and that is his creation of story time. Whatever time sequence there was in the actual history of Jesus' last days, and whatever temporal markers there were in PQ, the fact is that John has created his own time-shapes. Paul Ricoeur has shown how narratives have two dimensions: the episodic dimension and the configurative dimension. When the historian seeks to reconstruct the past in the form of a followable story, he is not content to create a sequence of episodes. Such a strategy would lead to him producing little more than an elaborate chronicle of uninterpreted events. The configurative dimension is the dimension which the historian is really looking for. Not content with merely evoking the logic of *chronos*, he seeks instead to transform a succession of events into a meaningful whole, to create a configuration out of a succession. This involves the conscious use of narrative strategies such as plot, characterization and themes. As Ricoeur puts it, 'By means of the plot, goals, causes, and chance are brought together within the temporal unity of a whole and complete action' (1984, p. ix). The thrust of Ricoeur's more recent work is that narrative is a device for transforming *chronos* time into meaningful time.

In composing his passion narrative, John has configured time; he has not composed a chronicle. Whilst there is an episodic dimension to John's story, there is also a powerful configurative dimension; episodes exist within the structure of the narrative, but they are richly interconnected and incorporated into a totality. Nothing illustrates this more clearly than John's creation and use of what I call his *passover plot*. There are a number of passover allusions in John 18–19 which support the argument that John wants us to see the death of Jesus as the final and sufficient passover sacrifice. The reference to the hyssop branch with the drugged wine on it in 19.29 recalls the hyssop branch of Exodus 12.22 which was used to sprinkle the blood of the passover lambs on the door-posts of the Israelites in Egypt. The OT citation in 19.36 seems to suggest a parallel between Jesus not having his legs broken and the importance of leaving the bones of the passover lamb intact and unbroken. But it is John's use of story time which most supports this identification of Jesus as the paschal lamb. There are three references to passover festivals in John, at 2.13, 6.4, and 11.55. Leon Morris speaks of 'the centrality of the passover' in John (1964, p. 72); J.K. Howard argues that 'the writer seems to be concerned with presenting Jesus as the perfect Paschal Victim' (1967, p. 330). In John 18–19, 'John sees the whole of this Passover symbolism reaching its climax' (p. 337). Three times we are told by John that the death of Jesus occurred on the day of Preparation (19.14, 19.31 and 19.42). As Howard says: 'the new Paschal Victim is led to the place of slaughter at the very moment when the priests are immolating the sacrificial lambs in the Temple (19.14). Just as the blood of the sacrificial victims was poured out, so also is the blood of Christ poured forth (19.34) ... and like the Paschal victim no bone of His body was broken' (p. 337).

In spite of Annie Jaubert's attempts to defend the historicity of

John's chronology here (1972), I believe that John's synchronization of the death of Jesus with the slaughter of the passover lambs is his creative contribution. John's use of time throughout the gospel is often symbolic, and this is no exception (Bruns, 1967). Here, Christology and chronology are inseparable. John configures time, and he does this through his use of narrative time-shapes. David Higdon has written a helpful introduction to the poetics of narrative time-shapes (1977), and it is his work – rather than the more complex work of Gerard Genette – that forms the background to the following interpretation of John's use of time. Higdon differentiates between four basic time-shapes in English fiction. He calls these process time, retrospective time, barrier time and polytemporal time. Process time is symbolized by a straight line moving from one point to another. It is a time-shape which stresses a process and its underlying causality, and it is manifested in precise dates and hours. Such 'persistent reminders of time keep the reader aware of movement and change, of a process gradually unfolding as the characters develop' (p. 5). Retrospective time, on the other hand, stresses being rather than becoming. It looks at how things were rather than things in process, and it is manifested when the narrator leads the reader momentarily out of the flux of time to consider the past. The barrier time-shape, on the other hand, looks to the future. Early on in a story an hour in the future is specified as the time by which a difficult task must be achieved, an adventure completed. This prescribed time-limit heightens and intensifies the action. Lastly, the polytemporal time-shape differs from all these and is manifested when a narrative has several time-lines running concurrently (the past and the present, the eternal and the temporal, etc.).

What is fascinating about John's story, and John 18–19 in particular, is the fact that John has used all these time-shapes in his configuration of events. In John's story of the death of Jesus we have process, retrospective, barrier and polytemporal time-shapes, so much so that it becomes clear that these shapes are to be found more ubiquitously than in English fiction alone. Let us look first of all at process time. In John 18–19 there are a number of references to precise dates and hours which create a sense of causality and which remind the reader of the passing of time. Whilst there are no explicit temporal markers in act one of the passion narrative, certain details function as time-indicators in an implicit way. The references to the lanterns and torches in 18.3 and the allusion to the charcoal fire in 18.18 imply that the events take place in the middle of the night. The allusion to the cock crowing in 18.27 implies that the process of events has moved on to the very early hours of the morning. In act two, we have a number of explicit temporal markers which increase the pace of the narrative and which heighten the reader's awareness of the flow of events. When Jesus is led before Pilate in 18.28 we learn that it is 'daybreak' (πρωΐ) – the last Roman division of the night between 3.0 and 6.0 a.m. As Brown puts it: 'One can interpret John to mean that the interrogation by Annas and the simultaneous denials by Peter came to an end about 3.0 a.m. ... that during the next three hour period Jesus was with Caiaphas, and that finally toward 6.0 a.m. Jesus was led to Pilate' (1966, Vol. II, p. 844). This trial lasted until 'the sixth hour' (19.14), i.e. until about noon. The date of the trial is described as 'the day of Preparation of Passover week' (19.14, 31, 42), i.e. the Friday before the sabbath. Finally, since this sabbath would have begun at 6.0 p.m., the crucifragium in 19.31ff. locates Jesus' death late in the afternoon.

The process time-shape is used throughout John 18–19, implicitly through references to lights and cocks crowing in act one, explicitly at two points in acts two (18.28 and 19.14), and explicitly at two points in act three (19.31, 42). These temporal markers (some signifying the hour of events, others signifying the day) keep the reader within the recognizable stream of chronological time. However, there are several moments when John takes the reader out of this chronological, process time in order to look back on some event already described in the story. These flashbacks are examples of the use of the retrospective time-shape and are, for the most part, couched in the form of explanatory parentheses. The first one is at 18.9, where the narrator, explaining the protective attitude of Jesus towards the disciples outside the garden, says: 'This happened so that the words he had spoken would be fulfilled: "I have not lost one of those you gave me"' (a flashback to John 17.12 and to 10.28–9). The second example of retrospective time is in 18.14, again an explanatory parenthesis, where the narrator reminds us that 'Caiaphas was the one who had advised the Jews that it would be good if one man died for the people' (a flashback to 11.45–53). Other examples of this time-shape are in 18.32 (where the narrator gives us a flashback to 12.32–4) and 19.39 (where the narrator gives us a flashback to 3.1ff., the meeting between Nicodemus and Jesus at night). In all four examples, the retrospective time-shape reminds the reader of an event earlier in the gospel.

If the process time-shape keeps the reader within the flow of chronologically arranged events, and if the retrospective time-shape functions to take the reader back into past story time, the barrier time-shape functions in John's story as a means of intensifying the sense of the impending approach of a predetermined time-limit for Jesus' work on earth. The sense of a prescribed time-limit for the action is created by the use of the noun ὥρα. This noun occurs 26 times, and in 10 instances it is used merely to indicate chronological time. An example of this tendency can be seen in 19.14, where the narrator informs us that it was the sixth hour (ὥρα). This is the kind of temporal marker we associate with process or chronological time. However, there are eight instances where ὥρα is used in order to evoke the sense of barrier time. In these eight instances (2.4, 7.30, 8.20, 12.23, 12.27, 13.1, 17.1, 19.27) ὥρα refers to the appointed hour or time of Jesus' return to the Father, after his completion of his work on the cross. In 13.1, ὥρα is used very clearly to create this sense of barrier time. Here the narrator says: 'It was just before the Passover Feast. Jesus knew that the time [ὥρα] had come for him to leave this world and go to the Father.' In 19.27, after the adoption scenario at the cross itself (the place of departure), the narrator says that 'from that time on [ὥρα], this disciple took her into his home'. Here ὥρα functions in the metaphorical rather than in the literal sense. It connotes the *kairos* of God's appointed time rather than the *chronos* of man's sequential time. This has to be the case for two reasons: first, if we take ὥρα literally in 19.27, then the BD could not be present to witness the event in 19.34; secondly, the word occurs close to Jesus' words about the completion of his task (19.30, which echoes 13.1). The word ὥρα in John's story creates a sense of barrier time and suspense.

John's storytelling skill can therefore be seen in the way that he combines process, retrospective and barrier time-shapes in his story of the death of Jesus. Process time gives the reader a sense of causality, retrospective time a sense of logic, barrier time a sense of anticipation. But it is John's use of the polytemporal time-shape which is most interesting. There are moments in John 18–19 where the reader is given the strong impression that a divine plot is emerging in the midst of human time. This impression is created primarily through the Old Testament testimonies in John 18–19. Four of the OT allusions in the passion narrative are in quotation form, and can be found in 19.24 ('they shared my garments among them, and cast lots for my clothing'), 19.29 ('I am thirsty'), 19.37a ('no bone of his shall be broken'), and 19.37b ('they shall look on him whom they pierced'). It is important to note that these testimonies are clustered together in the narrative of the crucifixion; they are absent in acts one and two, which depict the arrest and the trial of Jesus. The effect created by these testimonies is quite specific: it orientates the reader to an understanding of the crucifixion as a revelation of God's purpose in history. Everything that happens to Jesus at the cross is a fulfilment of aspects of the overall OT story. As C. H. Dodd pointed out, this thought is articulated in Acts 2.23, where Peter says, 'When Jesus had been given up to you, *by the deliberate will and plan of God*, you used heathen men to crucify and kill him' (1963, p. 31). The testimonies in act three from Psalm 21.19, Psalm 68.22, Psalm 33.21/Exodus 12.46 and Zech. 12.10 create the impression that the crucifixion of Jesus is both the greatest demonstration of human disorder and the supremest manifestation of divine providence. It is 'the pleromatic conformity' (Kermode, 1979, p. 111) between past prophecy and present event that creates this paradox.

John's creative use of the polytemporal time-shape in his passion narrative helps to underline two powerful truths: first of all, that the cross is the cruellest demonstration of the hatred, dissonance and fragmentation of human history; secondly, that this same event is the most 'meant' moment in space and time — that the real-life killing of the God-King is the denouement which reveals a profound narrativity within the apparent meaninglessness of life. Perhaps this is why, as Amos Wilder once said, 'the narrative mode is uniquely important in Christianity' (1964, p. 64). The NT theology indirectly reveals an understanding of God as the author of a world-story: 'God is an active and purposeful God and his action with and for men has a beginning, a middle and an end like any good story' (p. 64). This is why 'the new Christian speech inevitably took the form of a story' (p. 65). The narrativity of history called forth the narrative form. All the events surrounding Jesus and those who followed him were not seen as random episodes in the relentless flux of time but rather as important moments in the plot of history. 'The anecdotes about each such individual and many more have their significance in the fact that they are related to the total world-story from alpha to omega' (p. 65). Thus, Jesus' meetings with Nathaniel, Nicodemus, the woman at the well, the official, the cripple at Bethesda, the man born blind and Lazarus were not chance encounters but revelations of an emplotment within the tide of events. Such characters 'locate us in the very midst of the great story and plot of all time and space, and therefore relate us to the great dramatist and storyteller, God himself' (p. 65). The beauty of John's narrative history is this: that through the narrative form he recreates both a sense of the episodic nature of time and a sense of the teleological nature of history. John's story is, in the deepest sense, poetic history.

CONCLUSION

In *John as Storyteller*, I have sought to integrate various aspects of literary criticism which have tended to exist separately from one another. The first aspect of my integrative hermeneutic has involved the question of literary criticism and literary history. As I have pointed out, New criticism emphasized literary criticism over and against literary history. R.S. Crane, one of the leading New critics, drew a sharp distinction between the two, arguing that literary critics should concern themselves primarily with works of imaginative literature themselves, and not with 'generic and historical investigations' (1967, p. 17). It is this kind of thinking which lies behind Culpepper's *Anatomy* and indeed much contemporary NT narrative criticism. However, literary critics of the Bible need to realize that this is not the only viable paradigm for biblical criticism. René Wellek pointed out in the 1940s that theory, history and criticism 'implicate each other so thoroughly' that they must all be involved in the analysis of literary texts (McKnight, 1985, p. 3). In 1963, Wellek argued that the New critical focus upon the literary work of art as a 'verbal structure of a certain coherence and wholeness' should not involve 'a denial of the relevance of historical information for the business of poetic interpretation' (McKnight, 1985, p. 4). As McKnight has argued, this is not only a challenge to New criticism, but also 'a challenge to more recent structural views of and approaches to literary texts' (p. 4). What is needed, says McKnight, is a hermeneutic which does justice to the literary work 'while relating the work to external, historical, social and psychological factors' (pp. 4–5). In *John as Storyteller* I have sought to provide such a hermeneutic, examining John's story from the perspectives of literary criticism *and* literary history.

The second integrative aspect of my narrative hermeneutic has involved the four elements of literature. As has often been noticed, the practice of criticism has tended to prioritize one of the following aspects of a work of literature: the universe imitated in the work, the author, the work itself, and the reader. As M. Abrams pointed out in his seminal work, *The Mirror and the Lamp* (1958), the classical age prioritized the universe imitated in the work, the romantic age prioritized the author, the age of New criticism prioritized the work itself, and the present generation of reception and reader response theorists prioritize the reader (pp. 8–29). In *John as Storyteller*, all of these four elements have been treated together. I have examined the 'universe imitated in the work' in my concern to identify the referential value of John's story. I have examined the role and the artistry of the author in my emphasis upon the storyteller. I have also given much attention to the final form of John's story (the New critical focus on the work itself) and to the reader's role in perceiving the elusive connexity of fourth-gospel narrative (the reception focus on the reader). In respect to the four elements of literature, I have allowed none to be neglected. However, if I have wanted to give one of them an emphasis, it has been the role of the author of John's story. The title of this book is *John as Storyteller*. Such a title is a direct attack on the New-critical, exclusivist focus upon the literary text, and the structuralist murder of the author. In stressing the author, I have never at any point spoken of the gospel as the expression of the author's feelings (the expressive theory of the romantic theorists). Nor have I spoken of the gospel as something to be evaluated solely in terms of the author's intention (the intentional fallacy). I have merely stated the obvious: that John's story is the work of a masterful storyteller.

In the final analysis, it may be that the exact identity of this John who transformed sources into story will always elude us. There is something eminently appropriate about this. In a gospel whose narrative, whose eye-witness, whose hero and whose community all prove persistently elusive, there is something altogether proper about an elusive author. Perhaps the phrase 'John the elder' is the closest we are going to get to a name for the one who, between thirty and seventy years after the resurrection, composed and published the fourth gospel. Evidence extrinsic to the gospel has recently been provided by Martin Hengel for a more complete picture of the elder in *The Johannine Question* (1989), and it is doubtful whether much more can be added to what we read there. However, evidence *intrinsic* to the gospel demonstrates the following: that John was a person with an astonishing understanding of the power of the narrative form. What John the storyteller produces is an ironic, narrative tragedy with a style noticeable for its economy and connexity. More than that, the story he creates out of his sources is one which manages to fuse the two horizons of the past history of Jesus and the present history of the community by exploiting the social function of narrative discourse. In achieving this, John configures time into a plot which succeeds in evoking the true significance of Jesus of Nazareth both for his own generation and the generations to come. This is, by any standards, a quite brilliant literary achievement. It is my hope that *John as Storyteller* will pave the way for further studies on John's use of narrative. Of particular value will be studies devoted to the revelatory function of the narrative form. The next step from a book such as this must surely be to ask the following question: 'If John's story is revelatory, then how much of that sense of disclosure is due to John's exploitation of the narrative form?'

REFERENCES

Abrams, M.H. 1958. *The Mirror and the Lamp*. New York, Norton.

Alter, R. 1981. *The Art of Biblical Narrative*. New York, Basic Books.

Appold, M. 1976. *The Oneness Motif in the Fourth Gospel: Motif Analysis and Exegetical Probe into the Theology of John*. Tübingen, J.C. Mohr.

Auerbach, E. 1953. *Mimesis: The Representation of Reality in Western Literature*. Princeton, New Jersey, Princeton University Press.

Bailey, J.A. 1963. *The Traditions Common to the Gospels of Luke and John*. Leiden, E.J. Brill.

Barrett, C.K. 1978. *The Gospel According to St. John: An Introduction with Commentary and Notes on the Greek Text*. London, SPCK.

Barthes, R. 1977. *Image Music Text*. Trans. Stephen Heath. London, Fontana.

Barton, J. 1984. *Reading the Old Testament*. London, Darton, Longman & Todd.

Bauer, B. 1846. *Kritik der Evangelischen Geschichte des Johannes*. Leipzig, Owigand.

Baur, F.C. 1847. *Kritische Untersuchungen über die Kanonischen Evangelien*. Tübingen, L.F. Fues.

Beardslee, W. 1970, *Literary Criticism of the New Testament*. Philadelphia, Pennsylvania, Fortress Press.

Berger, P. and T. Luckmann. 1984. *The Social Construction of Reality*. Harmondsworth, Middlesex, Penguin.

Berke, B. 1982. *Tragic Thought and the Grammar of Tragic Myth*. Bloomington, Indiana Press.

Best, E. 1983. *Mark: The Gospel as Story*. Edinburgh, T. & T. Clark.

Bilezikian, G. 1977. *The Liberated Gospel: A Comparison of the Gospel of Mark and Greek Tragedy*. Grand Rapids, Michigan, Baker Book House.

Bligh, J. 1975. *The Sign of the Cross: The Passion and Resurrection of Jesus According to St John*. Slough, St Paul Publications.

Borgen, P. 1959. 'John and the Synoptics in the Passion Narrative', *NTS* 5. 246–59.

1965. *Bread from Heaven*. Leiden, NovT Supplements 10.

Boring, E. 1978. 'The Influence of Christian Prophecy on the Johannine Portrayal of the Paraclete', *NTS* 25. 113–23.

Bossmann, R. 1987. 'Authority and Tradition in First Century Judaism and Christianity', *BTB* 17. 3–9.

Bowen, C. 1930. 'The Fourth Gospel as Dramatic Material', *JBL* 49. 292–305.

Brémond, C. 1978. 'The Narrative Message', *Semeia* 10. 5–56.

Broer, I. 1983. 'Noch Einmal: Zur Religionsgeschichtlichen "Abteilung" von Jo 2.1–11', in *Studien zum NT und seiner Umwelt* 8. 103–23.

Brown, R.E. 1966. *The Gospel According to John.* Vols. I and II. London, Geoffrey Chapman.

1979. *The Community of the Beloved Disciple.* New York, Paulist Press.

Bruce, F.F. 1980. 'The Trial of Jesus in the Fourth Gospel', in *Gospel Perspectives*, ed. R.T. France and D. Wenham, Vol. I. Sheffield, JSOT Press, pp. 7–20.

Bruns, J.E. 1967. 'The Use of Time in the Fourth Gospel', *NTS* 13, 285–90.

Bultmann, R. 1971. *Die Geschichte der synoptischen Tradition.* Göttingen, Vandenhoeck.

1971. *The Gospel of John: A Commentary.* Trans. G.R. Beasley Murray et al. Oxford, Basil Blackwell.

Burke, K. 1941. *The Philosophy of Literary Form: Studies in Symbolic Action.* Baton Rouge, Louisiana, Louisiana State University Press.

1952. *A Grammar of Motives.* New York, Prentice-Hall.

Buse, I. 1957. 'St. John and the Marcan Passion Narrative', *NTS* 4. 215–19.

Cahill, P.J. 1982. 'Narrative Art in John IV', *Religious Studies Bulletin.* 2 (2). 41–8.

Carrier, H. 1965. *The Sociology of Religious Belonging.* London, Darton, Longman & Todd.

Chatman, S. 1978. *Story and Discourse: Narrative Structure in Fiction and Film.* Ithaca, New York, Cornell University Press.

Collingwood, R.G. 1953. *The Idea of History.* Oxford, Oxford University Press.

Connick, M. 1948. 'The Dramatic Character of the Fourth Gospel', *JBL* 67. 159–69.

Cornford, F. 1907. *Thucydides Mythistoricus.* London, Edward Arnold.

Crane, R.S. 1967. *The Idea of the Humanities and Other Essays.* Chicago, Illinois, Chicago University Press.

Crites, S. 1971. 'The Narrative Quality of Experience', *JAAR* 39. 291–311.

Crossan, J.D. 1980. 'A Structuralist Analysis of John 6', in *Orientation by Disorientation*, ed. R. Spencer. Pittsburgh, Pennsylvania, Pickwick Press, 235–52.

Culler, J. 1975. *Structuralist Poetics.* London, Routledge & Kegan Paul.

Culmann, O. 1976. *The Johannine Circle.* Trans. J. Bowden. London, SCM Press.

Culpepper, R.A. 1975. *The Johannine School: An Evaluation of the Johannine School Hypothesis Based on an Investigation of the Nature of Ancient Schools.* SBL dissertation series, no. 26. Missoula, Montana, Scholars Press.

1983. *Anatomy of the Fourth Gospel.* Philadelphia, Pennsylvania, Fortress Press.

Daiches, D. 1968. 'Character', in *Perspectives on Fiction*, ed. J. Calderwood and H. Toliver. London, Oxford University Press.

Dauer, A. 1967. 'Das Wort des Gekreuzigten an Seine Mutter und den Jünger', *BZ* 11. 222–39.

1972. *Die Passionsgeschichte im Johannesevangelium: Eine traditions- geschichtliche und theologische Untersuchung zu Joh. 18.1–19.30.* SANT 30. Munich, Kosel.

Deeks, D. 1968. 'The Structure of the Fourth Gospel'. *NTS* 15. 107–29.

De la Potterie, I. 1969. 'La Passion selon Jean', *As Seign* 21.21–34.

Dewey, K. 1980. 'Paroimiai in the Gospel of John', *Semeia* 17. 81–100.

Dibelius, M. 1934. *From Tradition to Gospel.* London, Ivor Nicholson, Ivor Nicholson & Watson.

Dodd, C.H. 1950. *About the Gospels.* Cambridge, Cambridge University Press.

1963. *Historical Tradition in the Fourth Gospel.* Cambridge, Cambridge University Press.

Dods, M. 1903. *The Gospel of John.* London, Hodder & Stoughton.

Domeris, W.H. 1983. 'The Johannine Drama', *Journal of Theology for Southern Africa* 42. 29–35.

Duke, P. 1985. *Irony in the Fourth Gospel.* Atlanta, Georgia, John Knox Press.

Du Rand, J.A. 1985. 'The Characterization of Jesus as Depicted in the Narrative of the Fourth Gospel', *Neotestamentica* 19. 18–36.

Eagleton, T. 1983. *Literary Theory.* Oxford, Basil Blackwell.

Edwards, H.E. 1953. *The Disciple Who Wrote These Things.* London, Clarke.

Ehrman, B.D. 1983. 'Jesus' Trial before Pilate: John 18.28–19.15', *BTB* 13 (4).

Eisler, R. 1938. *The Enigma of the Fourth Gospel.* London.

Eller, V. 1987. *The Beloved Disciple.* Grand Rapids, Michigan, Eerdmans.

Elliott, J.H. 1982. *A Home for the Homeless: A Sociological Exegesis of I Peter, Its Situation and Strategy.* London, SCM Press.

Ellis, P. 1984. *The Genius of John: A Composition-Critical Commentary on the Fourth Gospel.* Collegeville, Minnesota, Liturgical Press.

Fenton, J.C. 1961. *The Passion According to John.* London, SPCK.

Fergusson, F. 1949. *The Idea of a Theatre.* Princeton, New Jersey, Princeton University Press.

Filson, F. 1949. 'Who was the Beloved Disciple?', *JBL* 68, 83–8.

Flanagan, N. 1981. 'The Gospel of John as Drama', *The Bible Today* 19. 264–70.

Forster, E.M. 1962. *Aspects of the Novel.* New York, Penguin Books.

Fortna, R.T. 1970. *The Gospel of Signs: A Reconstruction of the Narrative Source Underlying the Fourth Gospel.* Cambridge, Cambridge University Press.

1989. *The Fourth Gospel and its Predecessor.* Edinburgh, T. & T. Clark.

Fowler, R.M. 1986. 'Who is "the Reader" in Reader Response Criticism?', *Semeia* 31. 5–26.

Frye, N. 1971. *Anatomy of Criticism.* Princeton, Princeton University Press.

Fuller, R.H. 1986. 'The Passion, Death and Resurrection of Jesus According to St. John', *Chicago Studies* 25 (1), 51–63.

Gallie, W.B. 1964. *Philosophy and the Historical Understanding.* London, Chatto & Windus.

Gardner-Smith, P. 1938. *Saint John and the Synoptic Gospels*. Cambridge, Cambridge University Press.

Garvie, A. E. n.d. *The Beloved Disciple*. London.

Giblin, C. H. 1980. 'Suggestion, Negative Response and Positive Action in St. John's Portrayal of Jesus', *NTS* 26. 197–211.

1984. 'Confrontations in John 18.1–27', *Biblica* 65. 210–31.

1986. 'John's Narration of the Hearing before Pilate', *Biblica* 67. 221–39.

Goguel, M. 1910. *Les Sources du récit Johannique de la Passion*. Paris, G. Fischbacher.

Grassi, J. 1986. 'The Role of Jesus' Mother in John's Gospel: A Reappraisal', *CBQ* 48. 67–80.

Greimas, A. J. 1966. *Semantique structurale*. Paris, Larousse.

1970. *Du sens*. Paris, Seuil.

Gunn, D. M. 1980. *The Fate of King Saul: An Interpretation of a Biblical Story*. JSOT Suppl. 14. Sheffield, JSOT Press.

Haenchen, E. 1970. 'History and Interpretation in the Johannine Passion Narrative', *Interpretation* 24. 198–219.

1984. *A Commentary on the Gospel of John*. 2 vols. Trans. R. W. Funk. Philadelphia, Pennsylvania, Fortress Press.

Hartman, L. 1984. 'An Attempt at a Text-Centred Exegesis of John 21', *Studia Theologia* 38. 29–45.

Hauerwas, S. 1981. *A Community of Character*. Notre Dame, Indiana, Notre Dame University Press.

Hawkes, T. 1977. *Structuralism and Semiotics*. London, Methuen.

Hengel, M. 1981. *The Charismatic Leader and his Followers*. New York, Crossroad.

1989. *The Johannine Question*. London, SCM Press.

Higdon, D. 1977. *Time and English Fiction*. New Jersey, Rowman & Littlefield.

Hirsch, E. 1936. *Das Vierte Evangelium*. Tübingen, Mohr-Siebeck.

Hirsch, E. D. 1967. *Validity in Interpretation*. New Haven, Connecticut, Yale University Press.

Hitchcock, F. R. M. 1923. 'Is the Fourth Gospel a Drama?', *Theology* 7. 307–17.

Holloway, R. 1961. *The Story of the Night*. London, Routledge & Kegan Paul.

Hoskyns, E. C. 1940. *The Gospel of John*. London, Marshall, Morgan & Scott.

Hotson, L. 1954. *The First Night of Twelfth Night*. London, Rupert Hart-Davis.

Howard, J. K. 1967. 'Passover and Eucharist in the Fourth Gospel', *SJT* 20. 330–37.

Humphreys, W. L. 1978. 'The Tragedy of King Saul', *SOT* 6. 18–27.

1985. *The Tragic Vision and the Hebrew Tradition*. Philadelphia, Pennsylvania, Fortress Press.

Jameson, F. 1972. *The Prison House of Language*. Princeton, New Jersey, Princeton University Press.

Jasper, D. 1987. *The New Testament and the Literary Imagination*. London, Macmillan.

Jaubert, A. 1972. 'The Calendar of Qumran and the Passion Narrative in John', in *John and Qumran*, ed. J.H. Charlesworth, London, Chapman, pp. 62–75.

Johnson, A.M. 1979. *Structuralism and Biblical Hermeneutics*. Allison Park, Pennsylvania, Pickwick Press.

Jonge, M. de 1977. *Jesus: Stranger from Heaven and Son of God*. Missoula, Montana, Scholars Press.

Kee, H.C. 1977. *Community of the New Age: Studies in Mark's Gospel*. Philadelphia, Pennsylvania, Westminster Press.

Kermode, F. 1979. *The Genesis of Secrecy*. Cambridge, Massachusetts, Harvard University Press.

Kimelman, R. 1981. 'Birkat Ha Minim and the Lack of Evidence for any Anti-Christian Jewish Prayer in Late Antiquity', in *Jewish And Christian Self-Definition*, ed. E.P. Sanders, Vol. II, London, SCM Press, 226–44.

Kingsbury, J.D. 1986. *Matthew as Story*. Philadelphia, Pennsylvania, Fortress Press.

Klein, H. 1976. 'Die lukanisch-johanneische Passionstradition', *Zeitschrift für die neutestamentliche Wissenschaft* 67. 155–86.

Kotzé, P.P.A. 1985. 'John and Reader's Response', *Neotestamentica* 19. 50–63.

Kreyenbuhl, R. 1900. *Das Evangelium der Wahrheit*. Berlin.

Kysar, R. 1975. *The Fourth Evangelist and his Gospel: An Examination of Contemporary Scholarship*. Minneapolis, Minnesota, Augsburg Publishing House.

Langkammer, H. 1968. 'Christ's Last Will and Testament (Jn 19.25–26) in the Interpretation of the Fathers of the Church and the Scholastics', *Antonianum* 43. 9–109.

Leach, E. 1969. *Genesis as Myth and Other Essays*. London, Jonathan Cape.

Leech, C. 1969. *Tragedy*. London, Methuen.

Lévi-Strauss, C. 1968. *Structural Anthropology*. London, Allen Lane.

Lightfoot, R.H. 1956. *Saint John's Gospel*. Ed. C.F. Evans. London, Oxford University Press.

Lindars, B. 1971. *Behind the Fourth Gospel*. London, SPCK.

1972. *St. John's Gospel*. London, Faber & Faber.

1977. 'The Passion in the Fourth Gospel', in *God's Christ and His People*, ed. J. Jervell and W. Meeks. Oslo, Oslo Universitetsforlaget, pp. 71–86.

1990. *John*. New Testament Guides. Sheffield, Sheffield Academic Press.

McKnight, E.V. 1978. *Meaning in Texts*. Philadelphia, Pennsylvania, Fortress Press.

1985. *The Bible and the Reader: An Introduction to Literary Criticism*. Philadelphia, Pennsylvania, Fortress Press.

Maddox, R. 1982. *The Purpose of Luke–Acts*. Edinburgh, T. & T. Clark.

Malbon, E. 1986. *Narrative Space and Mythic Meaning in Mark*. New York, Harper & Row.

Malina, B. 1985. 'The Gospel of John in Sociolinguistic Perspective', in *48th Colloquy of the Centre for Hermeneutical Studies*, ed. H. Waetjen, Berkeley, California, Centre for Hermeneutical Studies.

Mandelbaum, M. 1967. 'A Note on History as Narrative', *History and Theory* 6. 416–17.

Marsh, J. 1968. *Saint John*. Harmondsworth, Middlesex, Penguin.

Martyn, J. L. 1979. *History and Theology in the Fourth Gospel*. 2nd edn. Nashville, Tennessee, Abingdon Press.

Matera, F. J. 1987. 'The Plot of Matthew's Gospel', *CBQ* 49, 233–53.

Maynard, A. H. 1984. 'The Role of Peter in the Fourth Gospel', *NTS* 30. 531–48.

Meeks, W. 1972. 'The Man from Heaven in Johannine Sectarianism', in *The Interpretation of John*, ed. J. Ashton, London, SPCK (1986), pp. 141–73.

Mink, L. 1970. 'History and Fiction as Modes of Comprehension', *New Literary History* 1. 541–8.

1978. 'Narrative Form as Cognitive Instrument', in *The Writing of History*, ed. R. Canary. Madison, Wisconsin, Wisconsin University Press.

Moore, S. 1989. *Literary Criticism and the Gospels: The Theoretical Challenge*. New Haven, Yale University Press.

Morris, L. 1964. *The New Testament and Jewish Lectionaries*. London, Tyndale.

Muilenburg, J. 1932. 'Literary Form in the Fourth Gospel', *JBL* 51. 40–53.

Neirynck, F. 1979. *Jean et les synoptiques: Examen critique de l'exégèse de M. E. Boismard*. BETL 49. Louvain, Louvain University Press.

Newman, B. M. Jr. 1975. 'Some Observations regarding the Argument, Structure and Literary Characteristics of the Gospel of John', *Bible Trans.* 26. 234–9.

Nicholson, G. C. 1983. *Death as Departure*. Chico, California, Scholars Press.

Nickelsburg, G. W. E. 1980. 'The Genre and Function of the Markan Passion Narrative', *HTR* 73. 153–84.

Nuttall, A. D. 1980. *Overheard by God: Fiction and Prayer in Herbert, Milton, Dante and St John*. London, Methuen.

O'Day, G. 1986. *Revelation in the Fourth Gospel*. Philadelphia, Pennsylvania, Fortress Press.

Ohler, A. M. 1985. *Studying the Old Testament*. Edinburgh, T. & T. Clark.

Olsson, B. 1974. *Structure and Meaning in the Fourth Gospel: A Text-Linguistic Analysis of John 2.1–11 and 4.1–42*. Lund, C. Gleerup.

Palmer, R. 1969. *Hermeneutics*. Evanston, Illinois, Northwestern University Press.

Parker, P. 1955. 'Bethany Beyond Jordan', *JBL* 74. 257–61.

Patte, D. and A. Patte. 1976. *Structural Exegesis. From Theory to Practice*. Philadelphia, Pennsylvania, Fortress Press.

Perrin, N. 1972. 'The Evangelist as Author', *Biblical Research* 15. 5–18.

Petersen, N. 1978. *Literary Criticism for New Testament Critics*. Philadelphia, Pennsylvania, Fortress Press.

Pfister, F. 1937. 'Herakles and Christus', *Archiv für Religionswissenschaft* 34. 42–60.

Pfitzner, V. C. 1976. 'The Coronation of the King: Passion Narrative and Passion Theology in the Gospel of St. John', *Lutheran Theological Journal* 1–12.

Phillips, G. A. 1983. 'This is a Hard Saying. Who Can be a Listener to it? Creating a Reader in John 6', *Semeia* 26. 23–56.

Propp, V. 1928. *Morphology of the Folk-Tale*. Trans. L. Scott. Leningrad.

1978. 'Structure and History in the Study of the Fairy Tale', *Semeia* 10. 57–84.

Reinhartz, A. 1989a. 'Great Expectations: A Reader-Oriented Approach to Johannine Christology and Eschatology', *Literature and Theology* 3 (1). 61–76.

1989b. 'Jesus as Prophet: Predictive Prolepses in the Fourth Gospel', *JSNT* 36. 3–16.

Rensberger, D. 1989. *Overcoming the World: Politics and Community in the Gospel of John.* London, SPCK.

Rhoads, D. 1982. 'Narrative Criticism and the Gospel of Mark', *JAAR* 50. 411–34.

Rhoads, D. and Michie, D. 1982. *Mark as Story: An Introduction to the Narrative of a Gospel.* Philadelphia, Pennsylvania, Fortress Press.

Ricoeur, P. 1984. *Time and Narrative.* Vol. I. Chicago, Illinois, Chicago University Press.

1986. *Time and Narrative.* Vol. II. Chicago, Illinois, Chicago University Press.

Riley, W. 1985. 'Situating Biblical Narrative: Poetics and the Transmission of Community Values', *Proc. Ir. Blb. Assoc.* 9. 38–52.

Rimmon-Kenan, S. 1983. *Narrative Fiction: Contemporary Poetics.* London, Methuen.

Robinson, J. A. T. 1985. *The Priority of John.* London, SCM Press.

Ruckstuhl, E. 1951. *Die literarische Einheit des Johannesevangeliums.* Freiburg, Paulus Press.

Ruthven, K. K. 1976. *Myth.* London, Methuen.

Ryken, L. 1979. *Triumphs of the Imagination.* Leicester, Illinois, IVP.

Sands, P. C. 1932. *Literary Genius of the New Testament.* Oxford, Oxford University Press.

Saussure, F. de 1960. *Course in General Linguistics.* London, P. Owen.

Schenke, L. 1988. 'Der Dialog Jesus mit den Juden im Johannesevangelium', *NTS* 34 (4). 573–603.

Schiffman, L. H. 1981. 'At the Crossroads: Tannaitic Perspectives on the Jewish-Christian Schism', in *Jewish and Christian Self-Definition*, ed. E. P. Sanders, Vol. II, London and Philadelphia, SCM Press.

Schnackenburg, R. 1968, 1979, 1982. *The Gospel According to St. John.* 3 vols. New York, Herder & Herder.

Schniewind, J. 1914. *Die Parallelperikopen bei Lukas und Johannes.* Leipzig, Darmstadt.

Scholes, R., and R. Kellog. 1966. *The Nature of Narrative.* London, Oxford University Press.

1968. 'Plot in Narrative', in *Perspectives on Fiction*, ed. J. Calderwood and H. Toliver. London, Oxford University Press.

Schwank, B. 1964. 'Die ersten Gaben des Erhöhten Königs (19, 23–30)', *SeinSend* 29. 340–53.

Schwartz, E. 1907. 'Aporien im Vierten Evangelium', in *Nachrichten der Königlichen Gesellschaft der Wissenschaft zu Göttingen* 1. 347–72.

Schweizer, E. 1939. *Ego Eimi.* Göttingen, Vanderhoeck.

Scott, E. F. 1906. *The Fourth Gospel: Its Purpose and Theology.* Edinburgh, T. & T. Clark.

Scott, N. 1966. *The Broken Centre: Studies in the Theological Horizon of Modern Literature.* New Haven, Yale University Press.

1986. 'The Rediscovery of Story in Recent Theology', in *Art/Literature/ Religion*, JAAR Thematic Studies. Chico, California, Scholars Press.

Sloyan, G. 1988. *John.* Atlanta, Georgia, John Knox Press.

Smalley, S. 1978. *John: Evangelist and Interpreter.* Exeter, Paternoster Press.

Smith, D.M. 1965. *The Composition and Order of the Fourth Gospel.* New Haven, Connecticut, Yale University Press.

1987. *Johannine Christianity.* Edinburgh, T. & T. Clark.

Solages, Mgr de. 1979. *Jean et les Synoptiques.* Leiden, Brill.

Staley, J. 1988. *The Print's First Kiss: A Rhetorical Investigation of the Implied Reader in the Fourth Gospel.* SBL dissertation series no. 82. Atlanta, Georgia, Scholars Press.

Stanton, G. 1989. *The Gospels and Jesus.* Oxford, Oxford University Press.

Stauffer, E. 1960. *Jesus and His Story.* London, SCM Press.

Sternberg, M. 1985. *The Poetics of Biblical Narrative.* Bloomington, Indiana, Indiana University Press.

Strachan, R.H. 1925. *The Fourth Evangelist: Dramatist or Historian?* London.

1941. *The Fourth Gospel.* London, SCM Press.

Stroup, G. 1984. *The Promise of Narrative Theology.* London, SCM Press.

Talbert, C.H. 1970. 'Artistry and Theology: An Analysis of the Architecture of John 1.19–5.47', *CBQ* 32. 341–66.

Tannehill, R.C. 1977. 'The Disciples in Mark', *JR* 57. 386–405.

1979. 'The Gospel of Mark as Narrative Christology', *Semeia* 16. 57–97.

1984. 'The Composition of Acts 3–5: Narrative Development and Echo Effect', in *SBL Seminar Papers* 1984. Chico, California, Scholars Press, pp. 217–40.

1986. *The Narrative Unity of Luke–Acts.* Vol. I, Philadelphia, Pennsylvania, Fortress Press.

Theissen, G. 1978. *The First Followers of Jesus: A Sociological Analysis of Earliest Christianity.* London, SCM Press.

Thiselton, A.C. 1978. 'Structuralism and Biblical Studies', *ExpTimes* 89. 329–35.

Thompson, M. 1988. *The Humanity of Jesus in the Fourth Gospel.* Philadelphia, Pennsylvania, Fortress Press.

Tidball, D. 1983. *Sociology of the New Testament.* Exeter, Paternoster Press.

Torrance, T.F. 1985. 'Time in Scientific and Historical Research', unpublished seminar paper delivered at St John's College, Nottingham.

Trocmé, E. 1983. *The Passion as Liturgy.* London, SCM Press.

Via, D. 1975. *Kerygma and Comedy in the New Testament: A Structuralist Approach to Hermeneutics.* Philadelphia, Pennsylvania, Fortress Press.

Vorster W.S. 1985. 'Meaning and Reference', in *Text and Reality*, ed. B.C. Lategan. SBL, Atlanta, Georgia, pp. 27–66.

Wahlde, U. von. 1982. 'The Johannine Jews': A Critical Survey, *NTS* 28. 33–60.

1989. *The Earliest Version of John's Gospel.* Wilmington, Delaware, Michael Glazier.

Walhout, C. 1985. 'Texts and Actions', in *The Responsibility of Hermeneutics*, ed. C. Walhout *et al*. Exeter, Paternoster Press.

Wead, D. 1970. *Literary Devices in John's Gospel*. Basle, Friedrich Reinhart Kommissionsverlag.

Webster, E. C. 1982. 'Pattern in the Fourth Gospel', in *Art and Meaning*, ed. D. Clines and D. Gunn, Sheffield. JSOT Press, pp. 230–57.

Weeden, T. 1971. *Mark: Traditions in Conflict*. Philadelphia, Pennsylvania, Fortress Press.

Wellhausen, J. 1908. *Das Evangelium Johannis*. Berlin, G. Reimer.

Westcott, B. F. 1892. *The Gospel According to St. John*. London, John Murray.

White, H. 1973. *Metahistory*. London, Johns Hopkins University Press.

1978. 'The Historical Text as Literary Artifact', in *The Writing of History*, ed. R. Canary, Madison, Wisconsin, Wisconsin University Press.

1980. 'The Value of Narrativity in the Representation of Reality', *Critical Inquiry* 7. 5–27.

Wicker, B. 1975. *The Story-Shaped World: Fiction and Metaphysics*. London, Athlone Press.

Wilder, A. 1964. *Early Christian Rhetoric: The Language of the Gospel*. London, SCM Press.

Windisch, H. 1923. 'Der Johanneische Erzählungsstil', in *Gunkel Festschrift*. Göttingen, Vandenhoeck.

Winquist, C. E. 1978. *Homecoming: Interpretation, Transformation and Individualism*. Missoula, Montana, Scholars Press.

INDEX OF NAMES AND SUBJECTS